STUDIES IN WRITTEN LANGUAGE AND LITERACY

EDITORS
BRIAN STREET
King's College, London

LUDO VERHOEVEN
Nijmegen University

ASSOCIATE EDITORS
FLORIAN COULMAS
Chuo University, Tokyo

DANIEL WAGNER
University of Pennsylvania

EDITORIAL BOARD
F. Niyi Akinnaso (Temple University, Philadelphia)
David Barton (Lancaster University)
Paul Bertelson (Université Libre de Bruxelles)
Claire Blanche-Benveniste (Université de Provence)
Chander J. Daswani (India Council of Educational Research and Training)
Emilia Ferreiro (Instituto Polytecnico México)
Edward French (University of the Witwatersrand)
Uta Frith (Medical Research Council, London)
Harvey J. Graff (University of Texas at Dallas)
Hartmut Günther (Universität zu Köln)
David Olson (Ontario Institute for Studies in Education, Toronto)
Clotilde Pontecorvo (University of Rome)
Roger Säljo (Linköping University)
Michael Stubbs (Universität Trier)

AIM AND SCOPE

The aim of this series is to advance insight into the multifaceted character of written language, with special emphasis on its uses in different social and cultural settings. It combines interest in sociolinguistic and psycholinguistic accounts of the acquisition and transmission of literacy. The series focusses on descriptive and theoretical reports in areas such as language codification, cognitive models of written language use, written language acquisition in children and adults, the development and implementation of literacy campaigns, and literacy as a social marker relating to gender, ethnicity, and class. The series is intended to be multi-disciplinary, combining insights from linguistics, psychology, sociology, education, anthropology, and philosophy.

Volume 8

Edited by Carys Jones, Joan Turner and Brian Street
Students Writing in the University
Cultural and epistemological issues

STUDENTS WRITING IN THE UNIVERSITY
CULTURAL AND EPISTEMOLOGICAL ISSUES

Edited by

CARYS JONES
JOAN TURNER
BRIAN STREET
University of London

JOHN BENJAMINS PUBLISHING COMPANY
AMSTERDAM/PHILADELPHIA

∞™ The paper used in this publication meets the minimum requirements of American National Standard for Information Sciences — Permanence of Paper for Printed Library Materials, ANSI Z39.48-1984.

Cover design: Françoise Berserik

Library of Congress Cataloging-in-Publication Data

Students writing in the university : cultural and epistemological issues / edited by Carys Jones, Joan Turner, and Brian Street.
    p.   cm. -- (Studies in written language and literacy, ISSN 0929-7324 ; v. 8)
Includes bibliographical references and indexes.
1. English language--Rhetoric--Study and teaching--Great Britain. 2. Academic writing--Study and teaching--Great Britain. 3. College students--Great Britain--Social conditions. 4. College students--Great Britain--Language. I. Jones, Carys. II. Turner, Joan, 1951- . III. Street, Brian V. IV. Series.
PE1405.G7S78   1999
808'.042'071141--dc21   99-23670
ISBN 90 272 1801 3 (Eur.) / 1 55619 386 6 (US) (Hb; alk. paper)   CIP

© 1999 – John Benjamins B.V.
No part of this book may be reproduced in any form, by print, photoprint, microfilm, or any other means, without written permission from the publisher.

John Benjamins Publishing Co. • P.O.Box 75577 • 1070 AN Amsterdam • The Netherlands
John Benjamins North America • P.O.Box 27519 • Philadelphia PA 19118-0519 • USA

Table of Contents

Acknowledgements · vii

Information about the Authors · ix

Foreword · xiii

Introduction · xv
  Carys Jones, Joan Turner and Brian Street

SECTION A
Interacting with the Institution · 1

1. Foregrounding Background in Academic Learning · 5
   Monika Hermerschmidt

2. What do Students Really Say in Their Essays? Towards a descriptive framework for analysing student writing · 17
   Fiona English

3. The Student from Overseas and the British University: Finding a way to succeed · 37
   Carys Jones

4. On Not Disturbing "Our Group Peace": The plight of the visiting researcher · 61
   Graham Low and Latilla Woodburn

5. Writing Assignments on a PGCE (Secondary) Course: Two case studies · 81
   Brenda Gay, Carys Jones and Jane Jones

6. Academic Literacies and Learning in Higher Education: Constructing knowledge through texts and experience · 103
   Mary R. Lea

Section B
Mystery and Transparency in Academic Literacies   125

7. Whose 'Common Sense'? Essayist literacy and the institutional practice of mystery   127
   Theresa Lillis

8. Academic Literacy and the Discourse of Transparency   149
   Joan Turner

9. Inventing Academic Literacy: An American perspective   161
   Catherine Davidson and Alice Tomic

10. Agency and Subjectivity in Student Writing   171
    Mary Scott

11. Academic Literacies   193
    Brian V. Street

Index   229

Acknowledgements

Chapter 6, "Academic Literacies and Learning in Higher Education", was previously published in *Studies in the Education of Adults* Volume 30 Number 2, edited by Dr. Richard Edwards in October 1998. The editors would like to thank Dr. Edwards and the National Institute of Adult Continuing Education (England and Wales) for their kind permission to re-publication in the present volume.

Chapter 11, "Academic Literacies", was first published in 'Alternative Ways of Knowing: Literacies, Numeracies and Sciences'. edited by D. Baker, C. Fox and J. Clay in 1996. The editors would like to thank Falmer Press for their kind agreement to re-publication in the present volume. In addition the editors would like to thank OUP for kind permission to reprint pp. 107–110 of Social Anthropology Oxford University Press, 1964 by R. G. Lienhardt.

Brian Street would also like to thank the correspondents to that article, whose work is again published in the body of the piece, for their kind permission to re-publish in this context: Mary Lea; Shirley Franklin; Joan Turner; David Howes; David Russell; Sally Mitchell. That their names do not appear as co-authors is itself indicative of the power issues discussed in the article.

Information about the Authors

Catherine Davidson is the University Writing Coordinator at Richmond American International University in London. She teaches first year writing and creative writing and runs the Writing Across the Curriculum program. She has written about argument, the use of technology in teaching writing, and the multicultural writing classroom. Her first novel, The Priest Fainted, was published in 1998 in the US and the UK.

Fiona English heads the English Language Unit at the School of Oriental and African Studies (SOAS) in the University of London. She comes from a TEFL background and has been involved in teaching and teacher training over many years. Her work includes language and academic literacy with both international and British students. She has carried out investigations into children's use of language across the school curriculum and this has influenced much of her current research.

Brenda Gay is a Lecturer in Classics within the School of Education at King's College, London. She has wide experience in a variety of schools, having taught all age ranges from infants to unviersity students, as a Head of Classics and a Headmistress. Much of her research has been conducted in close co-operation with practitioners. Her interests include the linguistic analysis of disruptive incidents; gifted children; accountability in education and religion in the independent sector. She has published in these areas.

Monika Hermerschmidt is a PhD student at King's College, University of London. Her key research aim is to move towards a deep and complex understanding of learning as a social practice that is closely bound up with issues of language, identity, and power. In 1993 she obtained a Master's degree in English Language Teaching in London. She has taught English for Academic Purposes at Humboldt University in Berlin, and Principles of Writing classes at the American International University in London.

Carys Jones is a Lecturer in Language in Education, in the School of Education at King's College London. She has worked in the area of English for Academic Purposes with students from many different backgrounds and in a range of UK and other educational contexts. Her main area of research is in the development of second language use. She has also published about studies into the school experiences of minority ethnic teacher trainees and the role of language in learning.

Jane Jones is Head of MFL Initial Teacher Education in the School of Education, King's College London. She has taught languages in primary and secondary schools and co-ordinated several EU Socrates projects and research on language teaching issues, school management and European dimensions. She has published in international journals and edited several volumes on these topics.

Mary Lea is a Research Fellow in the Institute of Educational Technology at the Open University. She has worked in a variety of university environments, as both a practitioner and researcher, in the area of student writing in higher education. She is now looking at the implications of the use of new technology for student learning, with a specific focus upon computer conferencing and academic literacies.

Theresa Lillis has worked as a teacher for some fifteen years across a range of educational contexts — secondary, Further Education, Adult Education and Higher Education. She completed a PhD in 1998 on making meaning in academic writing and has published articles in the journals Language and Education and RaPAL (Research and Practice in Adult Literacy). She is currently working as a researcher/lecturer at Sheffield Hallam University and as a tutor with the Open University.

Graham Low is Senior Lecturer and Director of the English as a Foreign Language Unit at the University of York. His research interests are currently the use of metaphor, academic literacy and discourse aspects of research methodology. He is particularly interested in ways in which the results of language research can be used to help develop language teaching programmes.

Mary Scott is on the staff of the University of London Institute of Education where she is responsible for academic literacy across the Institute. She also offers an MA module in academic literacies and is the course leader of the MA Learning and Teaching of English. She has published papers on academic literacy and on the teaching of English, and has recently been involved, together with Professor Gunther Kress and Dr Nancy Lee, in a research project concerning undergraduate academic writing in universities in the UK and in Hong Kong.

INFORMATION ABOUT THE AUTHORS

Brian Street is Professor of Language in Education at King's College, London University and Visiting Professor of Education in the Graduate School of Education, University of Pennsylvania. He undertook anthropological fieldwork on literacy and education in Iran during the 1970's, and has since written and lectured extensively on literacy practices; in S. Africa, Australia, Canada, the US etc. He is best known for Literacy in Theory and Practice (C.U.P. 1985), edited Cross-Cultural Approaches to Literacy, (CUP 1993) and brought out a collection of his essays with Longman under the title Social Literacies (1995), which was cited in his receipt of the David S Russell award for distinguished research by the National Council for the Teaching of English in the US. He has written six books and published over 60 scholarly articles. He is currently concerned to link ethnographic-style research on the cultural dimension of literacy with contemporary debates in education.

Alice Tomic, Senior Lecturer, is Director of the English Language Development Program at Richmond, the American International University in London, where she has designed several innovative courses including a three-tiered English for Academic Purposes/Academic Writing programme for the university. Her research interests include using computers for teaching writing in intercultural communications. She has lectured and published on a wide, international scale and is an Editor of 'Language and Intercultural Communication'.

Joan Turner works at Goldsmiths College, University of London, where she is head of the English Language Unit. She has published on cross-cultural pragmatics, conventional metaphor, and academic literacy. Her current research interests include a genealogical perspective on academic conventions and emerging changes in the conventions of academic writing in the human sciences, interrelating with epistemological power shifts.

Latilla Woodburn is a part-time tutor in EFL in the English as a Foreign Language Unit, where she teaches a range of specialist support courses in English for Academic purposes. She is also a qualified and practicing counsellor, and has developed counselling approaches used to help the Unit's international students.

Foreword

The contributors to this book are members of LIHERG, Language in Higher Education Research Group. The research group developed from an awareness of the underlying issues concerning academic literacies, when viewed from the perspective of language and power.

On the one hand this perspective draws attention to the complex, language issues that arise in academic literacy practices in the contemporary academy where competing epistemologies and varying degrees of explicitness about what academic writing entails serve to confuse the student. On the other hand, such a focus highlights institutional marginalisation of academic writing as teaching, learning, and research practice. Discussions around those issues have led to this book.

Writing about academic writing is inevitably a reflexive process and this was heightened by the collaborative nature of the book's production. Notions of agency and subjectivity were not only analytical determinants but a heightened experience as each writer commented on others' work and had their own work commented on. Each voice met the interpretative dynamic of another's, mirroring the issues of who is writing for whom, who can say what, and how can/should it be said. Such issues themselves raise the larger questions of what counts as knowledge, how it is mediated by the rhetorical conventions of a particular culture, how far it can be produced and reproduced by the rhetorical conventions of different cultures, and to what extent the challenging of such rhetorical conventions is itself a crucial epistemological issue.

With the book, we hope to enjoin many others in its debates, including those who may never have thought they had any connection with them.

Introduction

Carys Jones   Joan Turner   Brian Street

Focus

With the expansion of higher education in a number of countries (UK; US; S. Africa etc.) attention is being focussed increasingly on the 'problems' students face in meeting the writing requirements of the academy. The present volume attempts to address these issues from a broader perspective than that evident in the dominant approaches where study skills are stressed at the expense of deeper, cultural and epistemological issues. Through detailed case studies of staff student encounters around the writing process, the authors bring to light underlying features of academic life that have tended to be taken for granted. This includes treating learning as a social practice rather than an individual act and giving voice to both tutors and students regarding their particular social as well as personal viewpoints on what is often framed and conceptualised for them by the institution. Although the data addressed includes 'problems' faced by overseas students and non-native English speakers in UK universities at both undergraduate and graduate level, the articles do not necessarily take at face value the dominant notion of 'problems'; rather they seek to locate the issue of student writing and faculty response in broader institutional contexts taking account of their cultural and epistemological underpinnings. This shifts attention away from the current concern with why students from 'non-traditional' backgrounds — whether in terms of class or country — do not easily access academic discourse, and instead asks less judgmental questions about 'what is going on' when students write in Higher Education and what are the underlying assumptions about knowledge and about tutor/student relations that inform such processes. Similarly, the papers in this volume raise broader questions about the issue of assessment of student writing, by both staff and students themselves; the significance of different domains of practice for how writing is construed, such as subject disciplines, English for Academic Purposes, Writing Across the Curriculum and other practices. The focus on relations between the parties involved — tutors, staff and administrators — shifts attention from 'blame' and from judgement towards understanding the social processes in which the production of texts and the deployment of different language registers take on significance. Finally, attention is directed not only to immediate participants involved in the writing process — tutors and students — but also to the institution as a whole as the context within which these practices are embedded. This approach also facilitates some comparison of attitudes towards academic writing in different institutional and national contexts and one article addresses this issue with respect to College writing in the UK and the US.

Cultural and Epistemological Issues

At the theoretical and methodological level the book breaks new ground by approaching the issues and case data as social and discursive practices and by raising the question of power relations and how to conceptualise and describe them. These debates are placed in the context of functional, cultural and critical approaches to the study of writing. In all of the papers, close linguistic and discourse analysis is related to broader social and institutional interpretations: the authors variously offer ways of addressing the relationship between agency and subjectivity on the one hand and the constitution of institutions through discursive practices on the other. A key argument throughout is that the level at which we should be rethinking higher education and its writing practices should not simply be that of skills and effectiveness but rather of epistemology — what counts as knowledge and who has authority over it; of identity — what the relation is between forms of writing and the constitution of self and agency; and of power — how partial and ideological positions and claims are presented as neutral and as given through the writing requirements and processes of feedback and assessment that make up academic activity. A number of the authors attend to the nature of mystery and transparency in such activity and the volume as a whole attempts to make visible what is often hidden, to provide a language and a method for penetrating the opaque surface of higher educational institutions and practices. One consequence of adopting such a broader, more theoretically based approach to student writing might be that the field of 'academic writing' support may be treated less as a remedial ghetto and taken more seriously as a central location in the construction of the academy itself and therefore as a major field of research and theory in its own right.

In terms of expectations of the academy and the contributions it can make, the issues involved are signalled as inevitably wide-ranging, deep, interlinked and crucially important to an evolutionary concept of higher education in an 'international' and 'intercultural' world. Through its discussions about students' writing, the book as a whole seeks to raise awareness of the changing nature of the academy in a global environment. The changes that are taking place in the composition of the student body and in the global links amongst knowledge workers can be viewed as a shift in the direction of 'cultural hybridity'. Instead of the academy representing itself as a homogenous and unified entity, to which outsiders must seek access through learning its ways, there is now more negotiation to be held between the particular institution's processes and discourses on the one hand and, on the other, the uniqueness of students' individual cultural and linguistic-related histories. In this new environment, the latter play a highly influential part in the institution's identity and the authors of this volume see this diversity as a source of enrichment. In this perspective, all the members of the academy are linked through their awareness of the institution of learning as an on-going, dynamic process to be shared by all those involved — administrators, lecturers, tutors and students — rather than as a given source of knowledge and regulations determined by a few in authority. This shared awareness entails a reciprocal understanding of others' world views as valuable in itself to the extent that fear of destabilisation of the individual and of the institution are perceived as, and are, non-threatening. The view of knowledge as process and of authority as multi-faceted suggests a different way of viewing the writing requirements of higher education and leads to new insights that might help explain the apparent 'problems' faced by some student writers as they encounter this changing environment.

The discussions, then, examine students' writing as a distinctive process set against institutional expectations: a process which is crucial to the nurturing of diverse intercultural perspectives. The authors' findings suggest that the university might be more open to change, to being shaped and reshaped by its various members. They highlight the need to avoid surface judgements being made about students' intentions through their writing and to search for deeper understandings. Some of the authors discuss how alternative perceptions of the issues can emerge and how misunderstandings of what writing means against this more complex background can be damaging. Lea, writing from the academic literacies approach outlined below, suggests two approaches to student writing amongst mature adults writing assignments for open University courses: the 'reformulation of texts' approach involves treating source texts as knowledge to be re presented in the students' own words; the challenging texts' approach involves the student relating their own experience and their other reading in the litertaure to the particular text in front of them, which often leads to questioning and challenging of the knowledge presented there. However, differences may arise here with the tutor, whose own view of the text and of how the student should represent it, may focus on the closeness of the writing to the source text rather than the struggles the student is making to challenge it. Such differences and sometimes misunderstandings associated with them — regarding what is knowledge, what is learning, what is writing — may lead to faculty and student frustration. Both English and Lillis, for instance, point out the damaging effects on students of misunderstandings about the often implicit requirements of the institution: they point out, for instance, how misunderstandings can occur in tasks such as the writing of assignments. English suggests that shared awareness is enhanced by discourse knowledge. She discusses how discourse is presented, then interpreted, in ways which differ from the intended meaning. Lillis shows how the validity of assessed essays can be challenged through the way questions are formulated and how students' struggles to interpret the question compounds their problems. Hermerschmidt, in her case-study, relates misunderstanding to power issues: she argues that opportunities for students to be understood by those in power are too few and too limited so that students become aware that they need to play a game which panders to the powerful rather than become wholly committed to developing their own academic paths. Scott too discusses how students become agents of their own subjectivity, aware of how they may be interpreted by others so that they develop their own hidden discourses. Gay, Jones & Jones present the perspectives of subject tutors as grounded in the cultural dominance of the institution, which can act to disempower students engaged in their studies. Davidson and Tomic signal how different cultural practices can be in their discussion of the US tradition in writing practices as contrasted with the British EAP culture.

English, Lillis, Low & Woodburn, and Jones, in their case-study approaches, all suggest that awareness is enhanced when opportunities are created for discussing intended and interpreted meanings. Low & Woodburn show how Grice's Co-operative Principle can be used to illuminate cultural problems of discourse. Jones discusses how a task-based approach might encourage problems of hidden discourse to be brought to the surface. Taking a more general stance, Turner argues that a shared understanding leads to a more critical awareness of the dominance and lack of transparency of institutional discourse. She highlights how traditional practices have deceptively developed a culture where awareness of hidden meanings of discourse has been discouraged and backgrounded. Street argues the case for acknowledging the complex epistemological issues which underlie students' writing as a process and product rather than as skills alone, as in much dominant discourse. His contribution consists of a series of disparate comments linked by their reference to a common stimulus — a short piece by Street on 'Academic Literacy'. This short piece was originally written as a result of his own experience of trying to make explicit to students his own assumptions about 'academic literacy'; it was circulated amongst groups of colleagues and at some workshops on the subject, and a number of people then responded in writing. These have been deliberately left in their original form rather than incorporated into Street's own summary, in order to draw attention to the genre and to force the reader to re-consider what we take for granted there, such as the traditional format and layout of the 'essay-text'. Focusing on this challenging note questions the very bases of what counts as 'writing' in the University: by locating the debate at the level of cultural and epistemological issues, the authors hope to provide a broader context in which to consider student writing both as a research issue and in terms of policy (cf. Creme & Lea 1997).

Models of Student Writing in Higher Education

Many of the authors in this volume draw upon the models of student writing provided in a recent paper by Lea & Street (1998), based on their research into perceptions of writing in some UK universities. Lea & Street distinguish between three models of student writing — study skills, academic socialisation and 'academic literacies' — and suggest that, whilst the narrow study skills approach has been generally superseded by a socialisation view, this too often still involves narrow interpretations of the learning process and the writing requirements associated with it. They advocate an academic literacies approach that allows a broader, more institutional and socially-sensitive understanding of the processes in which writing in higher education is embedded. The notion of academic literacies has been developed from the area of 'new literacy studies' as an attempt to draw out the implications of this approach for our understanding of issues of student learning. The three models (see Figure 1) are not mutually exclusive, and the authors who use them in this volume, like Lea & Street, would not want to view them in a simple linear time dimension, whereby one model supersedes or replaces the insights provided by the other. Rather, they would like to think that each model successively encapsulates the other, so that the academic socialisation perspective takes account of study skills but includes them in the broader context of the acculturation processes described below and likewise the academic literacies approach encapsulates the academic socialisation model, building on the insights developed there as well as the study skills view.

> **Models of Student Writing in Higher Education**
>
> - **Study Skills:**
> *student deficit*
> 'fix it'; atomised skills; surface language, grammar, spelling
> sources: behavioural and experimental psychology; programmed learning
>
> >*student writing as* technical and instrumental skill
>
> - **Academic socialisation:**
> *acculturation of students into academic discourse*
>
> inculcating students into new 'culture'; focus on student orientation to learning and interpretation of learning task e.g. 'deep', 'surface', 'strategic' learning; homogeneous 'culture'; lack of focus on institutional practices, change and power
>
> sources: social psychology; anthropology; constructivism
>
> >*student writing as* transparent medium of representation
>
> - **Academic literacies:**
> *students' negotiation of conflicting literacy practices*
>
> literacies as social practices; at level of epistemology and identities
> institutions as sites of/constituted in discourses and power
> variety of communicative repertoire e.g. genres, fields, disciplines;
> switching re: linguistic practices, social meanings and identities
>
> sources: 'New Literacy Studies'; Critical Discourse Analysis; Systemic Linguistics; Cultural Anthropology
> >*student writing as* constitutive and contested

Figure 1. (from Lea & Street 1998)

The academic literacies model, then, incorporates both of the other models into a more encompassing understanding of the nature of student writing within institutional practices, power relations and identities, as we explain below. This perspective, then, involves a hierarchical view of the relationship between the three models, privileging the 'academic literacies' approach conceptually but not sequentially. It follows from this view that, in teaching as well as in research, addressing specific skills issues around student writing, such as how to open or close an essay or whether to use the first person, takes on an entirely different meaning if the context is solely that of study skills, if the process is seen as part of academic socialisation or if it is viewed more broadly as an aspect of the whole institutional and epistemological context. We explicate each model in turn as a set of lenses through which to view the accounts of student writing presented in this volume, although as we argue below, not every author necessarily starts from here or themselves subscribes to the framework.

The study skills approach has assumed that literacy is a set of atomised skills which students have to learn and which are then transferable to other contexts. The focus is on attempts to 'fix' problems with student learning, which are treated as a kind of pathology. The theory of language on which it is based emphasises surface features, grammar and spelling. Its sources lie in behavioural psychology and training programmes and it conceptualises student writing as technical and instrumental. In recent years the crudity and insensitivity of this approach has led to refinement of the meaning of 'skills' involved and attention to broader issues of learning and social context, what Lea & Street (1998) have termed the academic socialisation approach.

From the academic socialisation perspective, the task of the tutor/advisor is to inculcate students into a new 'culture', that of the academy. The focus is on student orientation to learning and interpretation of learning tasks, through conceptualisation for instance of a distinction between 'deep' and 'surface' learning. The sources of this perspective lie in social psychology, in anthropology and in constructivist education. Although more sensitive to both the student as learner and to the cultural context, the approach could nevertheless be criticised on a number of grounds: it appears to assume that the academy is a relatively homogenous culture, whose norms and practices have simply to be learnt to provide access to the whole institution. Even though at some level disciplinary and departmental difference may be acknowledged, institutional practices, including processes of change and the exercise of power, are not sufficiently theorised. Despite the fact that contextual factors in student writing are recognised as important (Hounsell 1984; Taylor 1988) this approach tends to treat writing as a transparent medium of representation and so fails to address the deep language, literacy and discourse issues involved in the institutional production and representation of meaning.

The academic literacies approach sees literacies as social practices, in ways analogous to the cross-cultural accounts of literacies provided by researchers in the New Literacy Studies (Barton & Hamilton 1998; Barton 1994; Street 1984, 1993; Heath 1984). It views student writing and learning as issues at the level of epistemology and identities rather than skill or socialisation (Lea, this volume). An academic literacies approach views the institutions in which academic practices take place as constituted in, and as sites of, discourse and power. It sees the literacy demands of the curriculum as involving a variety of communicative practices, including genres, fields, and disciplines. From the student point of view a dominant feature of academic literacy practices is the requirement to switch practices between one setting and another, to deploy a repertoire of linguistic practices appropriate to each setting, and to handle the social meanings and identities that each evokes. This emphasis on identities and social meanings draws attention to deep affective and ideological conflicts in such switching and use of the linguistic repertoire. A student's personal identity — who am 'I' — may be challenged by the forms of writing required in different disciplines, notably prescriptions about the use of impersonal and passive forms as opposed to first person and active forms, and students may feel threatened and resistant — 'this isn't me' (Lea 1994; Ivanic 1998). The recognition of this level of engagement with student writing as opposed to the more straightforward study skills and academic socialisation approaches, or the focus on text types typical of the genre approach (Berkenkotter & Huckin 1995), comes, then, from the social and ideological orientation of the 'New Literacy Studies'. Allied to this is work in Critical Discourse Analysis, Systemic Linguistics and Cultural Anthropology which has come to see student writing as constitutive and contested rather than as skills or deficits. There is a growing body of literature based upon this approach, which suggests that one explanation for student writing problems might be the gaps between academic staff expectations and student interpretations of what is involved in student writing (Cohen 1993; Lea 1994; Lea & Street 1998; Bazerman 1988; Geisler 1994).

Mystery and Transparency

None of the authors in this volume adhere rigidly to any one model — rather the models facilitate understanding of the different dimensions of both research and practice in this area. But each paper in some ways demonstrates features of the different models as they work through particular institutional writing practices — whether giving a paper, writing an essay, taking an exam or interpreting tutor feedback. All of the papers recognise the extent to which such practices relate to underlying value systems, so that academic writing is seen not simply as a 'skill' but also as an expression of cultural values and beliefs and of epistemological standpoints that often remain hidden. Different authors approach these issues in different ways, and from different vantage points. A major point in the writing process at which such issues arise is in staff commentary and feedback on students' work. Lea, by using the academic literacies approach in her own research on adult students at the Open University, opens up aspects of assignment writing and faculty feedback that otherwise may not be noticed: for instance, the merging of students' own experiences from broader social contexts with the university's requirements involves issues of epistemology and of identity not always addressed in the two dominant models — skills and socialisation. Lillis, by her reference to the 'institutional practice of mystery', emphasises the extent to which the values that underlie faculty responses are often hidden from the student, while English notes their opacity for the L2 student struggling to gain more than borderline success in her essays. The cross-cultural dimension of how differing academic cultures affect the understanding of underlying evaluative criteria also features strongly in Low & Woodburn's account of a Japanese student's presentation of his research interests in a British university context. They show how transfer from his own cultural context can affect the success and reception of such performance. Jones similarly stresses the importance of helping L2 students negotiate the expectations of the academic community while developing their own self awareness, self esteem, and self assertion within that community. Hermerschmidt 'foregrounds' the frequent lack of acknowledgement of such aspects of student background and Lillis also underlines the feeling of students that their voice and experience are not taken into account.

The gap that some of the authors document between faculty and student expectations is partly explained by the way in which the culturally embedded nature of assessment and evaluation criteria can be so taken-for-granted that terms such as 'clarity', 'structure' and 'argument' which are used to signal them are left unexplicated. Turner refers to Polanyi's notion of 'tacit knowledge' to explain such non-explication, whilst Street's discussion with colleagues of 'academic literacies' also brings out theoretical and strategic issues regarding 'explicitness'. Lillis's illustration of what might seem a paradoxical confusion surrounding the injunction 'be explicit' combined with what she terms the 'monologic space' between tutor and student, whereby students are deterred from asking for clarification on such injunctions, further emphasises the need for a sustained focus on the gap between an institutionalised metalanguage of evaluation and the understanding of its epistemological, pedagogical, linguistic, and rhetorical assumptions.

It is such a sustained focus that the present book provides. It attempts to make visible, and to provide a language of description for, the processes that underlie student writing and student/staff relations around writing in the institutional contexts of modern higher education. Through detailed case studies of the kind developed here we might begin to 'see' more of what is going on in these contexts, to understand richer dimensions of the writing process and perhaps begin to explain some of the points of contestation and misunderstanding that underlie many of the difficulties associated with writing in the University.

References

Barton, D. 1994. *Literacy: An Introduction to the Ecology of Written Language.* London: Blackwell.
Barton, D. and Hamilton, M. 1998. *Local Literacies.* London: Routledge.
Bazerman, C. 1988. *Shaping Written Knowledge: The genre and activity of the experimental article in science.* Madison, WI: University of Wisconsin Press.
Berkenkotter, C. and Huckin, T. 1995. *Genre knowledge in disciplinary communication.* Mahwah, NJ: Lawrence Erlbaum.
Creme, P. and Lea, M. 1997. *Writing at University: A guide for students.* Milton Keynes: Open University Press.
Cohen, M. 1993. "Listening to Students' Voices: What university students tell us about how they can learn", Paper to Annual Meeting of AERA: Atlanta, GA.
Geisler, C. 1994. *Academic Literacy and the Nature of Expertise.* Mahwah, NJ: Lawrence Erlbaum.
Heath, S. B. 1984. *Ways with Words.* Cambridge: CUP.
Hounsell, D. 1988. "Towards an Anatomy of Academic Discourse: Meaning and context in the undergraduate essay." In Saljö, R. (ed.), *The Written World. Studies in Literate Thought and Action.* Berlin: Springer-Verlag.
Ivanic, R. 1998. *Writing and Identity: The discoursal construction of identity in academic writing.* Amsterdam/Philadelphia: John Benjamins.
Lea, M. 1994. "I Thought I Could Write Till I Came Here: Student writing in Higher Education." In Gibbs, G (ed.), *Improving Student Learning: Theory and Practice.* Oxford: OSCD.
Lea, M. and Street, B. 1998. "Student Writing and Staff Feedback in Higher Education: An academic literacies approach." *Studies in Higher Education* Vol, 23 (2): 157–172.
Street, B. 1984. *Literacy in Theory and Practice.* Cambridge: CUP.
Street, B. (ed.) 1993. *Cross-Cultural Approaches to Literacy.* Cambridge: CUP.
Taylor, G. et al. 1988. *Literacy by Degrees.* Milton Keynes: Society for Research in Higher Education/Open University.

SECTION A

Interacting with the Institution

Section A presents a range of issues through six case study approaches. The 'students' who feature in the case studies are at different stages of their academic careers, ranging from undergraduate level to a highly experienced Japanese researcher. The issues are to do with the ways in which they, as individuals, relate to their specific academic communities and work towards achieving their goals. The key concerns are grounded partly in different experiences and beliefs about what counts as knowledge and learning and about how knowledge is transmitted and shared; they are also to do with students' assumptions about the discoursal dominance of institutional ideology. All six chapters, either explicitly or implicitly, signal the complex, interwoven nature of these two aspects from different angles and within the institutional setting.

The authors examine the perspectives of individual students and of tutors functioning within the institution, highlighting their covert and sometimes conflicting nature. The depth of the problems come to be revealed and better understood through exploring the students' perceptions of their tasks. Scrutiny of single cases shows how tutors working with students on an individual basis can aim to narrow the gap between such perceptions and those of the institution. Possible ways forward are suggested. The process of studying is examined in different ways with a view to how students as individuals might, over time, become more empowered to address their particular needs through utilizing their own expertise and experiences. The authors show how an enhanced awareness can come about when opportunities over time are created for discussing intended and interpreted meanings.

Sometimes the issues foreground non-native English speakers from different countries, whose cultural and linguistic differences are often perceived to be more explicitly defined than those of native English speakers, thus tuning into an international dimension. However, problems to do with language, especially at the discourse level, it is claimed, are not exclusive to non-native speakers. The chapters describe such problems as they might appear on the surface and argue for the need to interpret them at deeper levels, with respect to the discoursal and institutional dimensions of student writing. For instance, it is suggested that the way language is used by the dominant discourse community perpetuates the so-called 'gap' between those 'in-the-know', the 'insiders', and others, 'outsiders'. Thus questions are posed about whether the academy values and appropriately addresses individual needs; whether or not it is a shared community of 'insiders' which expects individual 'outsiders' to adapt to its established framework; whether or not it recognises that students have their own diverse values and expectations that are intrinsically derived from a range of experiences but which may not resemble those of the institution. Further questions are raised about whether the ways in which students make extensive efforts to meet institutional challenges are misdirected, with or without assistance.

Each chapter constructs the gap in distinctive ways through examining what might lie behind individual students' attempts to negotiate their learning. Hermerschmidt, in Chapter 1, focuses on students' perceptions of functioning within the institution through utilizing her own past experiences as an 'outsider' student to analyse the different perspectives of two present 'outsiders'. She foregrounds the lack of acknowledgement, by the institution, of the students' own beliefs, educational and professional experiences and expertise, and argues that learning is not just an individual act but a social practice. The students' general concerns with issues of identity and power are discussed since, she suggests, it is these that direct them towards particular approaches to their own learning. She argues that institutions have set expectations of students which inhibit them from exploring and developing their identities as learners and pursuing their academic interests in their own ways.

English, in Chapter 2, considers how damaging the effects on students can be when misunderstandings occur concerning the expectations made of them in written assignments both by the students and by the tutors, who are 'in the know', in reading students' assignments. Her case study centres on one assignment written by a Japanese Masters level student. English shows that what seems clear at surface level in the text may serve to hide the real nature of the problems. In a detailed textual analysis, she discusses several ways in which the student's essay can be interpreted, which differ from the meaning that is probably intended. She examines the assignment for different layers of conceptualization that need to be gradually penetrated in order to arrive at a fair understanding of what is written, thus arguing the case for foregrounding discourse and content organization above discrete features of language in assessing students' essays. She concludes that her approach can help student and tutor to reach an enhanced, shared awareness of the student's needs and potential.

The issues she raises are reinforced in Chapter 3 by Jones, who suggests a pre-sessional strategy to overcome the problems of the gap perceived by students, particularly in the case of non-native speakers. Jones highlights the reciprocal, enriching dimension that can be nurtured within the academic context through cultural hybridity when the needs and experiences of students from overseas are seriously explored. She speculates about how the students themselves might be encouraged to circumvent the perceived dominant discourses of their institution through negotiating their learning. Her suggestion is to consider how implementing a task-based, familiarization programme in advance of the mainstream study context might enable students to enhance their understanding of the expectations made of them and help them to reflect on their own approaches to learning. In turn, she suggests that the students' responses could inform the effectiveness of such a programme.

In Chapter 4, Low & Woodburn show how the student's voice can directly lead towards successful learning. Their case study examines the needs of a Japanese researcher preparing oral presentations of his own work in an unfamiliar cultural context. They highlight key aspects of his strategic behaviour that drive his progress by discussing what interview transcripts reveal about his perceptions of his learning. They also examine the results interpretively by comparing the draft presentation script with another presenter's script and using Grice's Co-operative Principle as a system of analysis. Cultural and epistemological tensions are revealed through the persistent efforts made by the researcher to retain his own voice and at the same time be understood by his audience. Low & Woodburn show how various levels of language use can interweave during the process of developing communicative competence.

In Chapter 5, Gay, Jones & Jones consider the perspectives of one institution through presenting the voices of two mainstream tutors teaching on an intensive, initial teacher education course. The authors acknowledge a certain inevitability of the problems that arise on such a demanding programme and how these necessarily channel tutors' expectations of the students in their written assignments. The two tutors each describe their experiences with one student. The different approaches adopted by the two students to the process of writing their assignments impact on their degree of success. One case is a success story; the other is highly problematic in terms of the student's professional development. Taken-for-granted aspects of the course are challenged by her unanticipated reactions to the demands of the written assignments. Gay et al. conclude that written assignments are a product of certain non-linguistic processes which need to be positioned centrally to avoid pathologizing some students. The student's firm view that her limited language ability was at the heart of the problem prevented her from understanding and overcoming her weaknesses as perceived by her tutors.

In the last chapter of this section, Chapter 6, Lea takes an integrative perspective on these issues. She examines how mature students understand their studies in a distance learning setting and in relation to the institution's practices. She discusses two contrasting approaches, a 'reformulation' approach, where the students attempt to replicate the authority of the texts they read, and a 'challenge' approach, where the students attempt to engage dialogically with their reading by situating it within a broader framework, one that embraces their outside experiences and understandings. Feedback from their tutors, whose perceptions of assignments may contrast sharply with those of their students, leads her to conclude that the interaction between the learning texts, academic literacy practices and the broader and social contexts of learning is essential to understanding students' work.

Section A examines a variety of shared contexts of study, where the issues raised are specific to those contexts. Nevertheless, the common factor becomes clear: that by exploring individual perceptions of institutional learning in depth, the learning process as a whole provides rewarding insights and an enriched experience for all those involved. These signal pathways towards a more general in-depth examination of the issues suggesting that what has up till now been complacently ignored needs to be given a much more central focus.

CHAPTER 1

Foregrounding Background in Academic Learning

Monika Hermerschmidt

Introduction

Institutions of education aim to provide equal opportunities for the development of all students. Teachers and lecturers aim to treat students with respect, regardless of whether they are women or men, regardless of whether they are black or white, regardless of whether they do or do not worship a divine authority, regardless of whether they need special aids to do what the majority of students can do with ease, regardless of the personal circumstances of students. However,

> applied linguistic research has amply demonstrated (that) face to face interaction often perpetrates quite subtle forms of unintended bias and discrimination:
> it is important to avoid these in applied linguistics teaching (BAAL 1994: 6).

Classroom encounters are "unequal encounters" (Gumperz 1982) and face to face interaction in and outside of classrooms in educational institutions may, albeit unconsciously, be a source of inequality. Therefore, there appears to be a need to explore the relationship between the teaching practices that feel natural and familiar to teachers and lecturers and the practices that students have learned and that feel natural and familiar to them.

The chapter reports on research I have undertaken into how students on MA in Applied Linguistics programmes in some British universities conceptualise language and construct their identities and the institutional practices they encounter in their learning. A key research interest has been to explore how the expectations that are set up in institutions of higher education in Britain relate to the cultural processes and the educational and professional experience that students bring to their learning.

The study has grown out of my experience a few years ago of learning on an MA in English Language Teaching programme in a multi-cultural group in a

British university. As a former MA student, and currently still a student, I know how incompetent we feel when we struggle to get our writing done. There is a sense of not knowing how to say what we want to say. As a research student, however, my identity keeps shifting from being an insider to being an outsider. For my research project, I went back to observe classes on MA programmes, to conduct interviews with students, now being an outsider in the group of MA students. I do research "on" the group, and in my analysis, I can distance myself from being an MA student, and I use my own experience as a research tool.

The aim in the research was to understand more of the complexity of the relationship between language, identity and learning. As Hewitt (1992) put it, "that language and identity are frequently linked is commonly acknowledged but the depth and breadth of this linkage has hardly been recognised or tapped". My aim was to gain insight into learning as a social practice, and to help understand some aspects of the complex relationship between language and identity.

Complex Identities and Multiple Discourses

Entering higher education at undergraduate or postgraduate level is a step into institutions that have set expectations which have to be met by those coming in. Recent studies into academic learning (Ivanic 1992, 1997; Lea 1994, 1996; Lea & Street 1997; Mitchell 1994; Zamel 1995) have shown that there appears to be a gap between students' expectations and the expectations of educational institutions. Institutional practices construct identities for learners which may conflict with how students perceive their self as views of learning are contested and closely bound up with contested views of the role of language in education.

I want to suggest that there is a relationship between students' views of language and their views of what they can achieve on their courses. I want to argue that concepts of language, and the assumptions underlying those, need to be made explicit, as the concepts of language that students bring to their learning seem to affect the expectations they have about what it is they want to achieve. In other words, the views that individual students and institutions have about language constrain and limit, or enhance and extend, the learning that is going on.

The students I am studying are professionals; they are teachers. They know how to manage a classroom; but on their courses they are being assessed as students. These students think of themselves as proficient speakers of English, having taught English, and English being their field of study. But on their course what they say and write is being judged by the standards of the institution. These students are insiders who have been within educational institutions as learners, teachers, and administrators for most of their lives. But they are outsiders and newcomers to the institution they have come to; they are outsiders and newcomers to its culture and to its ways. The identity of these students is complex. However, in educational institutions students tend to get seen as a "bunch of students", and the experiences that students bring to their learning tend to be perceived as cultural "background".

The approach that I have taken is based on the following assumptions regarding language and learning and their link to identity and power. Firstly, learning is not just an individual act but a social practice. I explore views of learning and language from a "new literacy studies" perspective (Street 1984, 1995; Lea & Street 1997). According to Lea and Street (1997), institutional practices need to be understood as ways of doing that are situated in their social and cultural histories. Secondly, power operates at the level of discourse; therefore, views of language and learning are closely bound up with issues of power and identity. The site where the learning encounter takes place in classrooms, or through academic writing, is the site where identities get constructed. According to Foucault (1980), power is not monolithic. Individuals "are not only its inert or consenting target; they are always also the elements of its articulation" (p98). That is to say that learning encounters and identities are infused with and articulate the power relations of these sites, and they also construct these sites as sets of complex social relations. Thirdly, the discourse is based on the constructivist notion that social reality and social identity are constructions rather than "reality" or the "truth".

In this research I have chosen an ethnographic approach as it resists, although it cannot entirely avoid, preconceived ideas about what will be discovered by starting from field observation in the broadest sense, and narrowing down the focus of description and interpretation as data analysis and data collection proceed. The research focus emerged from the data. I have undertaken a substantial amount of classroom observation, and have collected a corpus of interview data with 12 students on MA programmes in the field of Applied Linguistics in two universities in London. At the time of interviewing, I was a student in one of them. I was sensitive to my status as a student, but also to the interviewees' status as students who were still being assessed on their courses. In my data analysis I address the implications of my shifting identities from being one of the group to pursuing my research agenda and constructing knowledge about the group as this research went on, and the ways in which this has facilitated but also limited this study. I will take that point up briefly at the end of this paper.

Two major strands of data analysis have emerged so far. One line of analysis, which I am going to illustrate in the next section, draws on the model that Lea and Street (1997) have developed of three approaches to student writing. According to Lea and Street, there are three main perspectives on student writing: the study skills approach, the academic socialisation model, and the academic literacies approach. With a *study skills approach* to writing, students are seen as needing the grammar, the spelling, and the skills to get their writing done. With an *academic socialisation approach,* institutional practices are seen as being monolithic with set rules and criteria that students need to learn if they want to get access to the academic discourse.

With an *academic literacies approach,* practices are seen as ways of doing, that are closely bound up with beliefs about how we know about the world; the literacy practices of the academy are seen as closely bound up with authority and power, and with our sense of identity and self. I do not suggest that these approaches to language are mutually exclusive. As Lea and Street (1998) put it,

> each model successively encapsulates the other, so that the academic socialisation perspective takes account of study skills but includes them in the broader context of the acculturation process and likewise the academic literacies approach encapsulates the academic socialisation model, building on the insights developed there as well as the study skills view. The academic literacies model, then, incorporates both of the other models into a more encompassing understanding of the nature of student writing within institutional practices, power relations and identities. (1998: 158)

All three perspectives can and, in fact, do co-exist and provide insights into staff and student interpretations of the nature of academic literacy practices.

Another line of data analysis draws on critical discourse analysis (Fairclough 1989, 1992) looking into questions of how students construct themselves and their day-to-day reality and how they are being constructed by educational institutions. As Lincoln and Guba (1985) pointed out, "data are the *constructions* offered by or in the sources; data analysis leads to a *reconstruction* of those constructions" (p. 332). This line of analysis will include an examination of the shifting power relations between interviewees and interviewer. Using the analytical categories of modality, topic control and control of agendas (Fairclough 1992), the analysis will show how meanings got mutually constructed in the interviews and that social phenomena derive their meanings from how they get defined by participants in particular social events.

Analysis and Findings

To illustrate that discourses shift and compete as students try to give meaning to institutional and to their own approaches to learning and writing, I am going to make reference to four interviews with two students:

Harry, a native speaker of English, a teacher of English who prior to being an MA student was a teacher of EFL, working in Spain and other European countries, and

Alison, a non-native speaker of English, an English language teacher in a secondary school in her home country Botswana.

I will also draw on my classroom observations. In my analysis, I apply the model of how to approach and understand issues of student learning in higher education that Lea and Street (1997) have developed. I am extending this model to include student speaking, in order to explore the different discourses that are available to students and upon which they draw in their interviews. Below I have used quotes from the interviews to show how the way students represent their learning experience can be explicated using Lea and Street's model.

"in an appropriate time and way"

The *study skills* approach to student writing they suggest is based on a model of language that emphasises grammar and spelling, and breaks language learning and language use into sets of oral and written skills that need to be mastered. Being an MA student, I had observed that some students were silent while others were talking a lot. I had also observed that students were trying to get their point across in an appropriate time and way. The preoccupation with trying to make a point "accurately" and in an "appropriate time and way", often having the result of not making the point at all, is closely linked to a theory of language that highlights the linguistic and communicative competence of speakers from a narrow technical perspective. This view is based on the assumption that all individual speakers acquire and use language in the same way, and language teaching is thus geared towards students attaining the varieties of competence they need to acquire the right way of writing and speaking. As a result, students who do not get their essays "right" get constructed as having a language problem. Students who, before they speak, think about how they are going to say what they want to say construct themselves, or get constructed, as being linguistically incompetent with reference to what is judged to be the norm. Dubin

(1989), however, suggests that communicative competence has come to have multiple meanings, and that this narrow perspective contrasts with a broader social view on communicative competence. Alison observed:

> ...Then maybe if they maybe come across a situation where somebody makes a grammatical error, they wouldn't maybe think that it's a way of totally disregarding that person as somebody who is not qualified to be on a course such as this, but just see it like something that can happen to anybody, because even people who are native speakers, they have their own weaknesses, and I think when it comes to maybe writing, you realise that there can be second language speakers who can write better than native speakers. (Alison, 2nd interview)

The view on writing, Alison is expressing here, is skills based. Writing is a skill that some students master better than others. At the same time, she observes and disapproves of the fact that overall competence of going through a Master's course is being questioned by some students on the basis of grammatical errors. It appears that Alison adopts a broad social perspective on communicative competence. In her view communicative competence is not about students learning single elements of communicative behaviour, but about students being competent to communicate their learning.

"it's a cultural thing"

The *academic socialisation* model of writing is based on the assumption that students need and want to learn what the norms and conventions are in the new academic culture they have come to. "Access" is a key notion in the academic socialisation model, assuming that academic literacy practices are static, fixed, and "out there" for students to learn and to adjust to. Criteria such as "originality of thought", "synthesis of views", "reference to relevant literature" and "argument" give labels to what is expected of student coursework to be judged as excellent and "appropriate".

Harry referred in his interview to the unease of a fellow student when she realised that, when she did contribute something, people were not paying any attention to what she was saying:

> It might be to do with the sort of expected discourse of contribution, as well. And if someone is, in the way they speak isn't expressing their ideas in the way that you are sort of expected to, ...then it might be that... people are not so sure about it... What's going on, ehm, I suppose, again, it's a cultural thing and what, the schema that if you have an English native speaker lecturer, a male white lecturer, and I'm a male white English speaking teacher, we are

> going to, we share a lot more, and we have both been to English universities, and we've both sort of been in English language teaching, so we know, you know, ... There is just some expectation of what to contribute, how to contribute... If somebody comes from outside that, has to learn that, I think. So, maybe, before they have learned it, it's possible that, you know, the person seems to be missing the point. (Harry, 2nd interview)

To Harry it is a "cultural thing". For him culture is an explanation for what he sees as somebody unsuccessfully trying to contribute to what was going on in class, yet "missing the point". As Harry said, there is some "expectation of what to contribute, how to contribute", and somebody who comes from outside the "culture" has to learn what is expected. Harry constructs the academic culture as given, as natural, as neutral and as coming with set rules that students need to learn if they want to belong to the academic world. He indicates how such "culture" seems natural to the subgroups of male, white English students, but he fails to realise that "if somebody comes from outside that, (and) has to learn that", thus albeit implicitly, those practices are not at all neutral, or given.

As Street (1991) has argued, "culture is an active process of meaning making and contest over definition, including its own definition" (p25). That is to say, in the context of this study, the definitions, norms, and categories we live by have been created by those having authority to define rules and guidelines so as to know who is in and who is out, who conforms and who does not, consciously or unconsciously. This may include both lecturers and students themselves as they internalise and validate rules. I asked Harry in the interview, whether it had happened to him that people were not paying attention when *he* was making a contribution. Harry said:

> Hmm, yeah, certainly, I mean, I have said things which I have realised I have missed the point completely... ...it's just, especially when you are making a point, when you are trying to make a point so simply, and it's quite a specialised technique, thinking about it, being able to make a snappy contribution in a sort of semi-lecture situation. (Harry, 2nd interview)

Students come to learn how to enter academic debates, but they conceptualise categories such as "contribution" in different ways: as "a sort of expected discourse of contribution", as "quite a specialised technique... being able to make a snappy contribution in a semi-lecture situation", as *being heard in class*, or as *being heard*, as a way of bringing one's own voice and authority into the argument. Even Harry as a "male white English speaking teacher" who has been to English universities does not get it "right" all the time. When Harry described what he does in his writing, he said:

...The switching into academic mode in writing, I find it quite natural;
but he also said:

> ... When I'm in a class, ...and I'm contributing, that isn't really me, I don't, I sort of almost feel that I switch into another way of being. (Harry, 2nd interview)

Harry "switches" into academic mode in writing, it seems, more confidently than he does when contributing in class, when he feels "that isn't really me". As a male white English student he has been inculcated into the ways of essay writing in English schools and universities and, as a result, they feel "quite natural" to him. He feels at home with the criteria that are expected for written work to be judged as excellent. But in a classroom situation, although he is familiar with the technique of making a "snappy contribution in a sort of semi-lecture situation", he feels he has to "switch into another way of being", too. He does not know how the talk is supposed to be going. He feels he is forced to present himself as if he was not himself:

> Harry: There is two models, as far as I see it, of teaching: one is that you are imparting knowledge, and one is that you are allowing students to discover things for themselves, or to make whatever knowledge that is relevant to them in this situation. And I think the idea of contributing is based on this, but I think it's such a half-hearted approach here... ...because in the end we'll be assessed on how much you've learned, yeah? You'd have to go *much* (stressed!) further in the direction of contribution... they pay lip-service to contributing, in the end they have lecture notes, which is what they want to get through, want to give to you, so I don't, so there is just not the possibility for, to bring things to the course, I mean.
> MH: Why do you think it is done only half-heartedly?
> Harry: Only half-heartedly. I think it's possibly an institutional thing.
> (Harry, 2nd interview)

Harry seems to have constructed institutional practices as an "institutional thing". As with "culture", he has placed the institution in a category that he sees as given. He has constructed institutional *processes* as being *things*, fixed and static. But neither in the way Harry has constructed the institution as a fixed "thing" nor in the way lecturers seem to only "half-heartedly" invite students to contribute, is there a sense of writing and of learning as being sites of knowledge making, where the experience of students can be valued and made part of the learning that is going on. Norms seem to have a gatekeeping and uniforming function. Fairclough (1992) has discussed "the appropriacy of appropriateness", addressing issues of power as underlying the norms we are expected to comply with. Institutional practices need to be conceptualised at the level of procedures that are in place to keep the gates where they are, and at the level of how particular subgroups of students struggle to demystify these procedures in order to belong to the academic community. It appears that institutional hegemony works beyond even the favoured subgroups of male white English students.

"such that I get a balanced idea"

With an *academic literacies* approach to learning, institutional practices are conceptualised as ways of doing, that are closely bound up with beliefs about *how* we know about the world. According to Gee (1990), "Discourses" need to be understood as ways of believing, behaving, and valuing that include not only early childhood experiences but also those of our chosen field(s) of interest. Discourses in different fields of study represent different ways of understanding. In her second interview, Alison refers to a situation in one of her classes when she tried to raise an issue:

> I was talking about the fact that in our universities we use English to teach Sitswana, you know, I was expecting us to maybe explore the topic more, I mean such that I get a balanced idea of maybe the argument for that, you know, and if it's something like that maybe somebody could have given me a point of view that would make me appreciate the situation as it is, or maybe we could have sort of debated it as a class, and maybe come up with something sound out of it... (Alison, 2nd interview)

Like Harry, Alison did not get what she wanted; she wanted her question to be explored, to be taken further; she wanted an opportunity to get to know different points of view and where they were coming from. Alison wanted to find out about different ways of understanding and interpreting the issue she had raised. Instead the lecture went on. Alison said in her interview about this incident:

> ...You end up telling yourself that everytime I have to say something no notice is taken of what I have to say, or people can afford to just say 'yes' and that is it. (Alison, 2nd interview)

With her question about the use of English to teach Sitswana in universities in her home country, Alison was trying to expand on the topic of the lecture, thereby putting something on the agenda that had not been on the lecturer's agenda. But the lecturer did not open up her agenda to Alison's question. She went on delivering the knowledge she wanted to impart to the students, making use of her social authority and institutional power, ignoring the weight and significance of Alison's question in *Alison's* learning agenda. Her agenda thus would be more in keeping with Street (1996) who has argued that the issue of how power can be transformed

> involves a transformation from the disciplinary and coercive forms it has taken on in modern society, so that it works instead in a positive way to bring out human potential and to harness creative energy (p13)

than with the position adopted by the lecturer in this case. When students have their experience and their questions not taken up, when institutional knowledge is being privileged over students' knowledge, students may have a sense of being "deprofessionalised" as Ivanic (1992) has found in her study of mature students. What is at stake for students is their self, their self as professionals, who want to bring into the debate what they know and take away some broader view to reflect on.

Applying the academic literacies approach to my own practice and writing, and taking up a point I made earlier about the implications of my shifting identities in this research from being one of the group to pursuing my research agenda as someone who is no longer an MA student, I would like to end this paper on a reflective note about my interviewing. I asked every student at the end of their interviews about what they thought their role had been in this research, and about my coming to their classes, hanging around and doing interviews. Here is what Harry said:

> Harry: My role, I don't think it's any more than just provide data, I must say. And I have been intrigued, I was intrigued by your coming on at first. I think that's when you got on to say you are writing about things, I was intrigued to know sort of what was your angle on the classroom. I suppose in some ways it's almost a bit disappointing that I am the provider of data (Hmm.), and I realise that you don't really want to sort of express too much of what you feel is going on, but I'd find that quite interesting as well.
>
> MH: Hmm. So what you are saying here, if I don't misinterpret it, you would like to get to know more about what I am thinking about all this (Yes.), if you had the chance to interview me.
>
> Harry: Hmm, or just to, to have a dialogue, yeah. (Harry, 2nd interview)

My being concerned about giving space, and time, and voice to the MA students during the interviews, about listening to what they had to say, seems to have prevented me from hearing that Harry had said he thought it would be interesting to hear my angle. On reflection, I would now. I did not then. At the time of interviewing I had some distance to being an MA student, I did not have enough distance to critically reflect on my own research practice. I did not yet see clearly enough that my assumptions about learning, which were well in place long before I started my research, have shaped and driven my observations, my questions, and the design of this study and that I could have safely shared my angle with the students as there is no "neutral" research frame. I could have shared my assumptions with the interviewees and their critical reflection could have added valuable data to this project.

Conclusion

I have argued that classrooms in academic institutions and academic writing are sites where identities get constructed and where knowledge is contested, and that learning encounters are infused with and construct power relations of these sites. I have applied Lea and Street's three models of student academic writing to my data on student's perceptions of their contributions to academic discourse in MA in Applied Linguistics classrooms. The model can help us to understand how teachers and students evaluate what is going on in these classrooms and in their writing on the basis of their learned norms. Using Lea and Street's academic literacies approach to writing as a lens through which to view what is going on in academic learning helps to conceptualise language in education in ways that bring issues of identity and power to the foreground, and to acknowledge that power relations are contested. Seeing difference as a resource in academic learning can provoke thought and generate reflection on common classroom practices and challenge simplistic assumptions about the nature of learning. Students who perceive their experience as not being valued might resign from the game rather than engage in and transform their learning as active participants.

References

BAAL. 1994. "Recommendations on Good Practice in Applied Linguistics." British Association for Applied Linguistics.

Dubin, F. 1989. "Situating Literacy Within Traditions of Communicative Competence." *Applied Linguistics* Vol. 10 (2): 171–181.

Fairclough, N. (ed.). 1992. *Critical Language Awareness*. London and New York: Longman.

Fairclough, N. 1992. "The Appropriacy of 'Appropriateness.'" In Fairclough, N. (ed.), *Critical Language Awareness*. London and New York: Longman.

Foucault, M. 1980. *Power/Knowledge: Selected Interviews and Other Writings 1972–77.* Brighton: Harvester.

Gee, J. 1990. *Social Linguistics and Literacies. Ideology in Discourse.* London: Taylor and Francis. (Second edition 1996).

Guba, E. and Lincoln, Y. 1985. *Naturalistic Inquiry.* Chicago: Sage Publications.

Gumperz, J. (ed.). 1982. *Language and Social Identity.* Cambridge: Cambridge University Press.

Hewitt, R. 1992. "Language, Youth and the Destabilisation of Ethnicity." Social Science Research Unit, Institute of Education, University of London.

Ivanic, R. 1992. "I is for Interpersonal: the Discoursal Construction of Writer Identities and the Teaching of Writing." Paper at Domains of Literacy Conference, U.L.I.E.

Ivanic, R. 1997. *Writing and Identity. The discoursal construction of identity in academic writing.* Amsterdam/Philadelphia: John Benjamins.

Lea, M. 1994. "I Thought I Could Write Till I Came Here: Student writing In Higher Education." In Gibbs, G (ed.), *Improving Student learning: Theory and practice.* Oxford: OSCD.

Lea, M. 1996. "Staff Feedback and Student Writing: Developing ways of knowing in Higher Education." Paper to Annual Meeting of AERA: New York.

Lea, M. and Street, B. V. 1997. *Student Writing and Staff Feedback in Higher Education: an Academic Literacies Approach.* Swindon: Economic and Social Research Council.

Lea, M. and Street, B. V. 1998. "Student Writing in Higher Education: an Academic Literacies Approach". In *Studies in Higher Education* Vol. 23 (2): 157–172.

Mitchell, S. 1994. *The Teaching and Learning of Argument in Sixth Forms and Higher Education.* Final Report University of Hull: Centre for Studies in Rhetoric.

Street, B. V. 1984. *Literacy in Theory and Practice.* Cambridge: CUP.

Street, B. V. 1991. "Culture is a Verb: Anthropological aspects of language and cultural process". Keynote Address to BAAL Annual Conference on Language and Culture.

Street, B. V. 1995. "Academic Literacies." In Baker, D., Fox, C. and Clay, J. (eds), *Challenging Ways of Knowing in Maths, Science and English.* Brighton/Philadelphia: Falmer Press.

Street, B. V. 1996. "Literacy and Power?" *Open Letter* Vol. 6 (2).

Zamel, V. 1995. "Strangers in Academia: The experience of faculty and ESL students across the curriculum." Centre for Culture and Community Studies Vol. 46 (4).

CHAPTER 2

What Do Students Really Say In Their Essays?
Towards a descriptive framework for analysing student writing

Fiona English

Introduction

My interest in this issue was originally aroused when I was working with a Japanese student doing a Masters degree in History. She could not understand why she was getting such consistently low grades in her coursework essays pointing out that she had read around the topics and had provided a considerable amount of information in responding to the essay questions set, including reference to the information given in lectures. Her use of English was largely accurate and her writing generally coherent. However, despite all of this she remained a border-line case.

All students, whether 'overseas' or 'home' status have to acquire new discourses in order to fit into the academic community. Mitchell (1994) describes the process of students moving from 'A' level to degree studies as being one of ' both acquiring a broader knowledge base and an increasingly specialised way of dealing with that knowledge.' (p. 195) The difference between an 'A' level student and a third year undergraduate is 'not so much an increased ability to argue [...] so much as an increased expertise in the discourse and disciplinary culture.' (p. 196)

Composition, rhetoric and argumentation have traditionally played a key role in Western education,[1] and argumentation in particular is valued highly for its associations with the concept of logical thinking, proofs and refutations. Swales (1990) discusses this at some length in his book 'Genre Analysis', tracing the origins of such a methodology to eighteenth century scientific discourse. But, while in the past students were explicitly taught about how to compose ideas in writing, such training is largely implicit today. Even where it is made explicit, it tends to take the form of skills training, where students are 'introduced' to the conventions and forms of so-called academic style in the expectation that they will then be able to produce appropriate written texts.[2] The problem is, however, that this approach can lead students to the conclusion that so long as they apply these conventions and styles, like some kind of template, they will be fulfilling the expectations of their readers. What is ignored is the need for students not simply to 'know' the conventions but rather begin to understand how these styles and conventions can be used to represent and construct students' own meanings.[3]

My work seeks to explore this idea of meaning making in the context of student writing in order to investigate what it is that students do in their essays to earn themselves praise or otherwise for their finished work. This study, which focuses on the work of a Japanese student, examines what could be called a gap between what the student feels is valuable and what is, in fact, valued by her reader and, by implication, the university institution. The methodological background to my work stems from the approach used in a UK wide project (Gorman et al. 1988, 1991), which analysed the discourse of school pupils' texts. My present involvement with international students in British Higher Education provides the practical context and the analysis I apply owes much to kind of close text analysis associated with functional linguistics (e.g. Halliday & Hasan 1976; Kress & Hodge 1983; Halliday 1985).

Context of the Study

In recent years there has been a rapid increase in the number of overseas students following degree programmes in the UK which has meant that Institutions are having to deal with a wide range of difficulties encountered by students from vastly different linguistic and cultural backgrounds.[4] This has, of course, been paralleled by a general expansion in university education in Britain and a widening of the catchment population which brings its own challenges to the 'received' expectations of academic culture. In this volume, Lillis discusses the experiences of 'non-traditional' university students and the mismatch between their understandings and those of their tutors. So, if 'home' students, who have the benefit of English language competence and of a broadly shared cultural and educational background, encounter difficulties in acquiring the 'ground rules' (Sheeran & Barnes 1991) then how much worse that experience must be for 'overseas' students who are also operating in a completely different language.

One reason why it is interesting to look at the work of Japanese students is that their essays are often singled out for criticism and much comment is made on the lack of argument or evaluation. To the British university tutor Japanese essays, particularly in the social sciences, often seem bland and unfocused with little or no analysis. In fact, these writers often appear to be 'absent' from their essays in the sense that there is no identifiable writer's 'voice' providing commentary or mediation. Departmental tutors often express a sense of unease about these students, unsure of where the problem lies. Their questions revolve around whether the unsatisfactory essay can be attributed to poor academic acumen, failure to understand the course content or, since they are international students, poor use of English. They often opt for the last and advise these students to take 'English language' classes in the hope that something can be done to sort the problem out.

Of course, these students do experience problems relating to their competence in English — but in its broadest sense where language proficiency interplays with discourse awareness, academic culture, academic literacy and, inevitably, course content itself. One of the main difficulties is in identifying the different elements that influence a student's overall performance. It is easy to attribute problems to general categories such as cultural background, or make stereotypical statements such as 'the Japanese never argue'. It is easy to tell students to take English classes or 'buy a grammar book' as more than one student has had written at the end of an essay. But without having a clear picture of the exact nature of the problem it is impossible to provide the information that the student really needs to understand what is going wrong.

The Study

One way of providing elucidation for the teacher and, of course, for the student concerned is described in the small study here which suggests a methodology that helps to identify some of those features of performance that might be contributing to the lack of success. The process can be very useful not only in locating some of the less obvious problems but also in revealing to the student what exactly is going on in the text, what meanings their writing is conveying and in what ways these can be interpreted or misinterpreted by the reader. Rather than focusing on what the text does not do, the emphasis is placed on what the text actually does.

My approach attempts to be descriptive in that I examine the text closely in order to ascertain what the writer is actually doing with her 'words', how the text is constructed in terms of its cohesive and thematic nature and how, therefore, it can be interpreted. By talking through the analysis during follow up tutorial it is possible to help the student writer recognise what kind of meanings the text conveys. This text-oriented approach highlights the role of language in the representation of meanings and can lead to valuable discussion about how students expect their 'words' to convey the meanings they wish to represent. It can also reveal the extent to which students writing in a foreign language transfer the function values of their own grammars and discourse management of their own rhetoric to, in this case, English.

The Student

The student involved in this study is following an undergraduate degree programme in Russian and East European Politics and History. She had spent four years in Britain firstly studying, successfully, for 'A' levels and subsequently undertaking a BA programme. She failed her first year university exams and her Department were concerned that it was her language skills which were letting her down. At their suggestion she decided to join an in-sessional English for Academic Purposes (EAP) programme while preparing to resit her exams the following year. Her level of English, as calculated by the IELTS test was 7 overall which is unconditionally acceptable for entry to most British universities, and indeed her use of English is largely accurate and fluent.

This student was having great difficulty in understanding how she had failed to produce what was expected of her. It emerged during the EAP programme that, despite all the comments from her Departmental tutors regarding the need for analysis, for her opinion, for reference to other sources, she still could not see how things were going so wrong.

She is certainly not unique among Japanese students and comments found at the end of her coursework essays are reflected in those on many Japanese student essays. These include observations such as:

"You don't give any evidence to show that ...";

"You were right to say that ... but you don't show how they were supposed to work.";

"You do not really answer the part of the question dealing with 'Why are there so few...";

"Too broad and not deep enough!"

I do not intend to enter discussion here on cultural differences. This is, of course, a crucial element in the study of 'writing across languages' (Connor & Kaplan 1987), but the focus of this paper is otherwise.

The Investigation

The text under discussion is a first year BA History course essay written at an early stage in the student's university career.

The essay is analysed under two main categories adapted from those employed in the national research project (Gorman et al. 1988, 1991) mentioned above. In that survey, analytic assessment schemes were devised based on the identification of criteria which seemed to have influenced the way in which experienced teachers holistically assessed pupil's writing. The aim was to investigate what it was about a text that was valued or not, so that the findings could be fed back into the school curriculum. The aim of my research is similar in that I seek to explore how the essay attracted the kinds of comment it received and how these comments can be translated into a form that the student can understand. In this study I focus on:

Content Organisation — relating to how the writer represents the materials involved. Here the attention is on the selection of ideas and information and on the writer's commentary or voice.

Discourse Organisation — relating to the management of ideas and the development of the argument. Here the focus is on cohesive relations, sequencing, paragraph development, and the overall structure of the text.

The essay question was: *Assess the respective weight of reasons for the Emancipation Edict of 1861.*[5]

The tutor's comment at the end of the essay is lengthy and detailed so I will only present the overview comment here. Comments made by the Departmental tutors can provide the kind of impressionistic evaluation which was employed in the school language surveys referred to above (Gorman et al. 1988, 1991). This information is an essential part of the process of investigation, since it provides a useful reference point. Close scrutiny of these comments and discussion with the student can reveal much about the gap between what the tutor wants and what the student understands by it.[6]

> What you have written is good and clearly expressed for the most part. You succeed in *listing* many of the factors that are often cited for the Emancipation of the serfs in 1861, and in presenting a good selection of information. However, your paper lacks a clearly stated thesis and argument. You need to

provide an introductory paragraph where you introduce and set out your argument — i.e. why *you think* serfs were emancipated. You should then present information and evidence supporting and developing your argument, as well as consider and rebut opposing arguments. The paper should then end with a concluding paragraph where you summarise why *you* think serfs were emancipated in 1861.

Your first and last paragraphs are good paragraphs in themselves but they do not introduce or conclude the paper. The topic of the paper was "*Assess* the respective weight of reasons..." Your paper "*Lists*... reasons"

On reading this student's essay myself, I too felt it lacked 'analysis', 'evaluation' and 'comment', as, indeed, did all her essays up to the time she joined us. What the student appeared to have been producing were *accounts of* rather than *accounts for* the events which constituted the focus of the questions. Despite the direct nature of the remarks from her tutor and meetings subsequently held, the student was still unable to produce the higher scoring essays she anticipated and still failed to understand why. This led me to look for a way to demonstrate firstly to myself and then to the student what was really going on in her essays.

The methodology illustrated below proved to be a very useful way of analysing the essay since it focused attention on what was actually 'said' and how it could be interpreted. By breaking it down into basic components it became possible to see problems that might otherwise have remained hidden, on a superficial reading, beneath the template type surface that I mentioned above.

Analysis

I shall provide two extracts from the essay to illustrate how such close analysis of the text can provide insights into the precise nature of the writing that the student is producing. Three forms of analysis are applied to the text. The first deals with the issue of topic and comment,[7] which is useful when considering how the student has managed both the content and the discourse. The second looks at the cohesive relationships within the text to see whether there is anything there that might contribute to confusion or misinterpretation by the reader. The third form of analysis investigates the propositions that can be derived from the text itself. In other words, it draws out the possible interpretations that can be made of what the writer has written. Each analysis is followed by a brief discussion which assesses the findings and gives an idea of the kind of discussion that can be held with the student during a tutorial session. The full text of the essay is appended.

The first stage was to type out the essay for myself in order to render it flexible for my own analytical procedures. This in itself is a valuable exercise in that it focuses the attention on what exactly is being said rather than, as is common, what the reader reads as being said. It will, perhaps, become clearer later on what I mean by this.

The next stage was to identify topics and comments/statements to see how the ideas were developed within each paragraph and then ultimately through the essay as a whole. This proved very useful in seeing how the student had managed the content, including quotations and references to other sources. It also helped to reveal the cohesive relationships in the text and the logical relationship between the ideas. Finally, I broke the text down into propositions and comments to see what exactly the student was saying about each topic and if there were more than one reading available.

The analytical stages are numbered (i) to (iii) and the layout is designed to highlight the different aspects being investigated. The key below should help to distinguish the different aspects of the text.

KEY	
Bold type	= topic
<u>Underlined</u>	= comment
*	= cohesive device (e.g. reference markers, discourse markers[8])
(usage)	= description of the actual usage of a chosen co-ordinator
(interpretation)	= reader's possible interpretation

<u>Extract 1</u>

'Serfdom was a fundamental element of Russia's social and political structure until the day of its abolition. While serfdom in Western Europe is associated with the Middle Ages, and the absence of centralised political authority, it existed in large areas of Eastern Europe until well into the nineteenth century with the centralised authority.'

Close examination of this first extract, which is the opening paragraph of the essay, demonstrates how descriptive analysis can provide explicit information about the cohesive nature of the student's text as well as aspects of organisation, focus of content and response to the assignment set. The opening paragraph of a British university essay is, of course, of great importance since it sets the tone for the whole text. It has to be both general and relevant in order to focus the reader on the issues in hand.

A first reading of this paragraph gives the impression that it is well written, logical and relevant. Indeed, it was awarded a tick by its 'official' reader. Closer analysis reveals, however, faults in logic which result from poor referencing and weaknesses in paragraph development. This is the kind of instance that I referred to earlier where the reader makes the logic fit despite faulty cohesion.

(i) <u>TOPIC AND COMMENT</u>
In this stage of the analysis I wanted to focus on the topic, the comment and certain cohesive devices, particularly reference and discourse markers, employed.

1) **Serfdom** was <u>a fundamental element of Russia's social and political structure until* the* day of its* abolition.</u>

2) While* **serfdom in western Europe** <u>is associated with the middle ages,</u>
and* <u>the absence of centralised political authority,</u>
it * <u>existed in large areas of Eastern Europe</u>
until* <u>well into the nineteenth century with* the centralised authority</u>.

(ii) <u>COHESIVE RELATIONSHIPS</u>
This is closely linked to the first stage and the logical relationship between the ideas is considered.

<u>Reference</u> –   1) its = serfdom('s)
                2) it = serfdom in Western Europe

<u>Co-ordination</u> –   1) until + event as time (non finite clause)
                    2) while (concessive — linking two finite clauses)
                    2) and (additive — linking two nominal groups)
                    2) until + time and circumstance (non finite clause)
                    2) with + nominal group

(iii) <u>PROPOSITIONS</u>
This stage focuses on the content — what is being said — and provides information on the way in which ideas are developed.

Serfdom
was a fundamental element in Russia's social and political structure
was abolished

Serfdom in Western Europe
is associated with the Middle Ages
is associated with the absence of centralised political authority
existed in large areas of Eastern Europe

existed in Eastern Europe until well into the 19th century
existed with the centralised authority

Discussion

This paragraph opens with a statement which makes implicit rather than explicit reference to the essay question ('serfdom' instead of 'emancipation'; 'until abolition' instead of 'Edict of 1861'). The two main propositions are logically co-ordinated by the conjunction 'until'. This statement seems both relevant and appropriate to the genre.

The second sentence, however, is a different matter. It suffers on two counts: (1) management of the content, and (2) management of the discourse.

(1) The opening statement to this paragraph anticipates an elaboration of the themes involved; some kind of explanation about how serfdom had been fundamental in the social and political structure of Russia, for instance. However, the second sentence introduces instead three *new* themes — that of the difference between Western and Eastern Europe, the sub-theme of the different historical contexts and the theme of centralised or non-centralised authority, none of which seem directly related either to the opening sentence or to the essay task set. The paragraph ultimately lacks unity and it is difficult to see which way the writer is planning to go.

(2) This second sentence also suffers as a result of cohesive weakness. Although an experienced reader will infer coherence, the logical organisation is ambiguous as follows.

The problem lies *either* in the use of 'it' in the second clause (referring as it does to the whole noun phrase 'serfdom in Western Europe' and therefore not appropriate to the completion of the second clause — 'Eastern Europe') *or* in the use of the noun phrase 'serfdom in Western Europe' instead of simply 'serfdom'. It could be argued that such critique is nit-picking but it is possible that these cohesive ambiguities could contribute to an overall impression of muddled thinking.

A further weakness in this sentence concerns the management of the various propositions. It is impossible to determine the relative prominence of the different points since the writer does not provide the necessary linguistic clues. If we assume that the topic is supposed to be Serfdom and not Serfdom in Western Europe, then we identify three pairs of propositions distributed between the two clauses Western/Eastern Europe, Middle Ages/well into the Nineteenth

Century, absence of centralised political authority/presence of centralised authority. Since the clause complex is led by the conjunction 'while' a comparison within the pairs is anticipated. But first the writer needs to decide which pair leads and which are elaboration. In other words, what is the main dichotomy being discussed? Is it the Eastern/Western distinction, the centralised/non centralised distinction or the historical division? In this particular case, the follow-up tutorial session allowed the student to realise how her words had led to the ambiguity and how such an ambiguity could disturb the reader's understanding.

Extract 2
This extract is the second paragraph of the essay and, as will be seen, it continues to reflect similar weaknesses to those found in the first paragraph. It is a longer and more content oriented paragraph and additional problems occur here particularly with reference to the focus and source of the content.

> Sentiment for emancipation had begun to grow among foresightful Russians: Nikolai Novikov and the Moscow freemasons had advocated serfdom's reform in the 1770s and 1780s. Alexander Radishchev had called for its abolition at the end of the decade. Radishchev wrote in his 'Journey from St Petersburg to Moscow as following "Do you not know the peril in which we stand and the destruction that threatens us? The more dilatory and obstinate we are about freeing [the serfs] from their bonds, the more violent their vengeance will be." Thanks in part to Radishchev's work and in part to the impact of the French Revolution, the question of emancipation had become sufficiently focused in the minds of enlightened Russians by the beginning of the nineteenth century for Alexander I to put an end to the practice of rewarding loyal service with gifts of peasants. In 1804, he had emancipated the peasants in Baltic provinces without land. As the reign of Nicholas I began, the assumption could remain that if Russia's serfs ever were to be emancipated, they would be freed without land as they had been in the Baltic provinces. The key to opening the new era would be the emancipation of 22,558,746 peasants.

(i) **TOPIC AND COMMENT**

1) **Sentiment for emancipation** had begun to grow among foresightful Russians:

2) Nikolai Novikov and the Moscow freemasons had advocated **serfdom's reform** in the 1770s and 1780s.

3) Alexander Radishchev had called for **its*** abolition at the end of the decade.

4) Radishchev wrote in his* 'Journey from St Petersburg to Moscow' as **following**

> "Do you not know the peril in which we stand and the destruction that threatens us? The more dilatory and obstinate we are about freeing [the serfs] from their bonds, the more violent their vengeance will be."

5) Thanks in part to* Radishchev's work and* in part to* the impact of the French Revolution,

the question of emancipation had become sufficiently focused in the minds of enlightened Russians by the beginning of the nineteenth century

for

Alexander I to put an end to the practice of rewarding loyal service with gifts of peasants.

6) In 1804, **he*** had emancipated the peasants in Baltic provinces without land.

7) As* the reign of Nicholas I began, **the assumption** could remain

That*

If* **Russia's serfs** ever were to be emancipated,

They* would be freed without land
    As* **they*** had been in the Baltic provinces.

8) the key to opening the new era would be **the emancipation of 22,558,746 peasants**.

(ii) COHESIVE RELATIONSHIPS

Reference   1) its = serfdom's reform
             2) his = 'Journey from St Petersburg to Moscow'
             3) he = Alexander
             4) they = Russia's serfs
             5) they = Russia's serfs

Co-ordination   1) Thanks in part to (resultative — non finite clause + nominal group)

28   FIONA ENGLISH

       2) and (linking two non finite clauses)
       3) in part to (resultative — non finite clause + nominal group, infer 'thanks in part')
       4) As (time — introducing clause complex)
       5) that (reporting conjunction — introducing dependent clause)
       6) if (condition — introducing finite clause)
       7) As (manner — introducing dependent clause)

(iii) <u>PROPOSITIONS</u>

sentiment for emancipation
had begun to grow
was evident among foresightful Russians:

(implicit — not among other Russians)

serfdom's reform
had been advocated by Nikolai Novikov and the Moscow freemasons
had been advocated in the 1770s and 1780s.
    Alexander Radischev
called for the abolition of **serfdom's reform** (necessarily interpreted as serfdom)
called for **serfdom's reform** at the end of the decade.
    Radishchev wrote in his 'Journey from St Petersburg' to Moscow as following

> "Do you not know the peril in which we stand and the destruction that threatens us? The more dilatory and obstinate we are about freeing [the serfs] from their bonds, the more violent their vengeance will be."

the question of emancipation
was thanks in part to Radishchev's work
was thanks in part to the impact of the French Revolution,
had become focused in the minds of enlightened Russians
had become 'focused [...] Russians' by the beginning of the nineteenth century
    This led to (sufficiently focused... for)

Alexander I put an end to a particular practice
this was the **practice to reward loyal service** by giving gifts to peasants

He (Alexander I)
emancipated the peasants in Baltic provinces in 1804
didn't allocate them any land

the reign of Nicholas I
began

an assumption
existed

Russia's serfs
might be emancipated,
might be freed
wouldn't get any land

They (Russia's serfs) **in the Baltic provinces**
had been freed
had not been allocated any land

the emancipation of 22,558,746 peasants
was the key to the new era

Discussion

The second paragraph introduces the topics of 'a desire for emancipation' and 'early stages in emancipation among certain sectors of Russian society.' There is no explicit link to the preceding paragraph although one could be inferred perhaps from the reference to abolition. The paragraph goes on to identify the main contributors to the move for emancipation, outlining major events in the run up to the Edict in 1861. There are eight different topics, and although some are probably expected to be alternative ways of expressing the same thing, it emphasises the impression that this is a list.

As in Extract 1, Extract 2 also suffers from ambiguity in its cohesiveness, particularly with referencing. Extract 1, for instance, requires the reader to infer 'abolition' rather than 'serfdom's reform' in order for the meaning to make sense. Similarly, in Extract 2 (Topic and Comment analysis 7) 'they' leads to the referent 'Russia's serfs' rather than what must by inference be either *serfs* in general or *Baltic* serfs.

Another important weakness is that the writer fails to make the best use of the sources she uses. She quotes, but she does so without citing her sources or fully contextualising them.

For example, a quotation from one of the protagonists on the events of the period is provided, but we are not told *who* he is, only what his name is. The content of the quote could have been made more relevant to the discussion had we been provided with an explicit rationale or context for its inclusion. Instead we are expected to infer, not only its relevance but also that the author of the quote, Radishchev, must be associated with the group of 'foresightful Russians' referred to earlier and that his 'work' played a role in the emancipation process ("Thanks in part to Radishchev's work ..."). Such inferencing is not particularly taxing on the reader but it again creates the impression that the essay is somehow unmanaged and lacking in analytical comment from the writer.

Throughout the whole essay, in fact, the writer does not make a single reference to the sources she has used, a point which was commented on by the course tutor. This is, of course, one of the great bones of contention, not just in terms of citation but also in identifying whose words are being used and where one quotation ends and another begins. Some of the phraseology used in this essay suggests quotation, e.g. 'the question of emancipation had been insufficiently focused in the minds of enlightened Russians', but it is difficult to be sure without being familiar with the reading resources used by the student. This is a very important aspect of the student essay and the oft mentioned issue of plagiarism, but I do not intend to discuss it in detail here. However, it is worth pointing out that the focus on language and phraseology can help to move the discussion away from the minefield of plagiarism, with all the connotations it implies, into the less sensitive realm of language.

A good example of this can be seen in the concluding part of the paragraph which seems to read as a comment and at first sight could appear to be an evaluation of the events.

> 'As the reign of Nicholas I began, the assumption could remain that if Russia's serfs ever were to be emancipated, they would be freed without land as they had been in the Baltic provinces. The key to opening the new era would be the emancipation of 22,558,746 peasants.'

The grammar it is couched in — conditional form 'if' implying speculation followed by a consequential result — seems to imply analysis. However, closer examination suggests that rather than being the essay writer's own evaluation of the events, it is further description presented in the discourse of a historical *narrative* which is designed to be read in a chronological sequence of unfolding events. The historical *essay*, by contrast, does not normally include speculative commentary about historical events. The results are already known as historical fact. Instead the motivations behind the event and the student's speculations about these motivations are more in keeping with the genre; in other words, the 'why' of the tutor's comments above and the 'assess' of the essay question itself. In fact, it is not until the final paragraph of the essay that any direct comment on the events is provided.[9]

The point here, though, is that by focusing on the language it is possible to show the student how the words she has used and the choices she has made about what information to include lead not to the analysis and evaluation desired but to recounting and representation of events alone. Questions, for instance, can be asked about the speculative nature of the text and whose speculations they are. With this particular student discussion revealed was that she had thought that the recounting was the analysis. She had understood that by using the words of the source text she would be, by implication, demonstrating that she too held those views. Or, to put it another way, she thought the 'facts' spoke for themselves.

Conclusions

This approach is obviously very time consuming in the context of a full teaching timetable, particularly if the explanations must be written out. However, it can provide deep insights into students' performance and, with such explicit feedback, the student can begin to see how to move forward. This kind of examination provides a means of describing what is meant by terms such as 'clarity', 'analysis' and 'evaluation' and how these may or may not be realised in a particular essay. The text of the essay provides the focus of discussion rather than the subject itself and allows the language specialist to give feedback which is both relevant and useful regardless of the discipline. This enables the student to understand how the way in which information is expressed greatly influences how that information will be read.

In this particular case the analysis of the essay revealed that the writer seemed to have acquired the linguistic and stylistic forms appropriate to the history essay genre, but had not really understood the principles behind these forms. She did not demonstrate a proper understanding of the purpose of citing sources or contextualising quotations thereby revealing a failure to appreciate the conventions surrounding the culture of academic writing: critique and evaluation, support and referencing. She had missed the point that central to an essay are the question, the manipulation of the content and most importantly the ability to make the content relevant in the context of a discussion.

The feedback tutorials based on the analysis enabled this student not only to see where she was going 'wrong' but also to know what to do about it. Perhaps the most important achievement was that she no longer felt she was paying lip service to the conventions which she had acquired, but finally understood the reasoning and purpose behind them.

Although this study focuses on the work of a Japanese student the methodology could be applied to the work of any student since it suggests a framework for analysing both the discourse and content organisation of student writing, an approach that can be applied to the analysis of student writing in general. I have now used the approach to good effect with many students of varying degrees of English language competence and academic literacy awareness. It seems that once students can see what their words do and how their meanings can be interpreted it is easier for them to see, not only how their work may be failing to meet the expectations of their departments, but also what they can do to resolve the problem. This approach is by no means a miracle cure, but it is a way of encouraging students to recognise that they can begin to take control of their writing.

Notes

1. Herrick & Damon (1899) provide an interesting example of the way in which composition used to be dealt with explicitly. The themes included parallel many of those discussed in recent literature, such as Swales (1990) and exercises dealing with organisation matters resemble, at least in concept, those found in more contemporary coursebooks such as Oshima & Hogue (1983).
2. Lea and Street (1998) discuss models of student writing in higher education including this kind of approach.
3. See Scott, in this volume, for further discussion.
4. Connor (1996) discusses many of the issues surrounding the cross-cultural aspects of writing in a second language. The book provides a valuable overview of research in the field.
5. In this volume Lillis discusses some of the problems students experience in attempting to interpret essay questions and their struggles not only to meet the expectations of their tutors but also to find out what those expectations are.
6. Lea & Street (1996) offer some valuable insights into the issue of departmental feedback on student essays in their paper 'Student Writing and Faculty Feedback in Higher Education: an Academic Literacies Approach'.
7. Lautamatti's 1978 work on the development of topic is of interest here, although my own approach was developed independently.
8. Use of 'the', 'a' and zero articles could be considered relevant here since they are also involved in the logical relationships within a text. However, I have chosen not to go into this here since there are other issues associated with their use, particularly by non-native writers in English.
9. Hinds (1983) has illustrated ways in which Japanese rhetorical style differs from United States English.

References

Connor, U. 1996. *Contrastive Rhetoric.* Cambridge: CUP.
Connor, U. and Kaplan, R. B. (eds). 1987. *Writing Across Languages: An analysis of L2 text* Harlow: Addison-Wesley.
Gorman, T. P., White, J., Brookes, R. G., Maclure, M. and Kispal, A. 1988. *Language Performance in Schools — Review of APU Language Monitoring 1979–1983).* London: HMSO.
Gorman, T. P., White, J., Brookes, R. G. and English, F. 1990. *Language for Learning.* London: Schools Examinations & Assessment Council.
Halliday, M. A. K. and Hasan, R. 1976. *Cohesion in English.* Harlow: Longman.
Halliday, M. A. K. 1985. *An Introduction to Functional Grammar.* London: Edward Arnold.
Herrick, R. and Damon, L. T. 1899. *New Composition and Rhetoric.* Scott, Foresman and Company.
Hinds, J. 1983. "Linguistic and Written Discourse in English and Japanese." In R. Kaplan (ed.), *Annual Review of Applied Linguistics* III: 78–84. Rowley MA: Newbury House.
Kress, G. and Hodge, R. 1979. *Language as Ideology.* London: Routledge and Kegan Paul.
Lautamatti, L. 1987. "Observations in the Development of Topic in Simplified Discourse." In Connor, U. and Kaplan, R. (eds), *Writing Across Languages,* 87–114. Harlow: Addison-Wesley.
Lea, M. and Street, B. V. 1998. "Student Writing in Higher Education: An academic literacies approach". In *Studies in Higher Education* Vol. 23 (2): 157–172.
Mitchell, S. 1994. The Teaching and Learning of Argument in Sixth Forms and Higher Education. University of Hull.
Oshima, A. and Hogue, A. 1983. *Writing Academic English.* Harlow: Addison Wesley.
Sheeran, Y. and Barnes, D. 1991. *School Writing.* Milton Keynes: Open University Press
Swales, J. 1990. *Genre Analysis — English in Academic Settings.* Cambridge: CUP.

Appendix

Full Text of Essay   *Year 1 BA Russian Studies*

Assess the respective weight of reasons for the Emancipation Edict of 1861

Serfdom was a fundamental element of Russia's social and political structure until the day of its abolition. While serfdom in Western Europe is associated with the Middle Ages, and the absence of centralised political authority, it existed in large areas of Eastern Europe until well into the nineteenth century with the centralised authority.

    Sentiment for emancipation had begun to grow among foresightful Russians: Nikolai Novikov and the Moscow freemasons had advocated serfdom's reform in the 1770s and 1780s. (source?)

Alexander Radishchev had called for its abolition at the end of the decade. Radishchev wrote in his 'Journey from St Petersburg to Moscow as following "Do you not know the peril in which we stand and the destruction that threatens us? The more dilatory and obstinate we are about freeing [the serfs] from their bonds, the more violent their vengeance will be." (source?) Thanks in part to Radishchev's work and in part to the impact of the French Revolution, the question of emancipation had become sufficiently focused in the minds of enlightened Russians by the beginning of the nineteenth century for Alexander I to put an end to the practice of rewarding loyal service with gifts of peasants. In 1804, he had emancipated the peasants in Baltic provinces without land. As the reign of Nicholas I began, the assumption could remain that if Russia's serfs ever were to be emancipated, they would be freed without land as they had been in the Baltic provinces. The key to opening the new era would be the emancipation of 22,558,746 peasants. (source?)

On March 30/April 11, 1856, Alexander II had made his first public pronouncement on the most important problem of his reign — the emancipation of serfs. he told the representatives of Moscow nobility "For the contradiction of certain unfounded reports I think it is necessary to tell you that I do not at present intend to abolish serfdom; but certainly, as you well know yourselves, the existing manner of owning serfs cannot remain unchanged. it is better to abolish serfdom from above than to await the time when it will begin to abolish itself from below. I request you, gentlemen, to consider how this may be achieved, and to submit my words to the nobility for their consideration." (source?) It was the Tsar's first pronouncement on the subject of serfdom and it had several significant features. While avoiding to mention his intention of abolishing serfdom, he at the same time, expressed his conviction that the existing system had to be changed. he tried to convince the Moscow nobility that necessary changes must be introduced from above, but at the same time called on his listeners to submit their suggestions for necessary changes. There was also an implied undertaking that the modification and eventual abolition of serfdom would be a gradual process rather than a single cataclysmic act. After the speech, the Ministry of the Interior was entrusted with the early work of preparing for emancipation and in January 1857 it set the Social Committee on Peasant Affairs to act as a forum for discussion of the serf problem.

His concession to the need of abolition had been a gradual one. Although the question of whether Alexander II was a liberator or not is controversial, it was he himself who, in the speech delivered in Moscow on March 30/April 11, 1856 to the Moscow nobility, pronounced the fateful words. In fact, as a member of his father's secret committees he had, on the whole, inclined to the side of the serf-owner. (source?) However, several factors led him to change his views.

One of the factors is the influence of abolitionists in his immediate circle. These included his wife, a German princess he consistently neglected and his mistress, Princess Alexandra Wologowsky. His aunt the Grand Duchess Elena Pavlovna was always a liberal. Her palace was a centre of liberal ideas, and she herself gave her protection to liberal officials such as N. A. Milyutin. Both his mother, a Hohenzollern princess, and an early tutor, the liberal romantic poet Zhukovsky, had encouraged him to be a liberal. His brother, the ultra liberal Grand Duke Constantine had become an ardent supporter of emancipation. Thus in his immediate circle, the Tsar was insistently pressed to 'take the plunge'.

A sentimental and humanitarian child of the romantic age, Alexander II had from his youth been receptive of the abolitionist arguments on humanitarian grounds like those of Turgenev's 'Sportsman Sketches' published in the late 1840s. He did indeed, have qualities that helped him to find his way out of the complex domestic and international political issues that confronted him. Among these qualities were his common sense, his capacity to size up a situation quickly and to grasp it as a whole, and his lack of fanaticism.

The defeat in the Crimean War was partly laid at the door of serfdom; a serf, it was argued, had less incentive to fight well than a free man. Thus Russia intended to produce political results by allowing for the development of a more efficient and better selected army by means of emancipation, and to allow Russia to regain her prestige as a European great power. However, this event played an important role not only in this context but also in humanitarian considerations among educated people and in peasant unrest.

Western influence was seen during the 1860s in educational reform and in moves to relax somewhat the impact of the censorship. As a result of the defeat in the Crimean War which had clearly demonstrated the West's superiority to Russia, the continued existence of a system of serfdom inside Russia served to emphasise Russia's backwardness and demonstrated contemporaries that Russia still had a long way to go before she reached the level of the West. Question of self-regard thus played a part in the determination of many educated Russians to see serfdom abolished. Amongst the nobility of the provinces there were a number of educated and generous landowners who were deeply patriotic and at the end of the Crimean War became convinced of the complete bankruptcy of the existing political and social structure and of the extreme necessity of radical reforms. The starting point for these would be the emancipation of the entire Russian people from serfdom, which assumed more and more the character of slavery, and the replacement of ** on the peasant and the compulsory labour by free work. The highly-educated and prosperous landowners who were part of this minority stood firmly for emancipation of the peasants with land and for the most rapid transition to free labour. Among them humanitarian considerations were certainly important. An eminent example is the Slavophil landowner A. I. Koshelyou. His argument, to which he gave the greatest emphasis, was that serfdom demoralises the landowners themselves: "This measure," he wrote, "is more necessary for the welfare of our class itself even than for the serfs. the abolition of the right to dispose of people like objects of like cattle is as much our liberation as theirs: for at present we are under the yoke of a law that destroys still more in us than in the serfs any human quality."

The peasantry presented a permanent latent challenge to the government, for memories of the great rural revolt led by Pugachev in the 1770s were still clear and the regime was well aware of the problems which a rebellion on a similar scale would pose. The riots, during the reign of Alexander II, were taken more seriously because they coincided with the lost war. The Crimean War had seen a increase in endemic peasant unrest provoked mainly by the levying of recruits, a fruitful source of many and varied abuses. Moreover, the existence of serfdom appeared to pose a threat to the stability of the regime itself and it is truc that peasant disturbances were on the increase during Nicholas I's reign. Between 1826 and 1854 there were an average of twenty-three cases a year which were sufficiently serious to be noted by the Ministry of Internal Affairs, but in the late 1850's this figure rose substantially. In 1858 there were as many as eighty-six occasions when peasant unrest needed action by 'higher government authorities ', rising to ninety in 1859 and one hundred and eight in 1860. Although some historians have argued that this does not seem plausible since these numbers appear to be small in relation to the total expanse of the Empire, Alexander II clearly expressed his fears on them in his famous speech to the Moscow nobility in 1856.

Russia's agricultural yields per unit remained firmly at the bottom of the table of European countries. Russia could produce only six hectolitres per acre of cereals whilst Britain and Holland achieved fourteen hectolitres, France and Prussia over nine, and Spain and Greece just over six, although her economy remained almost completely based on agriculture. This was the result of primitive agricultural methods and techniques which had hardly changed for centuries. Although the evidence of Russia's agricultural backwardness was clear, for contemporaries it could be blamed on serfdom. It was argued that serfdom prevented the emergence of a free and mobile labour force and thus restrained economic development, and that the enserfed peasant had no incentive to work harder or to use more advanced agricultural methods since the benefit which was obtained would go not to the peasant himself, but to the serf-owner. Moreover, the government had faced a state financial problem. Between 1853 and 1858, the overall deficit increased from fifty-two million silver rubles to 307. The famous economist Tangoborsky expressed the situation in a memorandum of January 1857, "It is necessary at once to take the most radical measures to diminish expenditures ... for otherwise bankruptcy is inevitable for the state." Alexander II also wrote to his brother the Grand Duke Constantine, a member of the finance committee, that he was extremely concerned about the states financial situation.

Although serfdom had no positive support in popular tradition, it persisted because of systematic support by the state. In other words, serfdom was so dependant upon political agencies that once the state proposed to withdraw its support, serfdom had little or no momentum to carry on.

CHAPTER 3

The Student from Overseas and the British University

Finding a way to succeed

Carys Jones

Introduction

Entering British tertiary education for the first time can be a daunting experience for many students. Often, their prime task is adjusting to a new learning environment. For some students, coming from British secondary school education, problems may arise from having to function according to what seems to be a less explicit agenda than before. Students coming from other educational settings, especially those whose mother tongue is not English, will have other expectations and concerns. Most students may be expecting the unfamiliar but in ways which may not be easily identifiable.

From the university's standpoint, the continuing upward trend in the number of students coming to study in the UK from other countries should be welcomed if the higher education institution (HEI) is to have a voice in an increasingly multi-cultural world where the concept of globalisation is taking a firm hold. In effect HEIs need to relate to a fast-changing world. The influence of students from diverse cultural backgrounds, as prophets of the nature of change, might be viewed as a valuable resource in enhancing the international dimension of the university. But this essentially depends on the development of a forward-looking, reciprocal relationship between student and institution that brings about intercultural exchange in covert and subtle ways.

The field of EAP (English for Academic Purposes), which offers a high level of well-seasoned, specialist support, guidance and teaching, has many years' experience of addressing problems encountered by NNS (non-native speaker) students, both before and during academic mainstream study, as described by Jordan (1997) and discussed by Swales (1990). However, a gap marking crucial differences between the two contexts, the EAP context and the main study context, too often persists because the support provided in the EAP context is discovered not to be transferable to the context for which it is targeted. The deep-end, speedy and unpredictable nature of mainstream study cannot be emulated. Hence the groundwork covered within the protective EAP environment is sometimes in vain. The intention of this chapter is to consider how students might be prepared in advance to cope with the unexpected.

The hallmark of success for any student at university is mastery of academic writing. Students are constantly required to write essays, for which they receive assessment marks. These make up their profile and thus are the main indicators of their eventual success. Yet the writing process is a much neglected area because too little recognition is given to the fact that it is a highly complex process. It is often perceived as an isolated exercise whereas, in reality, it is entirely integrated with all aspects of a student's academic life.

The way students set about their main academic studies at the outset can have a significant bearing on the quality of their performance throughout their courses and consequently determine their final results. If, in mainstream education, misunderstandings concerning staff/student expectations are allowed to fester for too long, the outcomes for students can be very damaging (see Lillis in this volume). The complex nature of the issues involved needs to be further examined, theoretically and practically.

The question addressed here is how to do this. How does it become possible to understand these complexities and how can students, particularly students from overseas, be helped to understand the context within which they find themselves so that they are enabled to develop a balanced and critical approach to their own learning and profit fully from their studies? One preparatory measure is considered in this chapter: an attempt to provide a simulated snapshot of the dynamics in mainstream study by focussing on academic writing within a task-based programme.

Although task-based language learning has been widely researched and discussed in recent years in the context of general second language development (for example see: Candlin & Murphy 1987; Skehan 1998; Gass & Crookes 1993a, 1993b; Long & Crookes 1991; Prabhu 1987; Robinson 1995; Wenden 1995), little is known about how and to what extent it might be effective in helping students become critical and independent participants of an academic community. Here the design and implementation of such a programme is discussed in respect of how to help students develop an awareness for the way they might address the expectations made of them in writing assignments. But first the issues affecting the performance of NNS students within the British university context are more closely examined.

Uncovering the Issues

All students have 'an integrative need' (Gardner & Lambert 1972) to establish and assert their identity within the institution as a community, not only in the sense of belonging as a member but also so as to have a stake in the way it functions. They need to engage with that community to improve their chances of fulfilling their academic potential.

Students from overseas, because of the high value attributed to studying in the UK within their own countries, often make considerable sacrifices when they come. Also, it is more than likely that they have practical constraints, particularly financial ones, and will understandably seek to complete their studies in the shortest time possible. Therefore, any British institution which accepts students from overseas is under a strong obligation to accommodate and address their needs. Conversely, the institution should itself be ready to adapt to the demands of the changing wider world that the students represent.

However, Lea and Street in their research (1998) paint a rather depressing picture of the inflexibility that exists within UK higher education institutional practices. Their findings suggest that students' individual practices are not normally valued, even though the need to do so might be recognised. Their recent study of undergraduate students' marked assignments revealed that assessment comments were often unclear and unhelpful for the students concerned. They concluded that, to all intents and purposes, students, regardless of cultural background, were being marginalised rather than being drawn into the university academic culture. They also argued that students need much clearer guidance than that evidenced in their research.

The same point is reinforced by Low's review of the literature concerning university teachers' marking of the assignments of NNS students. Low (1996) argues that, in respect of academic writing, NNS students are unlikely to have received any previous training in addressing the complexities of coping with British university academia. They are disadvantaged by having to operate within a culture which many of them perceive as too impenetrable to fully come to terms with. Also, their initial perceptions and degree of consciousness of the difficulties they are likely to encounter will vary because of the 'different epistemologies in which ... (they) are trained and in which their identities are rooted' (Cadman 1997: 3). For some students, the sociological and institutional nuances of academic literacy practices in their new environment will be foregrounded in the ways described by Lea and Street, i.e. a sense of deeply embedded cultural differences; for others it will be specifically focussed on understanding and meeting specific task demands. Students will address their assignments in uniquely different ways. Yet all are subject to the expectations prescribed by the institution.

English, in this volume, describes the experiences of one Japanese undergraduate who failed her first year of study at a British university, despite having done her A' levels in Britain, because she was unable to fully understand the purposes and requirements of assignment writing. It was not until her second year when she was first directed towards specialist writing support that her difficulties with writing were gradually uncovered, and then only through a fairly long, intensive and continuous process. Although this procedure achieved eventual success, it had taken a year for the student's work to be identified as unsatisfactory and another year for the writing specialist's intervention to take effect. From the student's point of view, it seems that little had been achieved during one full year of study.

The 'language' dimension

The pragmatic task of finding how to become accepted within their new community combined with how to achieve academic success is something that students often embark upon by trial and error, in ways that they cannot predict or prepare for in advance. NNS students sometimes perceive their difficulties to be centred in the nature of using English as a second language. The writing process for them may be dominated by their concerns with surface language features such as syntax, lexical choices and cohesive markers mapped onto the writing practices they know. Thus the process of writing can become distanced from their thought processes. This 'surface' approach (Ellis 1994) sometimes interplays with a 'deep' approach, where priority is given to communicating the intended meaning at the expense of structure such that both approaches may be reflected in the intertextuality of the written product.

Conversely, assignment markers too may take a surface approach to interpreting NNS students' essays by evaluating the seriousness of structural errors without taking into account interlanguage factors, such as mother-tongue interference (Selinker 1972). Or they may attempt to reformulate according to their own linguistic frameworks, and the literacy practices of the institution, thus possibly arriving at a serious misunderstanding of the student's intended meaning. What is involved in 'making meaning' (Halliday 1978) is, invariably, extremely complex. It concerns the student, the institution and the interaction of the student with the institution. Thus the underlying difficulties go far beyond the linguistic level and the issues involved are extremely difficult to unpack and articulate; they concern all students, not only NNS students.

As other chapters suggest in this volume, students often feel that their conceptual development is framed by the dominant culture of the university. Scott points out that students need to become empowered so as to become 'agents of their own learning'. Their focus, particularly for NNS students, needs to be on finding out how to communicate appropriately and effectively, through written and oral modes, in conceptually challenging contexts, and as individual, original and authoritative thinkers constructing their own learning. Empowerment in this sense depends on much more than linguistic ability. Strategic behaviour can also play a crucial role (Cohen 1993).

For all students, the communication of their thinking means that some language development is taking place. Second language development involves engaging with the language at different levels and types of consciousness (discussed in detail by Schmidt 1994 and McLaughlin 1990). While developing a familiarity with their academic environment, NNS students will need to develop an awareness of when to strategically reflect on the language they use in such a way that it aids rather than hinders their conceptual development and the fair representation of their thoughts. In other words, as Halliday (1978) advises, language needs to be thought of as having a central position as a tool, or an instrument, for communicating thought and the writing process can be regarded as essentially a dynamic and progressive interplay among the ideational, interpersonal and textual meanings. The function of language is to represent the intended meaning such that the reader interprets the message in the way the writer desires as far as possible. On the writer's part this involves the appropriate selection and organisation of content and language under the umbrella of the whole discoursal context within which the assignment is situated. As Lea and Street suggest, this context, or 'field of study', does not span the whole institution but has its own epistemology, one which defines its own subjectivity as to how the task is to be understood, interpreted and assessed.

How can guidance help?

The main indicator of a student's academic potential and success within the institution is the assessment of written assignments as products. The process of writing is given little, if any, attention. In the case study described by English, the Japanese student needed the writing support specialist to examine her on-course written assignment and to analyse it for its failure to make the grade. Although this procedure achieved eventual success, it seems that much time, energy and anxiety could have been saved had her problems been addressed at the outset. This attention to linking process and product seems to have been extremely valuable. Success came about gradually not suddenly.

The issue here is how NNS students can be helped to prepare adequately for their studies in advance so as to preempt such problems during their main studies. Stierer (1997) criticises for its limitations the context-independent, skills-based approach which is often used to help overseas NNS students with their writing in the UK and welcomes the more 'culturally-sensitive' approaches such as that followed by the well-established tradition: 'Writing Across the Curriculum' (WAC) in the US (see Davidson and Tomic, in this volume, and Swales 1990).

Lea and Street suggest that perspectives on providing support to students' writing, regardless of cultural and linguistic background, may be categorised in terms of three models: one focussing on study skills, which they view as student deficit; one on academic socialisation, where the task is 'to inculcate students' into the culture of the institution; and a third on academic literacies, where literacies are defined as 'social practices'. Certainly the skills-based model, as they argue, has many drawbacks. By focussing on itemised skills, students are diverted from developing their understanding of the main goal and how they can work towards it. The approach suggested here partly adopts what Lea and Street term the 'academic socialisation' model, which recognises that students bring with them their own expertise into their new study environment but that the dominant discourse of the institution is likely to prevail. It also draws on the third model suggested by Lea and Street, that of 'academic literacies', which values individual difference among students and highlights 'student writing and learning as issues at the level of epistemology and identities'. There needs to be provided 'a central place for individual differences' (Selinker 1972: 213) and the student as original thinkers with their own ways of knowing.

The reactions of every student to an unfamiliar setting are determined by crucial cognitive and affective factors, which are unlikely to be fully understood externally. By giving voice to NNS students about their experiences of writing within a restricted context, they are encouraged to become masters of their own learning through developing strategic competence in managing their writing tasks and in negotiating their own positions within the dominant culture. If conditions are created that encourage NNS students to work in this way the gap between their perceptions and the expectations made of them may be considerably narrowed (Cadman 1997: 12). Students need to gain an enhanced critical understanding of the requirements made of them and of how they can interact with those requirements. They need to develop a sense of ownership for what they write within the context of particular assignment goals and to interpret those goals to their own advantage. The problems of NNS students in this context have a distinctive dimension. What is immediately important to them could be less to do with understanding the dominant discourses of their field of study and more with enhancing their use of language so that it reflects the quality of their thinking. But behind this lies their need to develop the self-awareness, self-esteem and self-assertion that equip them with the means to negotiate their passages towards success. The role of the writing support specialist may be regarded as providing the conditions for this to take place. The question is then 'How?'

The rest of the chapter discusses one possible approach that took the form of a developmental programme and was implemented with a small group of students in advance of their mainstream studies.

A task-based instruction programme

The task-based programme described here was perceived as set within its own constructed cultural context, one which attempted to emulate key features of the future mainstream study context. It was intended to help NNS students become gradually familiar with that new learning context so that they would find their own ways of optimizing their learning and writing in English as their second language. Therefore the focus was on helping them to develop their language use within that context. The programme was designed to focus on the task, to foreground the students' learning while backgrounding the instructor and assessor, in accordance with findings of recent studies in task-based learning (Skehan 1998).

In order to develop appropriate strategies to improve their performance, the students were given opportunities to reflect on what they were doing in 'a cycle of analysis and synthesis' (Skehan 1996: 51) over the period of the programme. For each task they had to write an essay. Thus the programme consisted of a series of similar tasks, each supported by pre-task and post-task activities (as discussed by Long and Crookes 1992, and Wenden 1995) to help them analyse both the task demands and their own performances with an enhanced awareness and, in successive tasks and activities, to synthesise their work in relation to the task demands.

There were four main components of the programme that needed to be considered in its design: the task itself, the assessment of the students' performance in the task, the supporting pre-task and post-task activities and the series of tasks. These are now discussed in turn.

The task

The task was viewed as an instrument designed to help NNS students develop their writing. It did not focus on learning new linguistic structures but on developing effective strategies that would enable the students to draw on appropriate linguistic resources (Jones: 1982) in order to express their ideas effectively.

The main factors likely to influence NNS students' performance in a task might be considered as a framework for investigating language use. They can be broadly classified as external and internal. The external factors can be of two types: those which are socio-cultural — provided by the context; and those which are domain-specific — provided by the task. The internal factors would be those which describe the student's metacognitive, cognitive and affective behaviour and may not be entirely separable from one another (Schumann 1994). Metacognitive factors might include: a holistic view of the task demands, a view of self-competence and self-ability to perform the task, and the adoption of strategies deemed appropriate for improving performance (Cohen 1993). Two cognitive factors might be considered: linguistic level and communicative competence: conceptual level and knowledge (Bialystok 1990). Two affective factors might be considered: motivation and efficacy (Schunk 1995). Thus the students' strategic behaviour could be crucially important in determining their success and with the selection of appropriate strategies relying strongly on using metacognition.

The context of the task performance can be summarised as a process of 'familiarisation' (see Figure 1) where the written product would be assessed according to certain criteria, which will be discussed in the next section. This familiarisation process would need to:

a) encourage continual dynamic and interactive engagement and the development of appropriate language use within the task framework,

b) link each student's prior knowledge and experience from the past with their present and future concerns,

c) incorporate the possibility for students to develop a critical awareness both of the demands posed by the task within its controlled context and of how they individually relate to it.

The student factors outlined in Figure 1 need to be considered in the light of the type and demands of the task (Wenden 1995). According to Long and Crookes, 'little empirical support is yet available for the various proposed parameters of task classification and difficulty' (1992: 4). But generally, simple

Student Factors   Past → **Now** → Future
External
a) general: (socio-cultural)
b) domain-specific

Internal
a) metacognitive
   – holistic view of task demands
   – self-esteem linked to performance   **Familiarisation**
   – adoption of appropriate strategies
b) cognitive
   – linguistic level and communicative
   competence
   – conceptual level and knowledge
c) affective
   – motivation
   – efficacy

Figure 1: The student-task relationship

tasks provide clear though limited goals for language development with limited demands made of the student while complex tasks have less clear linguistically defined goals but make greater demands on the student's engagement. As Robinson claims, complex tasks are 'a spur to development regardless of the current stage of the learner'. Though the degree of cognitive load needs to be carefully considered:

> The greater the attentional, memory, and reasoning demands of tasks, the greater the cognitive load they impose on the learner. The additional cognitive effort expended by learners on more complex tasks, together with a perceived need for communicative resource expansion in order to successfully complete the task, will create the conditions for language development.... tasks can be too complex and impose too great a cognitive load on the learner, causing a deterioration in performance. (1995: 130–2).

In considering the nature of this complexity and the ways in which the task may be effective in helping NNS students with their academic writing two aspects appear to be important. The first, which has already been considered, is that preparing a written assignment involves linguistic and cognitive skills, which may or may not be separable. The second important aspect concerns the criteria used to assess the essay bearing in mind that writing an essay is undoubtedly a complex task.

Assessment criteria

Assessment criteria can have several important functions. Their standard function is to provide a valid and reliable indicator of the quality of a student's product. Achieving both validity and reliability is extremely difficult (Bachman 1990; Alderson & North 1991). The criteria are deemed valid if they assess those features they are intended to assess and for which the task is designed. They are deemed reliable if they produce consistent results. Achieving reliability in criterion-referenced testing is very difficult because some degree of subjectivity cannot be avoided. In the context described here, achieving as much validity as possible is highly desirable. Several authors in Alderson and North (1991) complain that it has too often been neglected in language testing.

The validity of assessment criteria can be enhanced if they serve to illuminate the purpose, type and demands of the task in relation to the students' own needs and goals. They can then not only signal the desired link between process and product but also provide an overall framework for the task in terms of what is entailed in the familiarization process. Therefore, in terms of practical use, they need to be accessible to students as well as to the assessor(s).

In complex tasks, the nature and extent of the student's progress is unlikely to be perceived externally in any atomized way and the criteria need to be holistic. Here, four main categories were used: one was for an overall impression and the other three were for content, organisation and language. These three were used as separate and inter-related indicators to assess how far each student was able to communicate successfully with the reader through the written essay.

The supporting pre-task and post-task activities

Skehan has pointed out the value of pre-task and post-task activities in 'manipulating the focus of the learner' (1996). Pre-task and post-task activities provide opportunities for students to seek clarification about task-related factors and discuss their own performance. Thus aspects of the students' performance and of the task itself can be the focus of attention (Schmidt 1994) at various levels e.g. identifying the demands of the task and the degree to which these have been met by the individual student. An enhanced awareness of these allows students to negotiate their own learning and have control over their own development.

Pre-task activities can reduce the difficulty of a task by providing the students with domain-specific knowledge: knowledge of the nature, demands and expectations of the task. This knowledge might be signalled in the assessment criteria in terms which raise the students' awareness to the task demands. Such activities are likely to alleviate any feelings of anxiety and enable the students to focus more confidently on performing the task.

Post-activities can have a variety of functions which might help the students to develop 'an empirical and introspective understanding' of the task demands (Faerch & Kasper 1987). As Schmidt (1990, 1992) and Skehan point out, they can work to develop students' confidence and independence as critical thinkers, enhance their perceptions of their own progress and of the task demands. Hence, post-task activities might usefully incorporate an opportunity for students to talk about their task performance and about the task itself, to go through the task again, to receive feedback on their performance and possibly to compare their experiences with each other. In other words, they can focus on all features of the writing process which may be missed by examining the product alone.

The series of tasks

The 'constant cycle of synthesis and analysis' advocated by Skehan can also be encouraged through the reiteration of the pre-task, task performance and post-task group of activities over a period of time. In this way students may come to use their metacognition to gain a deeper understanding of their strengths and weaknesses in relation to the context of the task and to select appropriate strategies for regulating their own behaviour (Zimmerman 1989).

The question of how the tasks could form a series needs to be considered in respect of similarity and difference. The tasks would need to have similar cognitive demands contained within fields of study relevant to the students' academic interests. But at the same time they would need to contain sufficient new elements to engage the students' interests (Plough & Gass 1993).

An example

The programme discussed here was designed to help a group of six Japanese students prepare for studying science at undergraduate level at a British university. It consisted of a series of five tasks and was conducted over a period of five months. In its aims to familiarize the students with a British academic culture, it attempted to preempt problems that might arise due to background influences. For example, in Japanese society group cohesion and collective behaviour are prioritized and the Japanese education system is still strongly influenced by Confucian thinking, where students are required to respect authority according to age and experience but are discouraged from projecting themselves as individuals (Jones 1997).

The Tasks

Each task had a standard format:
The students were required to write an essay about a given subject in accordance with a given instruction within three hours. Information about the topic was presented in an audio-visual and in a written textual form. No collaboration was allowed. A variety of English-English dictionaries were provided. The procedure was timed as follows:

10 mins:	Initial preparation	– thinking about the task instruction
10 mins:	Further preparation	– experimenting with planning the essay
20 mins:	Information input	– watching a video documentary – noting relevant information
10 mins:	Pause	– recalling and adding relevant information
30 mins:	Information input	– reading a text – noting relevant information
100 mins:	Final preparation	– planning, drafting and writing

But the topic, the task instruction and the information inputs were different for each task. The instruction was always differently formulated and the way the content was presented in the inputs (which were authentic documentaries and texts) varied. These differences meant that for each task performance the students needed to adopt a holistic approach specific to the task. The topics and the task instructions were:

Task	Topic	Instruction
1	Energy	Discuss the advantages and disadvantages of using the wind turbine as a means of supplying energy. Compare it with other means of supplying energy.
2	Water pollution	Describe the causes and effects of water pollution. Discuss how the chemist can help to improve the situation.
3	Space technology and travel	Concerning the use of satellites in space, why is the concept of **thrust** important to mankind? Discuss this with reference to the progress made between 1980 and 1991.
4	Darwin and evolution	Describe Darwin's theory of evolution. Discuss how it has contributed to further knowledge and change.
5	Genetics and genetic engineering	Discuss how the gene has led to important developments in science.

In each task, the students were guided methodologically. They were given a sheet of paper which had all the instructions showing the procedure with the suggested timings. (See the Appendix for an example.) They were encouraged to use a range of skills in preparing their essay. Although they had time work on their essays in their own ways, they were constrained by the fact that a complete essay, written in English, had to be handed in by the end of three hours. This means that selecting appropriate strategies was extremely important to their performing successfully.

The assessment criteria

Holistic criteria were used to assess the students' essays. As already mentioned, the four main categories were Overall Impression and three other categories: Content, Organisation and Language, which were further subcategorised as given below:

Overall impression
– an essay which fully addresses the task instruction

Content
– evidence of comprehesion of the task instruction and of the audiovisual and written information input
– relevance to the task instruction
– use of the information input and of knowledge and experience
– selection and elaboration of main points and details
– comprehensiveness

Organisation
– appropriate ordering of points, showing their relationships, distinguishing between main and subordinate points
– textual layout in paragraph distribution including an introduction and conclusion

Language
– accuracy in the use of lexical and grammatical patterns
– fluency in the range of expression and choice of lexis and grammar
– appropriateness of discourse including style, register and contextual genre
– intelligibility including coherence and presentation

The lowest and highest possible marks were set at 1 and 5 respectively.

Pre-task and post-task activities

One pre-task group session was held with the students in order to discuss the format of the task linked to the assessment criteria. However, the task instruction, the topic and the content of the information inputs were not divulged in advance of the task performance session.

Four post-task sessions were held during which the students could describe their experiences of doing the tasks and gain feedback on their written essays. The first session was an interview, when the students were asked for their first reactions to the task and to their own performances. During the second session, a group session, the whole task was discussed step by step from beginning to end. The third session was another interview, during which the students were given feedback on their essays and another opportunity to comment about doing the task. The fourth session was a short group session when the students were invited to compare notes about their experiences.

What happened? An overview

The product

In order to minimise the problems of reliability as far as possible, four markers were used. The students' marks for Task 1 and 5 essays, according to the four main categories of the assessment criteria, were as follows:

	Student	Takako	Natori	Satomi	Keiko	Masaki	Junsei
Task 1	Overall Impression	1.25	3.5	1.75	3.5	2.5	2.5
	Content	1.5	2.75	1.5	3.5	2.75	2.75
	Organisation	1	3	1.75	3.5	2.75	2
	Language	1.25	3.75	1.75	4	2.25	3
Task 5	Overall Impression	2	4	2.5	4	3.5	3.25
	Content	2.25	4	2.25	4	3.25	3.25
	Organisation	1.75	4	2.5	4	3.5	3.5
	Language	2.25	4	2.75	4	3.75	3.25

The students' Overall Impression marks for Task 1 ranged between 1.25 and 3.5. The marks for both Content and Organisation ranged between 1.5 and 3.5, for Language between 1.25 and 4. They suggest that there was a wide difference in the students' abilities to address these complex tasks

The students' Overall Impression marks for Task 5 ranged between 2 and 4. The marks for Content ranged between 2.25 and 4, for Organisation between 1.75 and 4, for Language between 2.25 and 4. They suggest that the gap in difference had not changed very much. The performance of the weaker students, Takako and Satomi, was still rather weak at the end. A certain amount of progress was evident by each student except for Keiko's performance in Language, which had not changed. The most progress seems to have been made by Masaki, whose Language mark had increased by 1.5.

The process: How the students viewed the tasks and what strategies they adopted

What follows is a summary of detailed discussions that were held during the pre-task and post-task sessions. The issues were raised many times and considered from a variety of different viewpoints.

Most of the students said they felt comfortable about the first topic — energy, because it was familiar, but not about the second topic — water pollution, which was not familiar. However, after both tasks, some students were concerned that they had not been able to understand all the information presented in the documentary either because there was too much, or because it was presented too quickly or because it was too difficult either conceptually or linguistically. Takako, Satomi and Junsei felt that, because time was so limited, a full twenty minutes allowed for thinking at the beginning was unnecessary and should have been allocated after the documentary had been shown. Natori raised a different point. In Task 2, he said that he had planned his essay during this thinking time using his own knowledge about sea pollution and was disconcerted to find that both information inputs only dealt with domestic water. He thought that what he had done was a mistake and decided to omit sea pollution from his essay. Satomi complained about the difficulty of finding information from both documentary and written text which was relevant.

Another concern of some students was the restricted amount of time they had overall. In several tasks, Takako's main concern was to finish her essay, regardless of its quality; after Task 1 she said how pleased she was that she had risen to the challenge and managed to complete. Masaki said that he spent too much time planning his essay and was unable to convert into writing what he had written in his plan.

By Task 3, which was about 'space', views were beginning to change. Some students began to focus more on the task instruction and less on the information inputs. Three students criticised the instruction for being too complicated, saying they had problems trying to make the connections among the different parts and deciding what 'thrust' meant. Junsei, Takako and Satomi all said they had enjoyed the documentary and the task instruction had not worried them. Keiko said that she had enjoyed learning about the topic although she found it hard and her scientific interests were in biology not physics. In Task 4, with the exception of Keiko and Natori, all the students found the instruction straightforward. Natori described at length why he thought it was ambiguously phrased and how he had struggled with it. He had only manage to write up half his essay: 'I can guess what is meant by further knowledge but what is meant by further change?' He and Keiko had, understandably, thought of 'further' as an adjective not a verb. Keiko also said that too much of the information input was relevant and it was difficult to know what to leave out. She said that she had decided not to worry but just enjoy the task. She became absorbed in reading the text in detail because she found it so interesting although this was not the main object of the exercise! Nevertheless, she wrote her essay without much deliberation and achieved her highest Overall Impression mark of all: 4.25.

It was evident that all the students had found Task 5 reasonably straightforward as well as interesting and absorbing. During the first interview, they were able to describe how genes are transmitted confidently, in some detail, and, interestingly, used some of the appropriate genre. Some students, in particular Natori, Keiko and Masaki, gave detailed and reflective answers about the ethics of genetic engineering when asked what they thought. This time, none of the students said they had problems with the task instruction and, by this stage, most students semed to have discovered how they could profitably use the 20 minutes thinking time at the beginning, making extensive use of the dictionaries and attempting a first plan of their essays.

It became evident that the students had realized they had to make strategic choices about their essays as a product: whether or not to complete at the expense of depth and breadth of content and at the expense of analysis; whether or not there was time for both draft and rewrite. For example, Natori finished Task 5 with five minutes to spare to check through his essay and gained an Overall Impression mark of 4.

In cases where the students had not understood revelant details from the information input sometimes the need to make decisions did not arise. This was often the case for Satomi, for whom the visual representation of information was very important because it compensated for her limited understanding of spoken English. The students often attempted to apply to the next task what they had learnt from the previous experience. In Task 2, some expressed disappointment because they predicted certain similarities with Task 1 which were not there. Thus the students learnt to expect the unexpected and to adopt strategies accordingly, though some more successfully than others. For example, having found Task 3 difficult, Junsei attempted Task 4 by relying very little on the input and instead used examples from his own knowledge and experience. He gained an Overall Impression mark of 3.25, which was higher than 3, his mark for Task 5.

Linking process with product

The students' comments during the post-tasks explained a great deal about their written work. Most significant were their comments about the time limit. For example, Masaki was able to explain why he handed in a plan as his product for Task 1. He was short of time. Satomi's comments explained why her Task 2 essay lacked relevance and intelligibility. She had spent too much time trying to understand the text. Keiko's comments explained why her Task 3 essay lacked coherence and organisation. Natori's comments explained why his Task 4 essay was very short and incomplete. Takako's comments explained why her Task 5 essay was not well organised and superficial.

Lessons learnt

The post-task sessions were revealing in several ways. Firstly, the students' comments pointed towards the weaknesses and strengths of the task design and of each task. They provided several insights about what the students could be expected to achieve within such a format; about how a task instruction might be interpreted; about the quality of the information input; about how it was perceived in relation to the task instruction. This provided an opportunity for modifications to be made to the design of succeeding tasks in the programme.

Secondly, the assessment criteria came to be used as terms of reference. The most discussed item was that of relevance to the task instruction, particularly in the later post-task sessions. Gradually, the students adjusted their strategies to accommodate the requirements as they were expressed in the criteria. This meant that the choice of assessment criteria became pivotal to their understanding of the expectations being made of them and to their strategic behaviour.

Thirdly, the time limit imposed certain restrictions on the students and, initally, these caused feelings of anxiety and stress. But, during the course of the programme, it seems that for some of the students these feelings gradually disappeared. Keiko, Junsei, Takako and Masaki described how they ceased to worry about what they could not achieve and attended more to their strengths and their perceptions of what was important as well as manageable. They realized that quick decisions had to be made during a task session. Clearly in task design, a carefully gauged balance between pressurised task situations and allowing time for reflection is an important consideration.

Fourthly, the opportunity to discuss the tasks seemed to help the students develop a more critical attitude to the demands being made of them and to their own choice of strategies. Time to reflect between tasks may also have been an important factor in the students using their metacognition to bring about changes in attitude and strategic behaviour.

Fifthly, the need to focus sharply on the task during the task session and on discussing performance afterwards meant that implicit language learning was taking place for these Japanese students. Those whose initial concerns were mainly with linguistic accuracy and presentation had necessarily to be modified both to take account of the other criteria and because of the limited amount of time. In the process, their language use developed subconsciously, both written and oral. This may have been due to the need to integrate thinking, listening, reading, writing and speaking skills, as well as other non-linguistic skills, as demanded by the tasks themselves and the post-task sessions.

Towards a task-based framework for narrowing the 'gap'

This study could be described as an exploration of how NNS students might be empowered to have a stake in their own learning. It demonstrated how close links between task designer, student and assessor could create a dynamic framework where the acceptance of continual change was being opened up. There was no polarisation of what was correct or permitted, rather a constant developmental process between all three. The assessment criteria anchored the various parts of the process. They were accepted, without question, by the students as indicators of a direction which they needed to take. In other words, their selection was crucially important with the proviso that, like the design of the tasks, they should be open to challenge.

With these thoughts in mind, a possible framework for a task-based programme can be envisaged. In developing students' academic writing, the assesment criteria could provide the link with the mainstream study context by signalling those features of academic writing perceived as crucial to the students' eventual success. They could be used to assess the students' written performance as well as encourage the students to participate actively in their own development. By featuring strongly in the pre-task and post-task discussions the criteria could provide the students with domain-specific knowledge, which in turn would guide them towards ways of reflecting on their learning and thus ways of enhancing their strategic competence. During the same sessions the students' performances could be discussed from different perspectives, providing a means of evaluating both task and assessment criteria. The students could be encouraged to reflect on their strengths and weaknesses between activities so as to adopt appropriate strategies and negotiate their own learning. Figure 2 below presents a framework showing the relationships between the task design and the assessment criteria.

To summarise, Figure 2 represents the pivotal significance of the relationships between the task design and the assessment criteria in a task-based programme intended for a specific purpose. The task design is informed by the nature of the target culture within which the students' aims are to achieve their maximum potential. The assessment criteria are designed to suggest to students how they might appropriately work towards achieving their academic goals. The post-tasks provide feedback which can usefully inform the evaluation of the task design and the design of the assessment criteria so that adaptations can be made to meet differences and changes in perspectives about academic writing tasks as well as about external and internal student factors. Thus, the assessment criteria

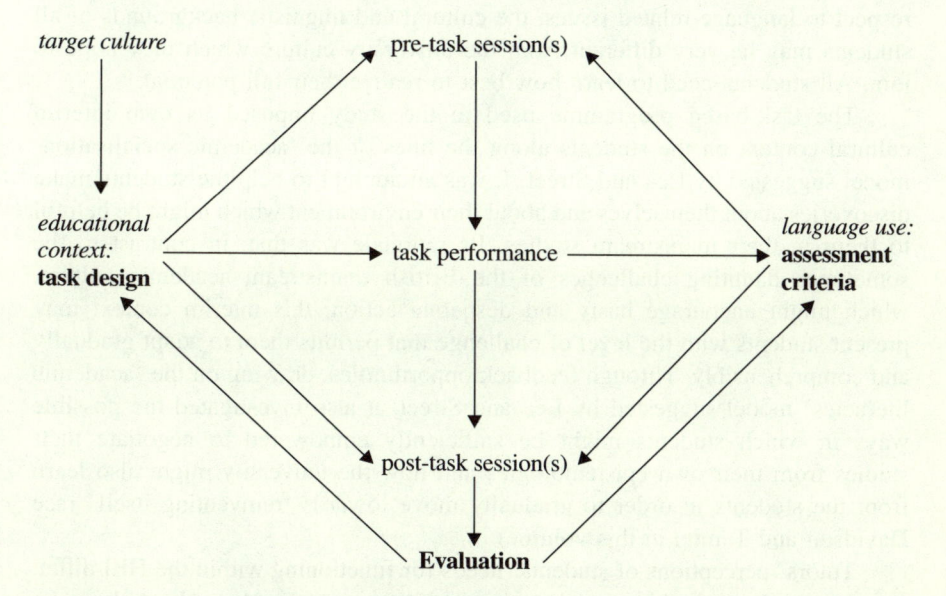

Figure 2: A framework for evaluating task-based instruction through implementing a series of tasks

become an instrument of formative value for the familiarization process that is bi-directional, between students and tutors.

Conclusion

Three ways forward have been discussed here to address the problems that NNS students may face during their studies in the UK higher education institution: firstly, implementing a series of appropriately designed task-based activites to enhance students' understanding of the process of adjusting to the university; secondly, a familiarisation process focussing not on discrete features of language and skills but on enhancing awareness and understanding of the interim task culture to encourage students to develop their strategic competence; thirdly, the nurturing of students' own academic positions as independent and original contributors to their own progress.

Hopefully, despite the limitations of a contrived context, the feedback from the Japanese students in the study described above has given some sense of the complexities which can arise for students when they are asked to write assignments. Although this chapter has foregrounded the needs of NNS students with respect to language-related issues, the cultural and linguistic backgrounds of all students may be very different from the university culture which they hope to join. All students need to learn how best to realize their full potential.

The task-based programme used in the study imposed its own interim cultural context on the students along the lines of the 'academic socialisation' model suggested by Lea and Street. It was an attempt to help the students make discoveries about themselves and about their environment which might be helpful to them in their mainstream studies. Its rationale was that, in contrast to the sometimes daunting challenges of the British mainstream academic culture, which might encourage hasty and desperate action, this interim context may present students with the level of challenge that permits them to adapt gradually and comprehensibly. Through feedback opportunities, drawing on the 'academic literacies' model suggested by Lea and Street, it also investigated the possible ways in which students might be sufficiently empowered to negotiate their studies from their own epistemologies and how the university might also learn from the students in order to gradually move towards 'reinventing itself' (see Davidson and Tomic, in this volume).

Tutors' perceptions of students' needs for functioning within the HEI differ. On a general level, this model suggests that a provisional needs analysis be drawn up at the outset to inform a set of assessment criteria and how tasks might be implemented. But this is not the end of the story. Ways have been discussed which might help to explore the complexities involved thus furthering a deeper understanding by both tutors and students so that, through a dynamic process of interaction, the possibility of modifying and refining the design might become accepted as the norm.

The context of this programme was a contrived cultural context which inevitably would create a gap between itself and the mainstream reality. It can be argued that written assignments themselves are specifically contextualized so that neither the subjectivity nor the dynamism of the academic institution can be fully emulated. However, the issues discussed in this chapter are grounded in the argument that the way students embark on their studies at the outset can determine the final outcomes. It is possible that in-depth preparation measures such as the programme suggested here, where students are given the opportunity to examine how they relate to their environment in a less exposed context, will have a far more positive impact on their overall performance and on their long-term development than an ad hoc deep-end strategy where their main concerns become reduced to survival within the institution. Crucial to the design is its flexibility in addressing new perspectives as they arise: perspectives about how both the student and the institution can positively interact with each other and with the changing demands of the wider world.

References

Alderson, J. C. and North, B. (eds). 1991. *Language Testing in the 1990's*. London: Macmillan.
Bachman, L. F. 1990. *Fudamental Concepts in Language Testing*. Oxford: OUP.
Bialystok, E. 1994. "Analysis and Control in the Development of Second Language Proficiency." *Studies in Second Language Acquisition* 16: 157–168.
Cadman, K. 1997. "Thesis Writing: A question of identity?" *English for Specific Purposes* 16 (1): 3–12
Candlin, C. and Murphy, D. 1987. *Language Learning Tasks*. Englewood Cliffs, NJ: Prentice Hall.
Cohen, M. 1993. "Listening to Students' Voices: What university students tell about how they learn." Paper presented at the annual meeting of *The American Educational Research Association* Atlanta, GA.
Ellis, R. 1994. *The Study of Second Language Acquisition*. Oxford: OUP.
English, F. 1996. "Japanese Students Writing in English: A descriptive analysis of students' essays. Paper presented at *Knowledge and Discourse* conference at the University of Hong Kong.

Faerch, C. and Kasper, G. 1987. *Introspection in Second Language Research.* Clevedon: Multilingual Matters
Foster, P. and Skehan, P. 1996. "The Influence of Planning and Task Type on Second Language Performance." *Studies in Second Languge Acquisition* 18: 299–323.
Gardner, R. and Lambert, W. 1972. *Attitudes and Motivation in Second Language Learning.* Rowley, Mass.: Newbury House.
Gass, S. and Crookes, G. (eds). 1993. *Tasks in a Pedagogical Context: Integrating theory and practice.* Clevedon: Multilingual Matters.
Gass, S. and Crookes, G. (eds). 1993a. *Tasks and Language Learning: Integrating theory and practice.* Clevedon: Multilingual Matters.
Gee, J. P. 1990. *Social Linguistics and Literacies.* London/Philadelphia: Falmer Press.
Halliday, M. A. K. 1985. *An Introduction to Functional Grammar.* London: Edward Arnold.
Halliday, M. A. K. 1978. *Language as Social Semiotic.* London: Edward Arnold.
Jones, C. 1997. "Emergent Internationalism? A case study." EAIE annual conference, Barcelona. Unpublished manuscript.
Jones, K. 1982. *Simulations in Language Teaching.* Cambridge: CUP.
Jones, S. 1993. "Cognitive Learning Styles: Does awareness help?" In *Language Awareness* 2 (3): 195–207.
Jordan, R. R. 1997. *English for Academic Purposes.* Cambridge: Cambridge Language Teaching Library.
Lea, M. 1994. "I Thought I Could Write Till I Came Here: Student Writing In Higher Education." In Gibbs, G (ed.), *Improving Student Learning: Theory and Practice.* Oxford: OSCD.
Lea, M. and Street, B. V. 1997. *Student Writing and Staff Feedback in Higher Education: An academic literacies approach.* Swindon: Economic and Social Research Council.
Lea, M. and Street, B. V. 1998. "Student Writing in Higher Education: An academic literacies approach." In *Studies in Higher Education* Vol. 23 (2): 157–172.
Long, M. and Crookes, G. 1991. "Three Approaches to Task-based Syllabus Design." *TESOL Quarterly* 26 (1): 27–55.
Low, G. 1996. "University Written Assignments and Complex Feedback Situations." Manuscript.
McLaughlin, B. 1990. "Restructuring". *Applied Liguistics* 11/2: 113–128.
Oxford, R. 1990. *Language Learning Strategies: What every teacher should know.* Rowley, MA: Newbury House.
Prabhu, N. S. 1987. *Second language pedagogy.* Oxford: OUP.
Purdie, N, Hattie, J. and Douglas, G. 1996. "Student Conceptions of Learning and Their Use of Self-Regulated Learning Strategies: A cross-cultural comparison." *Journal of Educational Psychology* 88 (1): 87–100.
Robinson, P. 1995. "Task Complexity and Second Language Narrative Discourse." *Language Learning* 45 (1): 99–140.

Rubin, J. 1990. "Study of Cognitive Processes in Second Language Learning." *Applied Linguistics* 11 (2): 117–131.

Schmidt, R. 1992. "Psychological Mechanisms Underlying Language Fluency." *Studies in Second Language Acquisition* 16: 357–385.

Schmidt, R. 1990. "The Role of Consciousness in Second Language Learning." *Applied Linguistics* 11 (2): 129–158.

Schumann, J. H. 1994. "Emotion and Cognition in Second Language Acquisition." *Studies in Second Language Acquisition* 16: 231–242.

Schunk, D. H. 1990. "Introduction to the Special Section on Motivation and Efficacy." *Journal of Applied Psychology* 82 (1): 3–6.

Skehan, P. 1998. *A Cognitive Approach to Language Learning.* Oxford: OUP.

Skehan, P. 1996. "A Framework for the Implementation of Task-based Instruction." *Applied Linguistics* 17 (1): 38–62.

Stierer, B. 1997. *Mastering Education: A preliminary analysis of academic literacy practices within masters-level courses in Education.* CLAC Occasional papers in communication: Open University.

Street, B. V. 1995. *Social Literacies.* Harlow: Longman.

Swales, J. 1990. *Genre Analysis: English in academic and research settings.* Cambridge: CUP.

Wenden, A. L. 1995. "Learner Training in Context: a Knowledge-based Approach. *System* 23 (2): 183–194.

Zimmerman, B. J. 1989. "A Social Cognitive View of Self-regulated Academic Learning." *Journal of Educational Psychology* 81 (3): 329–339.

Appendix: Task 1

You have ten minutes to read through this page.
You are expected to hand in several pieces of work at the end of this three hour session. The main one is a written essay. The other pieces of work are all items of preparation for it and are described below under 'Procedure'. The essay must be entirely in your own words. The time is limited and therefore you should allow yourself enough time for thinking, planning, reading and writing. Copying is not permitted.

You may use English-English dictionaries.

INSTRUCTION:
Use the video documentary 'Energy transfer devices' and the text 'The answer is blowing in the wind' to discuss the advantages and disadvantages of using the wind turbine as a means of supplying energy. Compare it with other means of supplying energy.
Use one or more diagrams to illustrate your answer.
You may also use your own knowledge and experience.

PROCEDURE: TIME

1. First read through this sheet very carefully and think about what you   10 mins
   have to do.
2. Think about the task. Try to answer it by writing down some notes   10 mins
   on the piece of paper provided.
3. You are now going to watch a video documentary called 'Energy   20 mins
   Transfer Devices'. Watch it carefully and look for the information
   which will help you with the task.
4. Write down what you can remember from the documentary.   10 mins
5. You are now going to have a text to read with the title 'The answer   30 mins
   is blowing in the wind'.
   Find the information you need to help you with the task. Take
   notes.
6. Use your notes and plan your essay.   1hr 30 mins
7. Write the first draft of your essay.
8. Write the final essay.

CHAPTER 4

On Not Disturbing "Our Group Peace"
The plight of the visiting researcher

Graham Low   Latilla Woodburn[1]

1. Introduction

Trying to discover what British university staff expect is not just a problem for international students; in some ways the problem is even more acute for visiting professors and researchers. While students are standardly given departmental booklets on 'How to study at University X', or can read numerous published study skill guides, visiting academics receive much less in the way of explicit advice. For example, very few university handbooks give them any useful information on how to establish an appropriate balance of friendliness and seriousness, how to flatter or argue with British academics without appearing rude or 'going over the top', how to bring to life or quieten down a British audience, or how to 'project' themselves in such a way that British academics will treat them as colleagues and peers. If the academics concerned have already mastered their home educational system, and achieved status and respect within that, then an unsuccessful seminar in a foreign context can easily lead, at least in their eyes, to an enormous loss of face and prestige.

The dimensions of the 'problem' that the visiting academic needs to solve are numerous and inter-related. While some of the difficulties are purely linguistic, in the narrow sense of the term (i.e. aspects of grammar, spelling or pronunciation), many relate to aspects of British university culture and to the inter-relationship between language and culture.

In this volume, English notes that "close analysis of student writing" (in her case, a university essay) can often serve to highlight significant cultural or rhetorical difficulties experienced by the writer, that might otherwise be overlooked. English extends her analysis at various points by mentioning supplementary data gathered from student interviews; in this paper we wish to take further this notion of combining textual information and reflections on the text by the writer, and to show that integrating data from several sources can sometimes indicate important points that would be hard to infer with much certainty from textual data alone (v. also Seedhouse 1996). Our proposal is that if some form of triangulation is introduced, such as by asking the writer to comment on his or her text (and thereby bringing the writer 'back into the equation' as Scott advocates in this volume), the combined result can show up the complex patterning underlying a text's creation, and disentangle in a reasonably precise way three things:

- attempts to **adapt** to the foreign culture,
- attempts to **retain and exploit** elements derived from one's L1 experience and
- relatively accidental linguistic detail/error.

To this end, we present a brief case study of a Japanese researcher's preparation for a talk to colleagues at a UK university. A case study approach has been chosen, as it allows us to focus in detail on different aspects of a single event and thereby to illustrate how the different types of data interact; our implicit contention is, however, that at a general level the linguistic and cultural problems faced by the researcher are not that atypical.

The paper is structured as follows. In the first part of the analysis (Section 5) we examine the nature of the preparation and consider why the researcher (whom we shall call M) did what he did. In the second part (Section 6) we employ Grice's four maxims for effective communication, in order to derive suggestions for ways in which M could improve his presentation. We do this by taking a roughly analogous text by Richard Feynman and comparing how he and M adhere to or 'violate/flout' the maxims. We end by examining what M actually did when he gave the talk. The presentation part of the talk appears from interviews with M to have been successful:

INTERVIEW EXTRACT 1
G   y.you have now finished the talk?
M   yeah, I finished it on the twenty first January
G   yeah(.) was it successful?
M   presentation itself, I think so
G   good (.) well, that's excellent
M   the questioning and the answering were very difficult for me (.) because (.) I, can't catch what the native speakers said

Our suggestion is that the success of the talk reflects successful learning by M.

2. Context of talk

The speaker, M, is a Personnel Management researcher at a Japanese university. In 1997, he was spending a year at a UK research centre as a visiting researcher and had been invited by a nearby university to give a talk about his work to staff and possibly one or two doctoral students. The talk formed part of a regular weekly programme of talks by guest speakers, and consisted of the traditional pattern of a presentation by the speaker, followed by a question and answer session. The power relationship was likely to be that of approximate equality, that is to say, talking to one's peers — indeed the speaker already knew several members of the audience and they had some familiarity with his research. Having said that, a possible power 'imbalance' was represented by the anticipated presence of a full professor (who had invited the speaker). M's talk was entitled: *Is Japanese Work Organization the Same as Teamworking?*

3. The data

M was keen to prepare for the talk and enrolled as a student on a one-week (25-hour) intensive course in Oral Presentations run by the EFL Unit at the University of York, and taught by one of the present authors (LW). The talk was given 'for real' one week after the York course. As part of the course, M prepared a partial script of his talk, and was given feedback by LW. In the intervening week, he appears to have asked other British academics about how best to give a research talk, and on the basis of the advice given, modified his script. The week after the talk, M agreed to be interviewed (by GDL) about his scripts and the talk. With his permission, the entire discussion was taped, and then transcribed. During the interview M also indicated the changes he made to his original, prepared script when he actually gave the talk. In addition to LW, two EFL teachers, labelled T1 and T2, were asked to react to the transcript of the talk; none read M's interview comments until they had reacted to the initial script.

The present paper is based primarily on M's original and final scripts and the interview data. For the sake of clarity, M's documents will be consistently referred to as 'scripts' and the term 'transcript' will be reserved for the record of the interview. The main transcription conventions are given in Appendix 1.

4. Literacy, criticality and risk reduction

It may be wondered at this point whether it is valid or reliable to explore an oral presentation on the basis of a written transcript and a post-hoc verbal report. We would, however, argue that, in this particular case, the exercise is both valid and reliable; moreover, the reasons why additionally serve to illustrate a number of interesting features about the data. The first 'fact' is that only a short part of the talk was scripted: namely the Preamble (which M called the "Before Introduction"), the Introduction and part of the Conclusion. The main body of the talk was given from notes and/or memory. The second fact is that M was very concerned to get the whole presentation exactly right, and rehearsed the talk at length (Extract 2). The Introduction seems to have represented a point of particular concern:

> INTERVIEW EXTRACT 2
> G how much practice *did* you do?
> M a:: more than (.) ten times, especially this (.) introduction area

One result of this extensive preparation and rehearsal was that M could remember every word of the transcript (including the parts which he had prepared, but did not in the event give) a week later. A second result was that he was very clear about why he had structured the transcript as he had, and why he ultimately omitted certain parts. *Post-hoc* verbal reports of language performance are often felt to be inaccurate, incomplete and highly reactive (e.g. Ericsson & Simon 1984; Cohen 1987; Haastrup 1987; Russo et al. 1989; Stratman & Hamp-Lyons 1994), but in this case the memory of the transcript was engraved upon M's mind and the interviewer avoided asking about unscripted details of the actual presentation.

Ironically, the extended preparation and rehearsal may have 'backfired' in a sense on M. He had, it seems (Extract 3, below), originally intended to transcribe his entire talk, but he spent so much time trying to write things down that he only managed to script the start and the end. Speaking as teachers, we assume that the absence of a script was probably a major contributory factor to the success of the talk!

> INTERVIEW EXTRACT 3
> M ... the main body, I (.) reform and reform (.) so I had, I didn't have enough time to (.) read the perfect draft

Our interpretation of Extract 2 in particular is that M considered the Introduction to be a 'critical point' of the discourse, since it forced him to take a clear position with respect to topics with which he was not familiar and which he considered 'problematic': namely British linguistic and cultural appropriateness.

M treated writing as "a resource" (Weinstein-Shr 1993: 277) which could be applied selectively to resolve a specific problem, whether or not that problem centrally involved writing. In this case, the problem section being the start and end of an oral talk, writing was *not* centrally involved. If correct, our interpretation dovetails neatly with what Street (1984, 1993: 7–12) called an "ideological model" of literacy — or literacies — which is premised on the view that people are active users and exploiters of literacy, not simply passive receptacles. However, Street's ideology view tends to focus on the use of literacy as implicated in power relationships and M's interview comments suggest that, though he was to some degree concerned with implications of power and face, these did not constitute his main reason for bringing writing to bear on the 'critical point' of his discourse:

> INTERVIEW EXTRACT 4
> G (1.5) why did you write, a script (.) and not use notes?
> M er:m, because (1) it is very difficult for (.) us, to speak the (.) s er exact English (2) so er yes, so (.) I have to write, draft (.) without draft, I s:
> ...
> M ... I oftly, make mistakes, fo er **sees:**, **s:ay**, or like that, or **I says**, or something like that, or plural and singular (.) so (.) and er, yes I (.) well, my purpose for coming, here [i.e. on the York course] is to, brush up my English (.) so, writing English makes (1) me, notice them (1) that point or, mistakes, of my poor English, so I write it down.

M is acutely sensitive that his English is less than perfect and uses writing, not so much to formulate ideas, or to manipulate power in a direct fashion, but more to highlight errors, which can then be eliminated in advance (to create "the perfect draft"). Thus writing is used to "minimise risk in communication" (Brown 1995: 29) in what M predicts is going to be a linguistic high-risk context. Writing thus implements a self-imposed "no gain without pain" strategy.

M's awareness of the negative view taken by UK listeners of people who read transcripts is evidenced by the following comment.

> INTERVIEW EXTRACT 5
> G [laughs] OK, so in pract, when you gave it, you actually, you *did* actually read it?
> M ye:, but er, I have to take eye contact with audience and I show OHP (.) and e:r (.) I have to time management, and I cut some parts (.) depending on the situation (.) so:

This is interesting, as it marks a conscious attempt to adapt to perceived UK norms, by exploiting behaviour (eye contact) and ancillary equipment (the OHP) to reduce the inappropriate effects of the script.

5. The initial script of the talk

'Before introduction'

There is a brief greeting section at the beginning. M appears to make reasonably clear right from the start what he is doing. There is thus an attempt at a 'thesis statement', though the precise academic topic is left till later. We will return to this point when we consider Grice's maxims.

> SCRIPT EXTRACT 1
> Good morning, everyone. First of all, I would like to express my gratitude to Professor Landsdown, Dr Oswald and all of you, for giving me such a nice opportunity to do a presentation and to discuss my research topic with you.

M then follows this with a joke aimed at himself. Humour is frequently used as an ice-breaking device in British and American talks, so M might be adapting to UK norms. On the other hand, the density of assumptions about Japanese culture might imply a degree of transfer from Japanese (though we have found little or no research on the use or non-use of humour within Japanese presentations).

> SCRIPT EXTRACT 2
> Before moving on to the main part of my presentation, let me introduce myself in brief. My name is Eiji Morita. My sir name "Morita" is famous for you, western people, especially for people interested in business world, because it is the same pronunciation as that of Mr Morita, the chairman of Sony, though my "Morita" in Kanji character is different from that of his.

The interview data (Extracts 6 & 7) make it clear that no transfer whatsoever is intended, with respect to either the content of the joke (the characters make the joke pointless in Japanese), or the fact of using a joke at all. M is thus using his own culture as an adaptation strategy.

> INTERVIEW EXTRACT 6
> G   but would you have made the joke? you could still Imake the joke
> M   Ioh no, no no
> G   you could still make the joke (.) why not?
> M   they don't accept it
> G   really?
> M   I think so

> INTERVIEW EXTRACT 7
> G   OK, well change it slightly (.) would you, if you were doing this in Japan, would you begin with a joke?
> M   no

G   why not?
M   as I said before, they (.) we *don't have* such a, cultural background to accept, joke
G   even in this situation where you're all researchers, you've all got doctorates? it's|
M | I think
G   the same sort of power relationship
M   I think *this* situation (.) *doesn't*, accept, such kind of joke rather than the general situation, like this (.) m:m (.) especially, at seminar, or at conference

M now moves on to relate details about himself and his life, and includes some information about education in Japan.

SCRIPT EXTRACT 3
I teach at K. University, Osaka, Japan and am currently a visiting researcher at the Greater Manchester Centre for Japanese Studies. I came to Manchester in April last year and will stay to the end of the coming March, since this opportunity is given as my sabbatical and as you know, in Japan school term starts in April and ends in March. Here, I have got opportunities to visit some manufacturing companies, both Japanese and British, and also interviewed British and Japanese managers, in order to know what is happening especially in work organization in the UK. However, today's presentation is not based on this research but on other researches I did in Japan.

INTERVIEW EXTRACT 8
G   now (.) again, if, if this was in Japan (.) w would you have given (.) a fairly extensive description of, about yourself and your movements?
M   m:::m yeah (1) if I: never (.) talked with, the audience or, I was invited to the (2) or, to the (.) how to say (.) yeah (1) d depending on the audience but er, I understand (.) they don't know me (.) very well, I may, introduce myself (.) and that, very, the, how to say (1) I take such a long, a long minute to, introduce myself
G   and you would talk about parts of your life, erm
M   mm if it, had relationship with my, research or my, today that day topic

SCRIPT EXTRACT 4
I think it would be better for me to tell you the reason why I come to this country, since it is closely related with my research interest. The reason I come here is that this country is the birth place of the Socio-Technical Systems theory developed by the Tavistock Institute in London.

The 'Before Introduction' ends with two lines of positive flattery about the culture of the audience.

SCRIPT EXTRACT 5
The encounter with it in my graduate days lead me to the academic world and it is not exaggerated to say that the encounter has made what I am today. I am very interested in it and, as I will mention this point later again, it gives my research a theoretical base. I would be very happy if you would kindly tell me, during the discussion time or after this session, how the STS theory is currently dealt with in British academic world or what impact the Tavistock Institute now has on academic and so on.
And I should never forget to say the second reason to come to the UK. It is because I like the United Kingdom and the British better than any other countries.

INTERVIEW EXTRACT 9
G   ... it then becomes an evaluation (.) and you were going to end this section (.) with (.) saying (.) well you know *this* is wonderful *that's* wonderful *everything's* wonderful
M   aahuh
G   is what you would again do in Japan? would you be expected to
M   yes I think this is what Japanese style (done?) this kind of joke
G   (3) but this is ser, this is serious, this is not
M   mm yeah (.) this is not a joke, but er if I was invited in Tokyo (.) I'm living (.) Osaka, different area in Japan (.) but but er, I come to Tokyo, thank you for inviting me to Tokyo, Tokyo is a very good place (.) like that, fine, I think I (.) I must, I must, *must*, no, I'm sure I say (.) such kind of er (.) great greetings, or something like that
G   and somewhere it is ex*pec*ted that you will say, that this is a very good place here
M   yeah

General reactions to the 'Before Introduction'

Overall, the most salient feature of the 'Before Introduction' is the fact that it does not appear to relate closely to the talk itself. In the interview, M himself noted that the script is a reflection of the Japanese tendency (see Seedhouse 1991) to work round to the main point:

INTERVIEW EXTRACT 10
M   yeah, in Japan we (.) we::, first we talk about the (.) you know, surface area or f [inbreath] not the not the core but er (1) how to say?
G   periphery?
M   yeah yeah periphery yeah (.) and er (.) slowly go to the core [laughs]
G   *how* slowly?

M   he::m depends on the situation, depends on the people, but er, oh: (1) we say, if I have given, three minutes, presentation (.) maybe (.) three minutes or five minutes (.) I spend, going not (...ing?)

This tendency is identical to what Young (1982) found with her group of Chinese businessmen. In Young's words, the text reflects "where the argument is coming from", rather than "where the argument is going to". Listening to the data, Young's native speakers of English were perplexed: "The main point was initially lost on them, because it lay buried in a mass of information". Stylistically, there was a lack of "clarity and forcefulness". "Worst of all, the lack of precision and the failure to address the point directly led to suspicions that the ... speakers were beating around the bush" (all refs, 1982: 79). This directly parallels the reactions of the York EFL teachers: "very unclear" (T1), "a lot of muddying of the waters" (T1), "just padding" (T2).

While there is certainly some evidence of transfer with respect to the length of the self-description and the need to flatter the audience, one must be careful not to exaggerate. Firstly, if either of us (GDL and LW) had been invited to speak at an overseas university, we would actively wish to say something nice about the location and the audience; the transfer lies perhaps in the extreme case formulation M chose to use (**never forget, better than any other countries**). Secondly, the comments above and the reactions of T1 and T2 might seem to be completely accounted for by Seedhouse's (1994: 7) comment that "Japanese argument follows an indirect cyclical pattern, and 'Japanese logic does not run in the straight lines of Western analytic thinking which emphasize the consecutive ordering of arguments'". A close analysis of M's script, however, lends only partial support to this conclusion. It is true that a degree of recycling takes place, when M repeatedly notes that his talk will be based on his research (a point which he will make again in the Introduction proper). There is also some indirectness, as when M describes research that he is not going to discuss. On the other hand, there is a clear line of progression through the section, where each chunk retains some of the previous chunk and then adds something new:

1   *M and his feelings, in the context of the people in the UK department*
2   *Describing M as a person*
3   *Describing M as a researcher*
4   *M as a researcher in the context of UK research*
5   *The UK's effect on M's feelings*

As can be seen, there is also a framing effect, as (5) harks back to (1), but this is not evidence of some sort of oriental circularity; boundary framing effects are common in 'Western' discourse, both spoken and written (v. Drew and Holt 1995: 125–6; Low 1997).

Introduction section

The Introduction begins with an explicit transition from preamble to "today's main". M then apologises for a very minor error in the title as advertised.

> SCRIPT EXTRACT 6
> So, let's move on to today's main.
> The title of today's presentation is "Is Japanese work organization the same as teamworking?" I sent to Dr Oswald a wrong title by E-mail, in which the word "teamworking" was divided into two words that means 'team, space and working'. I would like to apologize for my mistake and would like you to correct the title, using teamworking as one word.

Both T1 and T2 reacted identically to this section: "Omit. Irrelevant to presentation …" (T1) and "Is this necessary?". Why does M include it? It is not obvious from the script whether M felt that he was responding to Japanese traditions, or whether he considered this section to be adaptation to the worries of a Western research group. The interview data makes it clear that the need for exactness in all things is essentially transfer from the Japanese environment. M appears to argue that a difference in the title would represent him imposing something on the audience and that the audience might not be amused at finding a mismatch with what they thought they had agreed to. M happily shoulders all the blame for the problem, and since the minor error is formulated as an extreme case, the degree of blame shouldered is made to sound quite large.

> INTERVIEW EXTRACT 11
> G ... why did you think (.) it was wer, it was worth, saying?
> M becau:se (.) team*work*ing and team working, but teamwork er there are many many (.) words concerning (1) this style (.) this work style |in our field
> G |yeah
> M so:: summaries such are used team (.) working (1) but er, for me teamworking is, must be one word and it has (.) several words has er, special meaning, so
> G   mm
> G but if it's two words it doesn't make sense, in English (.) OK?
> M yes
> G one *one* word (.) makes perfect, hundred per cent sense
> M yes
> G two words (.) grammatically (.) it looks as though there's something wrong, it looks like a mistake
> M mm
> G now, the person (.) you e-mailed

M   yeah
G   was English
M   yes
G   so, they should've known (.)
M   uu:h
G   now, what you've said is, "it's not your mistake it's mine"
M   mm
G   why?
M   yeah even (.) this is also in, in Japanese situation (1) we have (.) it's a big mistake (.) the (.) difference (.) yeah (1) small differen:ce (.) yes, yes, it's a very tiny point I think, but er (.) in Japan (.) some researchers, say (.) official, your your title is like that, today's ver, today's handout is like that, that's the difference I think (over there?) so (.) very (.) small point very tiny point but er (.) we were, taught (.) by my (other?) supervisor (.) to (.) use the word exactly, very (1)
G   is it important because, I mea the title is (.) advertised publicly and
M   yes I think so because, people (.) audience come (.) decide whether come to my, presentation or not, by seeing the title
G   yes
M   s:o (.) I think (.) the title (.) is very important for, this kind of thing, yeah

Although M implies that his attention to minuscule detail represents transfer of cultural expectations, this is perhaps another context where one should be careful not to exaggerate. Doi (1992: 210) admittedly perceives attention to detail as a central characteristic stressed by the Japanese education system, noting that "the emphasis on academic 'preciseness' has taken precedence over the concern for individual growth and development of character and personality". To this might be added Bayne's (1996: 309) comment (about undergraduates) that, "the fear of mistakes and sense of risk felt by Japanese students is perhaps the single most debilitating feature of the Japanese EFL classroom". However, an alternative explanation seems possible. We have already noted M's desire for perfection and concern to eliminate all error. Hansen-Strain and Strain's (1990) comparative study of Japanese learners of English found that they experienced markedly greater anxiety than the other groups examined (including Chinese and Korean learners). We would accordingly suggest that M's error elimination and over-attention to detail can be just as easily explained by a perfectly understandable anxiety at the thought of looking a complete fool if the talk were to go wrong. The anxiety explanation would also help account for (a) why M joined the intensive course at York and (b) why (as will be shown below) he repeatedly referred in the interview to the need to create strategies designed to force his listeners to slow down their speed when asking questions at the end. As the interview demonstrated that M *did* lose the thread when I spoke too fast (unfortunately, the transcript does not indicate rate of delivery), his anxiety was in part related not so much to cultural transfer, but to a realistic evaluation of his own linguistic skills.

The apology is followed by a linearly sequenced summary of the structure of the talk, with each section flagged appropriately (**First I am going to talk about; Then I will move on to; Finally I sum up the research results by discussing**). There are periodic grammatical and semantic errors, but the structure is clear and Western oriented.

Conclusion section

The conclusion contains three terms whose genesis is unclear: **wrap up**, **selfish** and **offer**. None seem entirely appropriate, but the text by itself gives few clues about whether they are lexical errors due to selecting the wrong word from a dictionary, or whether more is at stake.

> SCRIPT EXTRACT. 7
> So that **wraps up** my presentation.
> I would be happy to do further explanation about what remains unclear for you and to take any question. I, however, would like you to accept my **selfish offer** that you would kindly speak slower than your natural speed because it is a little bit difficult for me to catch up with your normal speed.

The interview rapidly made it clear that **wraps up** came from a Japanese reference book based on American English. No style jump or conscious irony was involved, even though, as we have established, M was well aware of the 'British' view that injecting some humour into a talk is a 'good thing'... and that **offer** was a semantic error for something like **request**.

> INTERVIEW EXTRACT 12
> M yeah, the reason I (.) choose this word from the (.) textbook, I bought in Japan (.) and i, in Japan English (.) education (.) is based on, American English
> ...
> M so (.) I choose this phrase, from that book, so (.) that=s why I chose this word
>
> INTERVIEW EXTRACT 13
> G ... what did you mean by **offer**?
> M I (.) I just st, meaning, I (.) ask you (.) my asking is, please speak slower than usual

G   oh I see
M   yeah
G   so, perhaps in that case, this is (.) you=ve just got the wrong English word and you wanted (.) I don=t know, **request**
M   yes
G   perhaps (.) with with a request, you want *the:m* to do something (.) an offer means, *you're* going to do something
M   mm (.) so thi this is choice of words

The case with **selfish** is, however, quite different, though again no style jump or conscious self-irony is intended. **Selfish** involves pragmatic transfer from Japanese. It constitutes an attempt to request, but at the same time to lower the degree of imposition on the audience, by apologising for thinking of oneself too much. The word could, nevertheless, involve pragmatic transfer *and* represent a lexical error, inasmuch as selfishness, with its overtones of childish willfulness, being spoilt and perhaps even disobedience, is not a characteristic which we at least easily associate with 'giving a talk'. However, the interview makes it very clear that it is *not* a lexical error for a word such as, say, **personal**; **selfish** and 'wagamama' are perceived as having very similar meanings and connotations. This was confirmed by our checking Takahashi's Japanese-English Dictionary. The result becomes a curious mixture of intended translation and actual error!

INTERVIEW EXTRACT 14
M   yeah, **selfish** means that er (.) yes I asked, at the others to slow down your (.) usual pace, your natural pace (.) e:rm so, if I don=t ask such a (.) if I don't ask them (.) they can speak normal speed (.) but I ask them, to slow down their speed (.) speech, speak so (.) erm:, but *this* may be Japanese, in Japan I, we say, this (.) this is tra (.) direct translation from Japanese words
G   OK (.) keep explaining to me, if this was in Japanese, what, what would you actually be saying? Do you, sort of give it me in more words
M   ye:ah, mm (2.5) yes (.) by my asking (.) everybody have to (.) change their pace (.) because I ask them to speak slower, than usual, so (.) oh I feel I'm sorry (.) to disturb your, own usual, pace your usual, talking, so, that means **selfish**
G   how strong, in English, **selfish** is a very strong word (.)
M   mm
G   erm (.) and, you would use it, as (.) not quite an insult, but (.) it's a very very negative, statement about someone's behaviour, you are *not* supposed to be **selfish** it's a it's a very, bad thing to be (.) now, if you describe (.) what, your own behaviour as **selfish** you're making a very strong statement, about yourself
M   mm

> G so, what I'm saying is, if you do this in Japanese, is it a *very* strong statement in Japanese?
> M no no, not so strong (.) we all think it's
> G what is the, can you just write, what is the Japanese equivalent, do you want to write it?
> M yeah (6) **wagamama** (4)
> G I'm going to look this up in the dictionary 'cos we have some [both laugh]
> M so (1) my behaviour disturb, our (.) co-ordination or, my behaviour disturb (.) our group peace and collect, collectivity
> G OK, yes, so it *has* got the same idea as the English then, that it's disturbing other, what other people would like to do
> M yeah

This unwillingness to impose resembles M's shouldering an exaggerated burden concerning the error in the title and together may be seen as Brown and Levinson's 'negative politeness'. The need to praise the audience at the end of the 'Before Introduction' is perhaps more 'positive face', but remains close in spirit. Lebra (1987) relates politeness to the roles of 'standing out of the crowd' and silence in Japanese discourse, citing the Japanese proverb: "if the bird had not sung, it would not have been shot." This is very close to the remarks that Young's Chinese informants made about the role of the speaker in a group discourse. Not only should speakers refrain from making prestige-damaging statements, but they should also refrain from presumptuousness: "you are not considering the other members of the group. Thus you'd be hurting people by claiming something for yourself" (1985: 81). Condon (1986: 30, approvingly cited by Doi 1995) talks of this as 'shame': Japan is a "shame culture"; mothers train children by "appeals to the primary means of social control in the culture, shame". However, though M apologises in both the script (**I would like to apologise**) and — as part of his explanation — the interview (**I'm sorry**), neither show any obvious marks that we can see of a feeling of 'shame'. On the other hand, if acting out of 'shame' is intended to mean something less extreme, such as focusing on the *emotion* felt as a result of a problem, rather than (unemotionally) stating the *reason why* there is a problem (i.e. justifying it), then M's utterance can be almost entirely accounted for in terms of the Japanese, or rather "Japanist" 'world view' as described by Doi.

6. Grice and the problem of inferencing

The analysis thus far has focused on what M intended, and why his (initial) script looks as it does. However, this does not fully indicate why a British audience might feel unhappy, and it does not provide a useful basis for suggesting corrections that M might make.

In this last analytic section, we turn to Grice's Co-operative Principle and its four component maxims: of *quality, quantity, relevance* (or 'relation') and *manner*. We assume that the reader is familiar with them, but if not a summary may be found in Levinson (1983: 101–102). Grice's maxims appear to have been derived with a 'Western' speech community in mind and describe well the sort of terse, focused communication that formal university seminars involve. Whether they fit informal conversation is another matter, which we will not pursue here. Our starting point is that, to the best of our knowledge, neither M nor the audience had any 'secret' aims or intentions which they wished to realise via the guest lecture. We therefore feel justified in making the assumption that if Grice's maxims are not kept (or perceived to be kept), successful communication will break down in some way; breakdowns can range from minor misunderstandings to major failures to express an intended meaning.

What we want to do is to compare M's script with a published introduction to a set of lectures on physics by Richard Feynman (1985). Though not identical, the two contexts are sufficiently analogous for the comparison to be reasonably valid. Feynman's text is of particular interest because, structurally, Feynman adopts the same pattern as M, in that he has a 'lead-in' similar to the 'Before Introduction'. It is these two sections that we will compare: the lead-in and the 'Before Introduction'. Here is Feynman's lead-in:

> Alix Mautner was very curious about physics and often asked me to explain things to her. I would do all right, just as I do with a group of students at Caltech that come to me for an hour on Thursdays, but eventually I'd fail at what is to me the most interesting part: We would always get hung up on the crazy ideas of quantum mechanics. I told her I couldn't explain these ideas in an hour or an evening — it would take a long time — but I promised her that some day I'd prepare a set of lectures on the subject.
>
> I prepared some lectures, and I went to New Zealand to try them out — because New Zealand is far enough away that if they weren't successful, it would be all right! Well, the people in New Zealand thought they were okay, so I guess they're okay — at least for New Zealand! So here are the lectures I really prepared for Alix, but unfortunately I can't tell them to her directly, now.
>
> What I'd like to talk about is a part of physics that is known, rather than a part that is unknown. People are always asking for the latest developments in the unification of this theory with that theory, and they don't give us a chance to tell them about one of the theories that we know pretty well. They always want to know things that we don't know. So, rather than confound you

with a lot of half-cooked, partially analyzed theories, I would like to tell you about a subject that has been very thoroughly analyzed.

Feynman flouts the maxim of relevance with his first two words: a personal name unrelated in any obvious way to the topic of the lecture. The effect is to grab the audience's attention and to create a mild shock, or perhaps to stimulate questions such as 'What is this about?'. The maxim of manner is also flouted; Alix Mautner is obscure — it is not clear why she is mentioned so prominently. As Feynman develops his story about Alix, key phrases reappear: "interesting part", "quantum mechanics", "set of lectures on the subject". These 'leitmotivs' allow the audience to start to recover from their mild shock and, assuming that Feynman intends what he is saying to be relevant, they can infer the underlying coherence of the discourse. The words "So here are the lectures I really prepared for Alix" allow the audience to complete their inference — and enjoy Feynman's relaxed, jokey lead-in. A probable final inference would be: 'I prepared these lectures because I needed to find a way to explain fully a part of physics that I consider is really important'.

In his lead-in Feynman flouts another part of the maxim of manner, namely 'be brief' — however, he adheres to the sub-maxim 'be orderly' and this permits his audience to connect together the group of key phrases. Had Feynman also flouted the 'be orderly' requirement, our impression is that the audience would probably have given up in despair!

We may now turn to M's script, and examine how the 'Before Introduction' (see Script extracts 1 to 5 above) relates to Grice's maxims. The object is to locate points at which M departs from the maxims and to predict the likely effect on the audience. Feynman's lead-in section creates a particular relationship between speaker and audience — it is unexpected, not the norm, yet the audience is likely to understand its purpose without any real difficulty. However, our own reaction to reading M's 'Before Introduction' (i.e. *before* we undertook the analysis in the previous sections) was close to the reactions expressed by T1 and T2: a degree of disorientation, and uncertainty about M's intended aims. Like Feynman, M flouts the maxim of relevance. In the second paragraph (see Script extract 2), the reference to his own name (as part of the joke) is possibly interesting, but not connected in any obvious way with the subject of the talk. The references concerning when he came to Manchester also seem like blind alleys, down which the reader gets lost. The negative comment that, "today's presentation is *not* based on this research ..." at the end of the third paragraph again flouts the relevance maxim (*Why* is M telling us about this work?). In fact, the paragraph could also be said to break the maxim of manner, in that it is 'obscure'; T2 for example suggested that it was "too culturally based" and T1 asked "Does this cloud the issue?". Both second and third paragraphs could be said to be too long (at least for a British audience) and thus break another aspect of the maxim of manner.

In the final two paragraphs of the 'Before Introduction' (see Script extracts 4 & 5), the need to 'avoid obscurity' and the need to 'be brief' are again flouted. The reference to Socio-Technical Systems ("it gives my research a theoretical base") leads us to expect some development of this point by the speaker. However, not only is this expectation not met, but we are given almost the polar opposite: a request for information about STS from the audience. The result is that it is hard to infer a clear connection between the two points (T1 simply wrote "Is this relevant?" next to the second point).

By the end of the 'Before Introduction' the reader has an accumulated inferencing problem. Is the text intended to serve as a background to the theoretical position which will be adopted? Is the Before Introduction giving personal reasons for an interest in the area of research to be addressed? We have no real way to tell. The primary problem again seems to lie in the length of the digressions, which can easily signify to the British listener that the text concerned is of particular importance to the content of the paper to come. In Gricean terms, the combined effect of not being brief (i.e. the maxim of manner) is to violate the maxim of quantity ('Make your contribution as informative as is required for the current purposes of the exchange'). This combined effect makes it hard to make inferences which are "fundamental to our sense of coherence in discourse" (Levinson 1983: 107).

Both M and Feynman flout the Gricean maxims as a way of creating interest and expectations on the part of the audience. Moreover, the main rhetorical point of Feynman's Alix story and the use of a 'personal', highly interactive style is to create the expectation of a non-threatening, non-patronising explanation of research; our analysis in the earlier sections showed that M was most concerned to do exactly the same. Indeed, this accounts for much of what underlies M's desire not to "disturb our group peace and ... collectivity". So how is it that M's flouting of the Gricean maxims fail, but Feynman's appear to succeed? Apart from the question of length (which as we noted earlier is the locus of marked cultural differences), one major difference can perhaps be seen in the way M and Feynman treat negative information. M explains at length his research, then finishes the paragraph with the negative comment that what we have just learned is not going to be used. There is a brief coda that something else will be used, but that 'something else' is undefined and no amplification occurs in the next paragraph. The result is a disjointed, isolated text unit, which ends on an anti-climax. Feynman, on the other hand, ends Paragraph Two by saying that Alix cannot be the audience, but creates the *positive* implication that we as readers will benefit in her place. Paragraph Three also starts with a rejection (Feynman will discuss the "known" not the "unknown"), but the rest of the paragraph explains in a *positive* way why we as the new audience should not feel worried about receiving Alix's lectures. Feynman thus links negative comments to a positive line of argument and avoids the use of isolated text units.

7. What happened in practice: The talk M actually gave

The script, the interview data and the comparison with the Feynman lead-in have allowed us to plot reasonably accurately how M tried to prepare for his guest lecture, and have provided a basis for suggestions about how to improve it. It is to these that we now turn. As this is a success story, it has a simple and (appropriately) short ending; both the advice given to M and the solution adopted by M can be summarised very briefly.

Our advice was to omit all of the 'Before Introduction' except for the opening greeting. This would remove the isolated text units and over-long sections, thereby eliminating the accumulated inferencing problem. The intended adaptation device of the joke would also be lost, but this seemed a small price to pay.

As regards the Conclusion, we suggested modifying **wrap up** and omitting the whole paragraph concerning the **selfish offer**. It appears that several of M's British friends suggested the same changes and M took on board the need to be brief, concise, positive and only mildly polite.

We end with M's interview comments describing what he did. They illustrate, we believe, successful learning:

> INTERVIEW EXTRACT 15
> M ... this area, I *did*n't, speak this part (1) in the presentation [points to Paras 2&3 of "Before Introduction".], because, er time is, very (.) we don't have enough time, we didn't have enough time, and e:r (.) some, British (.) suggested me (.) British people, don't like this kind of introduction, like that (1) so, British people like, conci:se, conversation

> INTERVIEW EXTRACT 16
> M and er, the, and I (.) didn't use this phrase [**selfish offer**] (.) er (1.5) I don't remember but I change this: phrases (.) my my English friends, kindly changed this phrases (.) yes but, I don't remember what I said, but I, certainly change this area, but I s:aid, pleas:e s: speak slower than usual, because I can't catch (.) your, your natural speed (.) yes

Acknowledgments

Our thanks to Marianne Miller and Sarah Waud for their reactions to the script and above all to M, whose willingness to talk at length about his preparation work is greatly appreciated.

Note

1. The second author was the tutor on the course described and provided the initial draft of the speech act analyses which form the second part of the paper.

Appendix: Transcription conventions

italics	Heavy, especially contrastive stress.
,	Brief pause, frequently marking tone group or rhythm group boundary.
(.)	Pause of c. .5 second.
(1.5)	Pauses from 1 second upwards are timed to nearest half-second
[laughs]	Comment or explanation by GDL.
|	Interruption, or speaking concurrently.
?	GDL interpretation as a question. Generally rising pitch, or jump plus high fall.
is: e::r	Audible lengthening of vowel or consonant. Subjective values (:: is longer than :).

References

Bayne, K. 1996. "Three Strategies to Raise Levels of Learner Participation in Content-heavy Classrooms in Japan." *Dokkyo University Studies in Foreign Language Teaching* 15: 301–323.

Brown, G. 1995. *Speakers, Listeners and Communication.* Cambridge: CUP.

Cohen, A. D. 1987. "Using Verbal Reports in Research on Language Learning." In C. Faerch and G. Kaspar (eds), *Introspection in Second Language Research.* 82–95. Clevedon: Multilingual Matters.

Condon, J. C. 1986. *With Respect to the Japanese.* Tokyo: Yohan Publications.

Doi, K. 1992. "Reflections on Japanese Education". *The Journal of the College of Foreign Languages, Himeji Dokkyo University* 5: 203–214.

Doi, K. 1995. "Japanism as a Worldview: Cultural Idiosyncracies." *The Journal of the College of Foreign Languages,* Himeji Dokkyo University 8: 294–302.

Drew, P. and Holt, E. 1995. "Idiomatic Expressions and their Role in the Organisation of Topic Transition in Conversation." In M. Everaert, E.-J. van der Linden, A. Schenk and R. Schreuder (eds), *Idioms: Structural and Psychological Perspectives,* 117–132. Hillsdale, NJ: Lawrence Erlbaum,

Ericsson, K. A. and Simon, H. A. 1984. *Protocol Analysis: Verbal reports as data.* Cambridge, MA: MIT Press.

Feynman, R. P. 1985. *QED.* Harmondsworth: Penguin.

Haastrup, K. 1987. "Using Thinking Aloud and Retrospection to Uncover Learners' Lexical Inferencing Procedures." In C. Faerch and G. Kaspar (eds), *Introspection in Second Language Research,* 197–212. Clevedon: Multilingual Matters.

Hansen-Strain, L. and Strain, J. E. 1990. "Learning Styles of the Japanese Second Language Learner: Field Sensitivity, Cognitive Tempo, Test Anxiety, Modality Preference." *The Journal of the College of Foreign Languages,* Himeji Dokkyo University 3: 257–275.

Lebra, T. S. 1987. "The Cultural Significance of Silence in Japanese Communication." *Multilingua* 6(4): 343–354.

Levinson, S. 1983. *Pragmatics.* Cambridge: CUP.

Low, G. D. 1997. *Celebrations and SQUID Sandwiches: Figurative language and the management of non-core academic text.* Project report. University of York, EFL Unit.

Russo, J. E., Johnson, J. E. and Stephens, D. L. 1989. "The Validity of Verbal Protocols". *Memory and Cognition* 17(6): 759–769.

Seedhouse, P. 1991. "Problems of Oral Production with Japanese Learners". *Aston LSU Bulletin* 4: 20–24.

Seedhouse, P. 1994. *From Needs Analysis to Course Design.* Applied Language Research Paper 94/03. University of York, Department of Educational Studies.

Seedhouse, P. 1996. Learning Talk: A Study of the interactional organisation of the L2 classroom from a CA institutional discourse perspective. University of York: Unpublished D.Phil thesis.

Stratman, J. F. and Hamp-Lyons, E. 1994. "Reactivity in Concurrent Think-aloud Protocols: Issues for research." In P. Smagorinski (ed.), *Speaking About Writing,* 89–112. Beverley Hills, CA: Sage.

Street, B. V. 1984. *Literacy in Theory and Practice.* Cambridge: CUP.

Street, B. V. 1993. "Introduction: The new literacy studies." In B. Street (ed.), *Cross-Cultural Approaches to Literacy,* 1–21. Cambridge: CUP.

Takahashi, M. 1953. *Romanised English-Japanese, Japanese-English Dictionary.* Tokyo: Taisedo.

Weinstein-Shr, G. 1993. "Literacy and Social Process: A community in transition." In B. Street (ed.), *Cross-Cultural Approaches to Literacy,* 272–293. Cambridge: CUP.

Young, L. W-L. 1982. "Inscrutability Revisited." In J. Gumperz (ed.), *Language and Social Identity,* 72–84. Cambridge: CUP.

CHAPTER 5

Writing Assignments on a PGCE (Secondary) Course
Two case studies

Brenda Gay   Carys Jones   Jane Jones

Introduction

It is becoming increasingly clear that the problems of academic writing at university for some students need to be given much more attention than hitherto. Researchers and tutors who help students with their writing and the students themselves have raised concerns about a variety of underlying issues as they perceive them (Cohen 1993; Lea 1995; Low 1996). However, the perspectives of course tutors, who play a central role in their students' academic writing, are much more rarely presented. This chapter attempts to redress the balance. It examines two case studies, each of which presents the perspectives of a course tutor on one student's academic writing. The context is the writing of assignments during a one-year (secondary) Post-Graduate Certificate of Education (PGCE) course at a University Department of Education (UDE).

The professional development of teachers is multi-faceted and subject to severe time constraints. The course itself normally lasts only 36 weeks, of which 24 have to be spent in school leaving only 12 weeks for attendance at the UDE. Teaching is perceived as a demanding and challenging career and PGCE students are required to train under often very stressful conditions (Calderhead & Shorrock 1997). They are encouraged to develop their understanding of school teaching and learning through acquiring expertise in the classroom, through developing their understanding of secondary schools as educational and social institutions and through reflecting on their experiences in the light of theory. The daily pattern of life in schools is one of constant pressure while still further demands are made of the students by the UDE.

Becoming a teacher is perceived as an on-going, continual process, during which there is constant dialogue between theory and practice at different levels — from classroom practice to philosophical issues — to encourage reflection on practice (Schön 1987, 1983). In school, observations and experiences of classroom teaching practice are reinforced by feedback and discussions and students are required to write lesson evaluations. In the UDE, activities such as microteaching and practical presentations are discussed in the light of theoretical considerations. All written assignments are expected to draw directly on observation and experience and to be underpinned by theory. In order to qualify as teachers, students are assessed on their performance as teachers in the classroom and on their written assignments.

Students are accepted onto the course following consideration of their application forms, references and their performance at interview with the special subject tutor for their curriculum area. Briefly, candidates are required to display evidence of being suitably qualified and knowledgeable about their subject, being genuinely interested in teaching as a profession, having good communication skills and generally displaying the potential to become a good teacher. Additionally, the government has expressed a need for more science teachers and a need for more teachers from minority ethnic communities (Swann 1985). The scarcity of numbers of students wanting to become science teachers means that the qualifications of some science teacher trainees may be significantly lower than those of students training to become teachers in the humanities subject areas. Students vary greatly in their cultural and educational backgrounds as well as in how they perceive the demands of the course. This means that the range of ways in which students develop during the course and the variety of issues which have to be addressed are extremely wide and complex. In this particular UDE, students are required to reach a satisfactory standard on 3 major assignments during the course. Naturally, some students have an easier time than others depending on several factors: their past experiences; their initial understandings about their chosen profession, how they cope with the pressures which confront them; how they relate to their school communities during the course. These factors are the concern of their tutors whose role is to tap into their needs and provide appropriate support.

All students are designated at least one school tutor and two college course tutors (a subject tutor and a school policy issues tutor), who play a part both in providing guidance when necessary and in assessing the students' teaching and written performances. Because of the time constraints, students are assisted with preparing their three main written assignments in ways which are intended to be as efficient and effective as possible. At the beginning of the year they are asked to write a preliminary essay about their own school experiences so that any problems with writing can be detected and addressed early on in the course. Some students are advised to seek the support facility which is offered. The writing support tutor takes the student through a miniature academic writing course based on providing feedback on a sample of writing. The feedback is written and, after the student has had time to consider it, it is later discussed in a tutorial. The same procedure is repeated with further written samples until help is no longer required. The aim is that the student should develop an enhanced, critical understanding of his or her own writing in relation to the demands of the task. Detailed guidelines for each of the assignments are given in the student course handbook. For the first assessed assignment, which is a report on one aspect of the student's school experiences, hypothetical examples of suitable topics and recommended stages of preparing the assignments are outlined. A more detailed picture of what is expected in the assignment is given in an hour's oral presentation and reinforced with a handout. To summarise, the students have access to advice for writing from several sources: the handbook, the oral presentation and handouts, their school and college tutors, and the writing support tutor. In addition, the handbook contains a detailed description of the criteria used to assess all three essays. Internal agreement about the assessment is negotiated between marker and student as far as possible.

Research in recent years into the nature of the problems of academic writing encountered by some students has revealed a range of complexities. The perspectives of students about their own academic writing and of tutors who provide writing support have been particularly revealing. As both Lea and English in this volume show, students' perceptions of their own written work can sometimes differ greatly from the perceptions of those who assess their work. Sometimes students are surprised and disappointed to receive unexpectedly low marks for their written assignments. Writing support tutors also suggest that there may be a lack of communication between subject tutors and their students leading to misunderstandings about expectations (Lea & Street 1998). As Ivanic points out, the values and practices of the academic cultural context are difficult for students to grasp (1994) and students may try too hard to please their course tutors. Sometimes students are worried about having to construct another identity for themselves in the effort to try and please their tutor (Street 1994; Turner & Hiraga 1996). In doing so, they may lose sight of the focus of the assignment resulting in poor content organisation, poor discourse organisation and inappropriate language use (Gorman, Gubb & Price 1987).

The perceptions of course tutors who are primarily responsible for assessing students' written assignments in higher education have also been investigated (Lea, in this volume; Lea & Street 1998) but not explored in great detail nor with respect to any one course: nor has the provision of guidelines. Here two distinctive case studies from the PGCE course at one UDE are considered in order to provide a more composite picture of the problems. Each case study presents the perceptions of one PGCE course tutor about the assignment writing of one tutee.

Two case studies

The two case studies demonstrate how the tutors each consider the processes of assignment writing and evaluate the written assignment of one of their student tutees. In Case Study A, Nadège, whose mother tongue is French, has been educated in France and is training to become a teacher of MFL (Modern Foreign Languages). Her work is being evaluated by her UDE subject tutor, Jane. In Case Study B, Romatu is from North Africa, where she has received most of her education up to degree level. She is now living in Britain and training to be a science teacher. Her work is being evaluated by her UDE school policy issues tutor, Brenda. The many years' experience of teaching and of teacher training on the PGCE course of both tutors is evident in the discussions.

The tutors give their perspectives of the student's writing abilities in relation to the course criteria. The two case studies are strikingly different. However, the purpose of examining these two cases is not to highlight comparisons and contrasts but to identify those features which do emerge as important for the tutors in their consideration of the written assignments of the two students. The range of differences serves to reveal the complexities involved.

A brief summary of two different scenarios

In Case Study A, Jane describes what importance is given to language-related difficulties that may be encountered by a French native speaker wanting to qualify as a teacher in Britain. She discusses in some detail several examples of errors taken from Nadège's assignment. She also argues for the importance of examining performance errors in relation to the assignment. She describes it as 'written in near flawless English' and as 'a considerable achievement in linguistic terms'. Her overall assessment is: 'I had no problem in assigning a clear pass to this student.' On a more general level Jane draws attention to how cultural differences can account for problems with assignment writing, notably issues which are important to the educational ethos and the taken-for-granted conventions of essay structure, both of which could be alien to the student's own educational background. She argues that a detailed analysis of the errors in an assignment can greatly benefit the students concerned, can contribute towards 'the fairest evaluation of a student's written performance' and can be used in the wider educational context to beneficial effect.

In Case Study B, Brenda, without having the same degree of general knowledge about African countries as Jane has about France, draws on her own and other colleagues' specific knowledge of Romatu. She describes how Romatu was accepted on to the course and how she forms her first impressions of this student. In order to evaluate Romatu's written work, Brenda finds it necessary to consider a wide range of factors about her because it is not discrete errors which she finds worrying but the whole framework surrounding her assignment. Brenda suggests, like Jane, that any language-related issues are embedded within cultural considerations which may explain the way Romatu approaches her task. Brenda describes Romatu as lively and intelligent during discussions, but as not appearing to think and work independently, as mistakenly equating 'hard work with success' and identifying her problems 'as language problems'. More generally, she argues that Romatu's approach 'raises a number of questions concerning the expectations of students from different cultures about the nature of academic discourse and about responsibility for their own learning.'

Both tutors mention that cultural issues have a significant impact on students' frameworks in the way they address their writing tasks and in how they write. The differences highlighted by these two scenarios can clearly be accounted for by several factors: the tutors' different roles; the need to draw on different professional resources; the students' different subject orientations and their backgrounds. These factors determined those features deemed significant by the tutors in writing assignments. They will now be examined in more detail through the tutors' own comments.

Case Study A

To situate and evaluate Nadège's performance, Jane draws directly on her expert knowledge of the course and of how French PGCE students, who have been through the French school system of education, speak and write in English. She begins by describing in some depth the demands of the PGCE course in relation to how students are accepted thus giving some idea of the standards expected of Nadège:

> French native speakers often consider themselves to be potentially the best teachers of their native tongue as a foreign language, on account of their native

fluency, or so they claim in their application forms. Admissions tutors will be aware that this potential strength is far often outweighed by a range of other factors. These factors include, crucially, an inability to perceive the difficulty of their native tongue as the target language for the secondary-age pupil. At interview, a range of topics, designed to elicit knowledge on both general educational issues and on language issues, is covered. In fact, the interview process has evolved in such a way that the interview is probably a tougher test for native speakers since not only is their level of general communicative competence being tested but the ability to enter into professional discourse along with its attendant specialised vocabulary, meanings and jargon. Those whose first language is English find this difficult enough but can usually negotiate it satisfactorily.

In addition to other qualities which are being sought in a potential teacher, this hurdle is an effective indicator as to whether the student will be able to participate fully in the broad professional training base. These will take place almost exclusively in English in terms of dialogue with colleagues, in professional training activities and in written assignments, which will need to be written in English. As a result only the most capable linguists get through interview screening. This is entirely in line with the institutional requirement for a high level of linguistic competence in two foreign languages and a language profile which must always include good English as appropriate to post-graduate study and, indeed, for future employability in the British education system.

Jane points out here that the problem of using 'professional discourse' is not due to the language itself but to the ways in which it is used within the institution. This supports the claim made by Street (1996), and discussed by Turner in this volume, that writing is never 'a transparent medium of representation'.

Jane goes on to describe her knowledge of typical language difficulties encountered by French native speakers in using English as follows:

I generally find that a good command of spoken English is usually reflected in a good standard of written English. However, there is often slippage between the two since errors which cannot be detected in speech, such as plural endings in French, may be evidenced in writing.

and then describes how the French educational context is taken into consideration, both for its merits and demerits, when evaluating assignments written by French students on the PGCE course:

In reflective writing, the French native speaker often writes in a way which imbues the whole text with a tangible cultural flavour. ... This may be evidenced by cultural distance and obvious difficulty in relating to a topic. Pastoral care, the topic under consideration in this assignment, for example, does not exist as a concept in France, French teachers being primarily subject teachers, the pastoral role being reduced to routine class monitoring. Asking a French native to comprehend pastoral duties requires a massive cultural leap which may lead to infelicitous linguistic expression.

Another cultural phenomenon, a welcome one on the whole, is the near certainty that the French native will present her/his work in classic style on the thèse, antithèse, synthèse model, reflecting the ingrainedness of the academic literacy of the country, and will structure it in terms of layout, with clear subsections, subdivisions and subtitles. Both of these aspects can have a somewhat stilted effect but clarity of thought, if not originality, and coherence of organisation are guaranteed. It is an entirely acceptable and instantly recognizable construct of academic writing. Indeed, it is a model often adopted by students who have taken 'A' level French where they are frequently taught to write essays on this model, a practice often further refined on a Language first degree course.

In this case study Jane discusses one assignment written by Nadège which reinforces her high expectations of the writing of French PGCE students. It seems that the high standard of Nadège's assignment means that the content and structure are not problematic. In general terms, Jane is not worried about lack of originality or stilted writing but is concerned about the acceptability of discrete linguistic features. She strongly recommends applying a system of error analysis to help understand the seriousness of errors:

> I will identify and examine a range of errors in her assignment, seeking to categorise and analyse the errors and to discuss the effect on the quality of the whole assignment and the influence on the tutor's assessment. I find Richards' (1985) interpretations of Selinker's descriptions of interlanguage characteristics and the five processes identified as central to second language learning particularly appropriate at this level of language use and in this particular context. The five processes which Selinker identifies are: 'language transfer' (erroneously, as 'interference'), 'transfer-of-training' (errors deriving from the teaching method), 'strategies of learning', 'strategies of communication' and the 'reorganization of linguistic materials' ('overgeneralisation' in the case of incorrect 'reorganization'). Modern linguists are sensitive to such processes which can, in part, explain appropriate language use and successful learning as well as error, since they all have resonance within the present widespread acceptance and understanding of communicative methodology.

Jane attributes most errors to 'language transfer or interference, caused by transfer of grammatical or other elements from the native language to the target language'. The features she highlights are to do with structure, lexical choice, spelling and 'performance errors': 'unsystematic errors which Richards claims are normal aspects of language use and may relate to factors such as memory and length of utterance.' She illustrates the emphasis she places on expecting linguistic accuracy from an MFL student teacher by providing a comprehensive list of errors, which she analyses in detail:

A Range of Errors
Many of the errors can be described as instances of language transfer or interference, caused by transfer of grammatical, or other, elements from the native language to the target language. Examples from the aforementioned assignment (in italics) include the following:

- *for more able pupils, the prompt of vocabulary could be removed.*

Here the French word order as in 'la plume de ma tante' requires reversal in English to the equivalent of 'my aunt's pen'. Position of verbal structure is the reason for the awkwardness in the next example:

- *the school has established a specific description of what should be the pastoral duties*

Again, the verbal qualifier is wrongly placed as it is in the following:

- *they accepted more easily the difficult tasks*

Some obvious misspellings can clearly be explained by interference as in the very common spelling errors of *'responsable'*, *'negociate'* and *'differenciate'*. Whilst the latter two are newer in terms of common linguistic currency in French education jargon, the spelling for 'responsible' is a well known chestnut which is very difficult to eradicate.

Whilst in the domain of spelling, the student consistently misspells 'practice' as a noun starting with *'Teaching Practise'* on the title page and on several occasions thereafter. This error cannot readily be traced to the French 'pratique' and she joins the ranks of the many who cannot distinguish between the noun and the verb. There is a curious one-off use of a hybrid-type spelling in the next example:

- *a survey like this would necessit interviewing.*

'Necessit' is certainly closer to the French but is, I believe, an uninformed guess on the part of the student.

Overgeneralisation may explain the student's consistent use of inappropriate plurals as in:

- *monitor their progresses and behaviours* and in *teachers don't receive any trainings.*

Whereas French logic dictates, for example, one training per teacher, the student may have been influenced by the tendency in English to mark plurals. She may, for example, have learnt a phrase such as 'the children took off their coats' (the French allocates one coat per childe) and generalized from this model.

There are also examples of performance errors, unsystematic errors which Richards' claims are normal aspects of language use and may relate to factors such as memory and length of utterance. The next example demonstrates this:

- *pastoral care seems to have been a long tradition in the British education system and one of the implementation which symbolises the most this aspect of education is the presence of the form tutor.*

The meaning is, I would contend, clear but there are several awkwardnesses which may have been avoided if, for example, she had written this in two sentences.

- *Authentic weather forecast was recorded on a French radio.*

This, in fact, gives the opposite meaning to that intended. She does actually mean that a recording was made from the radio; the French 'de' is open to various interpretations and she has selected wrongly from the 'embarras du choix'.

- *The vocabulary used was familiar with them.*

This, as with the previous error, is a failure to communicate in the target language and probably reflects the stage and limits of the student's interlingual competence (Selinker 1974). There are other examples of this phenomenon of weakness of expression which is evidenced in certain statements where the meaning is clear but where there is an obvious incorrect choice of vocabulary. Examples of this are as follows:

- *point out the verbs are irregular verbs and therefore they don't build their future like the other verbs* and *the variety of materials is large.*

Jane's comments reveal how she is able to apply her knowledge of French usage to evaluating Nadège's errors and consequently to assess the degree of tolerance in each case. She also discusses the challenges associated with error analysis when inappropriate uses of semantic usage seem idiosyncratic in nature and are unclassifiable:

> In spite of the helpful categories and taxonomies of error and error-making processes, now well established in the field of contrastive and error analysis, sometimes errors just defy simple pigeon-holing. I quote this from a most diligent of students:
> - *The last exercise can vary from a low level to a highest one as it is a teacher's creation.*
>
> My expert judgement of this is that I do not have a clue as to what she is trying to say but I enjoyed the challenge of thinking about it. It lacks coherence of meaning and yet there is a meaning of a sort. It obviously has something to do with levels of difficulty and possibly to do with the exercise being designed by the teacher. I have a sort of understanding which relates to differentiated learning. She is, in other words, trying to make a point about how teachers can create a purpose-designed activity which caters for a wide range of pupil ability and, in this case, provides opportunities for differentiated outcomes. In any case, the odd sentence like this does not destroy either her intended meaning or my overall comprehension of the whole piece. I am,

however, curious to know whether the student was satisfied with what she had written in English or was her expression the best linguistic fit. She faces, in effect, a double bind of firstly needing to render her thoughts from French to English and then to attempt to evaluate the linguistic and semantic correctness. This is a common problem with students who have undergone a sustained period of schooling in another system, usually that of their native tongue and culture. It is a problem which usually presents itself as an authentic learning opportunity for the student who, invariably, finds the extended pastoral dimension of the teacher's role an enlightened one.

Finally, in totally idiosyncratic vein, perhaps imbued with a sense of French revolutionary fervour she states:
- *In school X, the structure is a horizontal rolling system' ... On the other hand, the head of Lower/Upper school doesn't roll with the form tutors:*

which is, I contend, a magnificent but probably unintentional piece of imagery, mirroring the recent revolution in schools.

Jane's familiarity with the language use of French students and her belief in the importance of error analysis are constantly foregrounded in her evaluation of Nadège's work. She then goes on to make recommendations for the PGCE course concerning MFL teacher trainees. She highlights the two-fold importance of error analysis in this situation suggesting that it could be profitably transferred to the school classroom:

> In conclusion, it seems to me such a student would benefit immensely if she were to be given the opportunity to discuss and learn from a detailed analysis of her errors. From the tutor's point of view, it would be helpful to have an awareness of the nature of the error to better evaluate the effect of apparent grammatical error and loss of meaning in the assignment as a whole. ....
>
> A thorough examination of error type and impact leads to the fairest evaluation of a student's written performance. Furthermore, it is an approach which could be adapted for and adopted in MFL secondary classrooms to the benefit of younger language learners. This teacher and her contemporaries could apply a similar rigour to the work of pupils to mutual advantage in terms of evaluating teaching and learning performance.

Jane's concern is with 'the fairest evaluation' of MFL student teachers' assignments. Her earlier comments suggest that although discourse and cultural factors may be influential in their writing, they are unlikely to be central considerations in the success of a student wishing to become an MFL teacher. A student educated under the French school system may hold a contrasting notion of an 'essay' in respect of structure, cohesion and lay-out but, for Jane, the main consideration is language features in terms of the error-types that she has described.

Case Study B

In evaluating Romatu's assignment writing about school policy issues, Brenda finds it necessary to situate her work within a much broader context than that of the assignment itself. Because of her own educational background, school policy issues may not be a familiar concept for Romatu and it might be difficult for her to gain the depth of understanding required to explore them critically. Consequently, as Brenda implies, her own task as tutor is less straightforward. In addition, as a student with a science background, Romatu may have had comparatively few opportunities to develop any expertise in academic writing.

Brenda examines any information available to her in order to become better acquainted with Romatu and thus arrive at a fair evaluation of her work. For example, from Romatu's application form, she notes that she:

> is a mature student aged 34 ... educated in a school in an African country where English was the language of instruction, although it was not her first language. ... She graduated from a university in Africa in 1986 with a third class degree in a science-related subject. ... In the same country Romatu taught at a tutorial College. She came to England six years ago and continued to be involved in projects to help maintain her own culture and also worked as a volunteer at her children's primary school. ... In her application she highlighted her Sunday School teaching and voluntary work with African children in this country. The reference from her university tutor described the projects on which she worked and emphasised that she was "a highly reliable young lady, intelligent, responsive and hardworking". At interview she came across as lively, articulate and intelligent.

Romatu's 'third class degree' and her university tutors' comments, which emphasize hard work rather than academic attainment, lead Brenda to conclude that she 'is not an academic high flier.' Nevertheless, at interview there was sufficient evidence of her potential to become a good teacher for her to be accepted on to the course. For example, she is clearly committed to contributing to children's development within her own, familiar community using her expertise derived from past practice. Brenda also notes:

> Although English was not her first language, throughout her secondary schooling Romatu studied in English both at school in Africa and at college in England. This suggests she had experience of using written and spoken English for both everyday and academic purposes.

and comments about Romatu's use of language in her first written assignment set by her subject tutor in the UDE:

> Romatu's subject tutor identified certain problems, viz. a lack of analysis and evaluation as well as some fairly minor grammar difficulties, and advised her to seek help from the academic writing support tutor. My own analysis of the language in her first piece of written work suggests that whilst there were some errors, she did not have significant difficulties apart from one instance when the word order was rather clumsy. In describing the primary school she wrote, "X is an infant and primary school where pupils are equally mixed in eight classes." Since this was probably an attempt to use educational terminology it is likely that lack of familiarity with the terms made her uncertain of the correct means of expression, rather than she was having difficulty in manipulating language per se. On the whole, however, this assignment was a fluent and coherent piece of writing.

In linguistic terms, Brenda's comments are favourable. The language difficulties are less to do with grammar than with making appropriate linguistic choices, which, being context-dependent, is understandably difficult for Romatu. From this assignment, Brenda makes an important observation about her which is reinforced on closer acquaintance during the course:

> Whereas she had been asked to write about her own school experiences which would have required some reflections, Romatu had instead chosen to give an account of her week's observation in a primary school, which did not require analytic skills or background reading.

Brenda again strongly indicates that Romatu does indeed have problems but that they cannot be directly attributed with any certainty to poor linguistic competence. Rather they are to do with her level of analysis. This first essay, which did show that she could 'write' fairly competently at a descriptive level, caused some concern at that point in the course. She did not appear to be aware of or to understand that other expectations were being made of her, such as her professional engagement and the ability to discuss and reflect.

Brenda considers other aspects of Romatu's work: for example, from observing her during tutorial group sessions:

> Romatu was always keen to participate in discussions and showed a caring and concerned attitude for pupil welfare. However, her comments were always very much related to her own experiences and she did not move towards a more abstract level of argument. Her perspective on life seemed bounded by her family commitments; religious activities and the promotion of her own culture within her ethnic group.

This again reinforces Brenda's view that other, possibly cultural, differences play a significant part in Romatu's academic work. Brenda's description of how Romatu approached and managed the first written assigment elaborates on this point.

More serious problems came to light when she embarked on her second written assignment: a major, compulsory report which students undertake in the first term, based on both experience in school and the subjects studied in College in the school policy issues sessions. Students are expected to select an issue and examine it in the context of their teaching practice school. The report should include primary data collection and, whilst a substantial amount of background reading is not expected, it is anticipated that the student will use knowledge of recent and relevant literature on the chosen subject to make an informed analysis of practice in that area in the school.

Brenda goes on to describe the way in which Romatu worked and the concerns she felt about the factors that seemed to be preventing her from making any significant progress with the assignment.

Romatu began to seek help from several sources. She turned to me as her School policy issues tutor in College, although students are not expected to seek tutorial support from College in planning and writing this assignment. During my first tutorial with her, it became apparent that, although Romatu was undoubtedly a very conscientious student, she had a number of difficulties. The first stemmed from an over-reliance on her mentor in school in defining the area for study and devising appropriate techniques for data collection. Indeed it emerged that several teachers in the school had given considerable help, although Romatu claimed that she had received very little help from the school. Secondly, she seemed to attribute her difficulties to language problems that arose from the fact that English was her second language.

Thirdly, despite the written guidelines and the presentation, Romatu had neither noted nor internalised the information. It then emerged that she did not understand how to set about the task of collecting and analysing data. I found it necessary to go through the guidelines carefully with her before she felt more confident about the nature of the task. She now appeared to understand the requirement that this was an independent study and that, whilst she could expect help from the school to the extent of allowing her to set up a small investigative project and in making available relevant school documentation, the onus was on her to define and investigate her chosen area.

Romatu decided to investigate Special Needs provision in her school and at a second tutorial talked in an articulate manner about Special Needs, showing that she had engaged with the issue. However, it seemed that she had been so much at a loss when it came to devising appropriate methods of data collection, that the school's Special Needs Co-ordinator (SENCO) had drawn up the list of questions for her to ask the SENCO! This seemed to reflect a fundamental lack of interrogative skills coupled with certain expectations of the amount of help to which she was entitled, contrary to the autonomy expected of a student on a post-graduate course.

At this crucially important point in the course, leading up to submission of the first major assigment, Romatu's progress is beginning to cause concern. In order to prepare this assignment, all PGCE students are expected to quickly adopt certain methodological skills and practices, which research students, in contrast, are able to develop over time through the provision of training courses. The PGCE course, of necessity, is so tightly organized that students have to rely on the guidelines given at the beginning of the course, from which they need to extract what is relevant for their own purposes, and on a limited amount of tutorial help. They need to find a way of synthesizing their research interests with some methodology and with the accommodations of the school where they are placed. For some students, like Romatu, such expectations may not be fully appreciated.

Brenda continues:

> At this tutorial I gave some advice on writing the report and Romatu submitted a first draft. Her reading seemed to have been restricted to the school's policy document. I advised her to read more widely and to make sure that she was asking sufficiently searching questions to gain some useful material. The completed report fell short of the criteria in a number of respects. It lacked a theoretical basis thus reflecting an inability to exploit the library as a source for background reading. Nor did the report locate her school's practice in a wider educational context. Extensive quotations were used but she had not extracted and analysed information in order to form her own judgements. A large proportion of the report was taken up with extracts copied from the School's policy document. The format used in presenting the data was that of question followed by answer. This allowed little scope for reflection and analysis in an ongoing manner. She made no attempt either to tie together her arguments at the end or formulate some general conclusions. In terms of actual layout the report was very clearly presented and good use had been made of IT. There were far fewer grammatical errors than in the first assignment, possibly due to efficient use of the spell check and grammar check functions. However, too much information was presented in bullet points rather than continuous prose which again meant that ideas were not developed. The main cause for concern was the fact that much of the advice given and the issues discussed in my two tutorials was not reflected in the writing. Romatu's report was returned as unsatisfactory and she was asked to rewrite it.

It seems that, despite her extensive preparation for the assignment and the substantial amount of help she had enlisted, Romatu was still unable to develop a critical approach in the ways expected of her. Brenda's comments upon her reactions to the assessment serve to illuminate further the depth of the problems involved:

> Romatu said that failure was unfair as she had put a great deal of work into this assignment. Hard work seemed to be equated with success. She also

regarded her family commitments as a reason why leniency should be shown. In fact she had spent a considerable amount of time on the task but had not used this time productively. Secondly, Romatu exhibited a high level of dependency upon her tutors in College and her mentor in school and did not seem willing or able to accept responsibility for her own learning. This was apparent again when her report was returned; she enlisted the help of two other tutors and of one of those who had originally helped her. Whilst Romatu defined her problems in purely language terms, it was clear that these were not a significant factor in her failure to produce a piece of work of the required standard. .... Romatu appeared to feel that time spent seeking help from a variety of tutors would best aid her learning, rather than utilising this help effectively and internalising the advice given. Nevertheless her perception was that she did not receive much help. In this way, a great deal of time and effort was used unproductively.

Brenda strongly suggests that Romatu's perceptions are very different from those of her UDE tutors about the amount of help she was getting and about the nature of her problems. Romatu was not meeting the course expectations and could not appreciate how or why. She did not seem to understand that, fundamentally, what appeared to be lacking was her personal and professional engagement. She seemed neither to have any conception of 'the required standard' nor to have developed the ability to analyze and reflect during the first half of this intensive course. Brenda implies that finding a constructive way forward is problematic. She reaches the following appraisal about Romatu:

> Overall her symptoms of a reluctance to work independently could arise from a number of causes: her lack of confidence in her own intellectual abilities; poor time management arising from her many preoccupations with her family and community, particularly with her involvements in projects centred on her own culture; an inability to take responsibility for her own professional development; failure to understand her position as a PGCE student and the lack of appreciation of the inequity vis a vis her fellow students of her excessive reliance on tutors.

By the time Brenda has reached these conclusions about Romatu, twenty-four weeks of the course have already passed and only twelve remain. It is conceivable that Romatu has had too little opportunity and practice to develop professionally according to her needs. Despite the attention she has received, she has not been able to adopt the appropriate strategies, which might have helped her develop her own intellectual framework. Her written performance could be viewed as symptomatic of a failure to make the necessary cultural and conceptual jump thus resulting in her feeling distanced from the course and unable to gain control over her own learning.

Brenda stresses the importance of 'knowing' Romatu in order both to understand how she approached the course and to efficiently address her needs. Crucially, Brenda has had to acquire this knowledge through the experience of working with her:

> The fact that Romatu was conscientious, hardworking, sought advice and apparently understood the ways of approaching the task raises a number of questions concerning the expectations of students from different cultures about the nature of academic discourse and about responsibility for their own learning.
>
> At a personal level, Romatu presents as being a well-motivated, friendly and eager student, one who seems harassed by the competing demands of her family and the course. This latter problem however is one that may be experienced by a student in a similar position from any cultural background.

Another issue emerges here. Brenda suggests that it is not unusual for students to encounter problems exacerbated partly by cultural factors and partly by personal, practical pressures such as financial considerations, or family commitments. It seems that, in Romatu's case, these impinged on her in such a way that her own professional resources were not effectively tapped in spite of the extensive efforts made to encourage students to become confident, independent and critical teachers. Here such efforts may be embedded within an approach based on what Lea and Street describe as an 'academic socialisation' model, where the students are expected to acculturate to the standard norms of the PGCE course without their own voices being heard. Perhaps what is needed in such situations, they suggest, is a more 'sensitive bridging' approach, where students' starting positions are given more purchase.

About Romatu, Brenda concludes:

> There seems to be a fundamental mismatch between Romatu's perceptions of the demands of a post-graduate course and the expectations of the UDE. These were not detected during the acceptance procedure but soon began to emerge. Despite several efforts by tutors to assist Romatu develop a more mature attitude to study and her high motivation to succeed, Romatu was unable to accommodate her intellectual framework to these demands.

Romatu's performance on the PGCE course is not perceived favourably. Nevertheless, her problems signal a range of complexities concerning individual students, which cannot be addressed on the course. Brenda ends by making a plea for further investigation 'to determine the extent to which each of these factors can be linked with cultural differences in academic standards and expectations.'

Two different 'academic writing' worlds

In these two case studies, Jane and Brenda highlight the wide range of diverse experiences for students following this PGCE course. Two different worlds are described from which complex and varied experiences can be inferred for tutors as well as students.

Jane describes the MFL teacher education world where procedures and standards seem well-established and function smoothly. Students like Nadège, who are accepted on to the course, are assumed to have an implicit understanding of what is entailed in writing an assignment at the outset, to possess a high standard of linguistic awareness and expertise, and to be confident about their writing. 'Academic writing' to this world means attending to language at the textual and clausal levels of acceptable and appropriate representation of the intended meaning (Halliday 1978). Jane's view is that some cultural differences, such as the French essay model with its clearly presented structure, can be viewed positively and accommodated within the course.

Brenda describes a very different aspect of teacher education where, for the minority ethnic student wishing to become a science teacher, procedures and standards seem to be constantly and persistently challenged. The learning process here has a strongly bi-directional quality, involving tutor as well as student. Brenda discovers that the past experiences of science graduates educated in another country can lead to a serious mismatch of expectations between tutors and students on a British PGCE course.

Both Jane and Brenda signal the importance of knowing as much about their students as possible. They evaluate their students' work using the resources available to them. The students' writing is unpacked only in so far as their knowledge of the students allows. In these two case studies the task is much easier for Jane, with her knowledge of the French education system and of French student teachers, than it is for Brenda. For her, closer acquaintance over time is essentially the only means of gaining a fair evaluation of Romatu's performance.

The experience of this PGCE course is that students vary considerably both in their initial understandings of what is entailed and in how well they adapt and achieve. Hence predictions of success are extremely difficult to make. 'Academic writing' holds different connotations for different students. For some, it is not perceived to be a problem. For some, it may be regarded as an area where grammatical and lexical choices, spelling, punctuation and graphics are the sole considerations. Problems are loosely attributed to linguistic inadequacies. However, some students embarking on the course are unfamiliar with a variety of nuances in writing assignments due to lack of opportunity and practice. They need to explore and examine how they themselves can address their tasks in relation to the expectations made of them (Scott, Chapter 7). However, this imposes extra demands within an already over-burdened course framework.

Taken-for-grantedness

The two scenarios illustrate two senses of the taken-for-grantedness that prevails in the British tertiary academic context. What is assumed is well-summarised in opposite ways by the two tutors: Jane in describing her expectations of MFL student teachers which dictate their progress; Brenda in her description of Romatu's short-comings summarised as a 'reluctance to work independently'.

For Jane, assumptions about the use of language are made which need to be addressed. In the case of MFL teacher trainees, with many years of schooling in French and English essay writing, a high standard of linguistic expression as well as some cultural understanding of the assignment writing procedure are assumed and, ideally, distinctive linguistic errors are tolerated only to a limited degree. French native speaker students are expected to respect these attendant values as the yardstick for their own professional credibility. Hence, feedback on errors in written assignments is considered to be extremely valuable for the individual student concerned. In the broader context, discussion on errors is thought to help develop pedagogical thinking.

Brenda's comments on the way Romatu approaches her assignment suggest that more could be done for student teachers from minority ethnic backgrounds to enhance their awareness and understanding of what is entailed in 'professional development'. In Case Study B, 'academic writing' is an abstract concept which may be assumed to be unproblematic initially. It may need to be unpacked in the light of the whole rationale behind the assignment, however helpful the guidelines appear to be. Brenda abstracts from her appraisal of Romatu some taken-for-granted ways of PGCE students working on the process of assignment writing. They can be summarised as follows:
– that advice given is internalised and utilised effectively,
– that the issues discussed are reflected in the writing,
– that the time preparing the assignment is used productively,
– that hard work is not equated with success,
– that research methodology is understood and applied reflectively,
– that data can be related to 'argument' and 'conclusions' (cf. p. x),
– that, above all, students are expected to become autonomous learners, who

work independently of their tutors in both the UDE and their school and come to accept responsibility for their own learning.

These aspects provide an alternative perspective on the process of professional development. It could be that what is entailed becomes apparent and realisable only in specific instances, when the abstract is translated into and applied in actual situations. Then the objectives may be open to different interpretations depending on individual perspectives. Thus the issue of taken-for-granted knowledge becomes a matter of awareness-raising. How this knowledge is individually interpreted and addressed begs investigation.

Ownership

The PGCE course is characterized by an interplay between theory and practice. The demands made of the students to address the practice of classroom teaching overtly involve their personal engagement while the more covert demands of assignment writing may be 'a tacit process' (Mitchell 1994), a task which provides opportunity for thought to develop through reflecting on practice. Whereas the essentially complementary nature of the two parts may be apparent to some students like Nadège, for others, like Romatu, possibly very restricted connections are made. Jane perceives Nadège as having no difficulty combining the two demands despite her lack of knowledge and experience in the field of pastoral care due to her French educational background. Brenda perceives Romatu as initially giving the appearance of encountering no difficulty though in reality as facing many serious problems due to her lack of awareness and ability to make the necessary links. She learns that Romatu's energetic and enthusiastic strategies to seek help in order to produce a written assignment are not realistic.

The pressures of the course may work to hinder some students from adopting a reflective approach to their practice. There may be degrees of difference in the extent to which students perceive the need to become personally engaged in writing their assignments and allow themselves to do so. For some this type of personal engagement may be automatic: an intrinsic part of their desire to teach. For others it may not be viewed as important. A lack of personal engagement in the writing process may mean that no sense of ownership for the product is developed. Arguably, a crucial ingredient of professional development may be missing. Perhaps the most important taken-for-granted aspect of a student's approach to writing assignments is that the written product belongs to that student including all that this entails: a personal and professional engagement with the practice of teaching; a willingness to question, challenge and understand issues; a unique perception of how the issues are interpreted.

The issue of taken-for-granted knowledge also raises the question of the tutor's role in familiarising the student with what is required in terms of research practice.

The Research Dimension

The problems encountered by some PGCE students with the writing of assignments give rise to a practical issue which may serve to undermine the whole academic ethos of the course: the question of how much importance should be given to this component. The links between the theory and practice of teaching are at best tenuous in such pressurised conditions. For many students, the immediacy of the classroom situation may serve to background any writing task, particularly on such an intensive course. For some, the links are grasped automatically. For others, the opposite is true.

The problems discussed in Case Study B signal the crucial importance of some training in research methodology since the students' conceptual entré into the world of teaching is partly nurtured through action research, which frames the writing task. Two concepts might usefully guide students' metacognition: firstly that the framework of an assignment may be defined by a set of questions and secondly that asking the questions entails complex theoretical and methodological issues. Through foregrounding the research issues, the writing process may be more easily channelled which may not only alleviate some students' problems with academic writing. It may also help them become more professionally engaged in the writing process, developing a sense of ownership and responsibility over their writing as well as a professional identity.

Conclusion

The perspectives of two mainstream tutors about their students' academic writing have been presented and important issues have emerged which might otherwise have remained hidden. They are to do with the taken-for-grantedness of some aspects of assignment writing and of research practice. It is arguable that the difficulties encountered by some students might be preempted if these aspects were considered in more depth, and that a heightened awareness could serve to enrich perceptions of what is entailed in the process of developing a professional identity as a teacher.

The two case studies show that the experience of writing can be markedly different for each and every student. Some students automatically address their assignments with clear ideas of how to proceed. They are culturally well-oriented; they assume autonomy from the start and encounter very few serious problems. For others, each step of the process needs to be systematically understood as a part of a whole. Viewed in this way, the task becomes much more complex. Though some of these students too may have a smooth journey, some may not. Their voices may not be heard by their tutors nor even articulated in terms that can be fully understood.

The process of becoming a teacher appears to comprise a constant series of challenges and hurdles. Students are unlikely to conform to a rigid, predictable pattern so that tutors' perceptions of their needs in writing assignments may well be frequently challenged. School practices as well as students' conceptions of their needs constantly demand new interpretations, which must impact on the course itself. In this context, the temptation might be to minimize the importance of written assignments and of the academic writing process. However, to do so would ignore a crucial aspect of the development of students into truly competent teachers as educators, as hopefully strongly suggested by this chapter.

References

Arndt, V. 1987. "First and Foreign Language Composing: a Protocol-based Study." *Written Language* BAAL/CILT 2: 114–129.
Ballard, B. and Clanchy, J. 1988. "Literacy in the University: An "anthropological" approach." In G. Taylor et al., *Literacy by Degrees*. Milton Keynes: Open University Press.
Berger, P. L. and Luckmann, T. 1967. *The Social Construction of Reality: A treatise in the sociology of knowledge*. Harmondsworth: Penguin.
Calderhead, J. and Shorrock, S. B. 1997. *Understanding Teacher Education*. Brighton/Philadelphia: Falmer Press.
Carr, M. 1997. "The Uses of Literacy in Teacher Education." B*ritish Journal of Educational Studies* 45(1): 53–68.
Cohen, M. L. 1993 "Listening to Students' Voices: What university students tell us about how they learn." Paper presented at *Annual Meeting of the American Educational Research Association*, Atlanta GA.
Gee, J. P. 1990 *Social Linguistics and Literacies*. London: Taylor & Francis. (Second edition: 1996).

Gorman, T., Gubb, J. and Price, E. 1987. "The Study of Written Composition in England and Wales." An account of a study conducted between 1981 and 1983, under the auspices of *The International Association for the Evaluation of Educational Achievement.* Windsor: NFER-Nelson.

Halliday, M. A. K. 1978. *Language as Social Semiotic.* London: Edward Arnold.

Ivanic, R. 1994. "I is for Interpersonal: Discoursal Construction of Writer Identities and the Teaching of Writing." *Linguistics and Education* 6: 3–15.

Lea, M. 1995. "'I Thought I Could Write Till I Came Here.' Student writing in Higher Education." In Gibbs, G. (ed.) *Improving Student Learning: Theory and Practice.* Oxford OSCD.

Lea, M. and Street, B. V. 1989. "Student Writing in Higher Education and Staff Feedback: an Academic Literacies Approach." *Studies in Higher Education* 23(2): 157–72.

Low, G. 1996. University Written Assignments and Complex Feedback Situations. Manuscript.

Mitchell, S. 1994. *The Teaching and Learning of Argument in Sixth Forms and Higher Education*: The Leverhulme Trust/The University of Hull.

Moore, A. 1996. "'Masking the Fissure': Some thoughts on competences, reflection and 'closure' in initial teacher education." *British Journal of Educational Studies* 44(2): 200–211.

Richards, J. C. 1985. *The Context of Language Teaching.* Cambridge: CUP.

Schön, D. A. 1987. *Educating the Reflective Practitioner: Toward a new design for teaching and learning in the professions.* San Francisco: Jossey-Bass.

Schön, D. A. 1983. *The Reflective Practitioner.* London: Temple Smith.

Selinker, L. 1974. "Interlanguage." In Schuman, J. H and Stenson, N. (eds.), *New Frontiers in Second Language Learning.* Rowley, MA: Newbury House.

Street, B. V. 1996. "Academic Literacies." In D. Baker, J. Clay and C.Fox (eds), *Challenging Ways of Knowing,* 101–134. Brighton/Philadelphia: The Falmer Press.

Swann Report. 1985. *Education for All.* London HMSO.

Turner, J. M. and Hiraga, M. K. 1996. "Elaborating Elaboration in Academic Tutorials: Changing cultural assumptions." *Change and Language* BAAL/Multilingual Matters 10: 131–140.

CHAPTER 6

Academic Literacies and Learning in Higher Education
Constructing knowledge through texts and experience

Mary R. Lea

Introduction

Drawing on research carried out with adult distance learners, this paper suggests that theoretical perspectives on student learning in today's higher education have tended to ignore the role of academic literacy practices in constituting knowledge in university settings. Although extensive research has been undertaken on the student's experience of learning and the contextual nature of this learning (Gibbs 1994; Marton et al. 1997), in this body of work not much attention has been paid to the role of language in constructing academic knowledge. When issues of language use are examined, then, until recently, they have tended to be presented in terms of 'learning academic discourses', a set of discrete categories, which, with the right teaching approaches, students can confidently expect to master. Such approaches appear to take little account of the way in which, for students, issues of personhood and identity are embedded in both language use and literacy practices within the academy. Contrasting literacy practices are themselves important elements of the process of knowledge making that takes place as students negotiate course requirements. In this respect academic literacy can be viewed as a mediating domain between adult students' wider cultural worlds and the final pieces of written work that they hand in for assessment. Using a case study of one particular student from the project, the paper draws on the theoretical frame of academic literacy to reveal two differing approaches that students are adopting towards their learning: the reformulation approach and the challenge approach. It highlights the need to understand these contrasting approaches in relation to the process of assessment.

The data is taken from a research project carried out at the Open University UK, which examined the study experiences of adult distance learners as they progressed from foundation level courses in social science and technology to first and second level courses in a variety of different subject areas. The project was concerned with the interaction of study with adult lives and looked at the ways in which students were attempting to construct academic knowledge, within particular social and cultural contexts, as they progressed through their studies. Although the research on which this particular paper is based is specifically about the experiences of adult *distance* learners, I believe that it also raises questions about the ways in which adults construct knowledge in all sectors of today's higher education. Additionally, it raises concerns which affect all students in higher education and not just adult students.

Theoretical perspectives

It is now widely understood through research on student learning that knowledge is constructed through the learner's experience of learning. A major area of such research developed within the 'phenomenographic' tradition, by Marton et al. (1997), is concerned to understand learning from the learner's perspective and the importance of the student interpretation of the learning task. This phenomenographic research, so called because it is interested to explore how learners describe and understand learning tasks rather than merely explain what students do, has been concerned with identifying the characteristics of different conceptions of learning.

Lave and Wenger (1991) are concerned less with student learning but with adult learning in a variety of cultural contexts; they challenge the transmission and assimilation model of learning in which individual learners are seen to internalise knowledge. Drawing on different examples of adult learning, they suggest that learning is about what they call 'legitimate peripheral participation' in communities of practice. Successful learning takes place when students are able to grasp the practices that they need to master to become full, rather than peripheral, members of the community. They outline the relationship between identities, knowing and social membership and highlight the importance of discourse and talk in communities of practice. Similarly, Saljö (1996) considers discursive practices in relation to both broader learning contexts and to the concept of 'understanding'; he also emphasises the relevance of shared social practices.

This paper takes a complementary approach to these other contextual approaches to student learning but is more concerned with the conflicts and contradictions that are experienced by students as they negotiate academic knowledge in relation to the more familiar worlds of work, community and home which they know and understand so well. Whilst acknowledging, in common with other authors who are concerned with adult student learning, that knowledge is not transmitted but constructed through students' interactions with specific learning contexts, the theoretical frames used in this paper are based upon the 'New Literacy Studies'. I want to suggest that a central part of the learning process for students is concerned not just with the struggle between other familiar 'ways of knowing' and 'academic ways of knowing', but with the different literacy practices that are associated with these. This is about more than just a conflict between everyday and academic discourses as Laurillard's work suggests (1993). She makes the distinction between experiential knowledge and everyday experience and articulated knowledge which relies upon exposition, argument and interpretation. Academic discourses embody the latter form of knowledge in contrast to the discourses of everyday experience. For Laurillard academic learning is a way of experiencing the world but it is conceptually distinct from other forms of everyday knowledge because it is concerned with 'second order' descriptions and experience of the world. This paper suggests that in order to make more sense of adult learning in higher education we need to blur the distinction being made here between these two distinct types of knowledge.

The particular research project reported upon here illustrates how adult learning — through students engaging with new and unfamiliar literacy practices — is often concerned with contesting and challenging these supposedly 'academic ways of knowing' and interweaving prior knowledge and ways of writing and reading texts with course requirements. In this sense 'academic knowledge' and 'everyday knowledge' are not conceptually distinct. In fact, what is important in terms of understanding adult learning is understanding the relationship between the textual representation of academic genres in writing and reading, and students' own personal construction of knowledge in a specific context. Language is not merely the transparent medium through which students learn about academic ways of thinking, which an 'acculturation into academic discourse' model of student learning would have us believe. Language and associated literacy practices actually construct and constitute knowledge in specific ways which frequently conflict with adult students' other experiences of constructing their own world knowledge. What is learnt for one course, or for a specific tutor or course is a particular way of viewing the world which students negotiate through their writing.

Literacy studies and approaches to learning

Developments in the 'New Literacy Studies'(Street 1984; Barton 1994), in school and workplace settings, have moved away from models which focus on the educational and cognitive aspects of writing and reading, and are concerned with the cultural and social characteristics of literacy. Literacy is therefore concerned with the social practices which surround the use of the written word. Street (1984) contrasts an 'autonomous' model of literacy, with an 'ideological' model. He suggest that an 'autonomous' model makes universal claims for literacy which are related to beliefs in fundamental cognitive differences between literate and non-literate groups in society, and further that this position relates becoming literate to the development of logical thought and abstraction. In contrast, he proposes an 'ideological' model which moves away from a cognitive understanding of literacy and focuses on the social relationships that surround particular literacy practices and the institutions in which these are taking place. In this sense literacy is understood within both the contexts and the ideologies in which a set of particular literacy practices are embedded. It is necessary to consider the social contexts within which any literacy event is occurring, and to realise the meanings that are produced for individuals who are engaged in any process of reading and writing.

This approach which conceptualises literacy as a social practice has more recently been applied to higher education settings (Lea & Street 1998). Learning at university involves adapting to new ways of knowing: new ways of understanding, interpreting and organising knowledge. Practices of academic literacy are central processes through which students learn new subjects and develop their knowledge about new areas of study. Meanings are not simply given by the texts that students encounter during their studies but are created through a particular set of literacy practices. Lea & Street (1998) have identified how, in the past, educational research into student learning in higher education has tended to fall into two main areas: those informed by models based on the acquisition of core study skills and those which see learning as being concerned with academic socialization, learning disciplinary genres and acquiring the discourse. They suggest that as a consequence two different models seem to have emerged in approaches to and research around student learning in general, and student writing in particular. The study skills model of writing focuses on 'surface' features of language form in terms of grammar, punctuation, spelling etc. In this sense writing is considered a technical skill, the basic and generic features of which are seen as transferable from one context to another. This is being increasingly replaced by what they suggest is an 'academic socialization' model of writing in which students are encouraged to learn the textual conventions of disciplinary discourses, the written genres, for example, 'how to write in history'. This approach appears to be based upon the assumption that language, and hence writing, is a transparent medium of representation and that particular disciplinary forms are merely reflected in, rather than constructed by, written texts. Lea & Street point out that more recently research has begun to point towards and address the complexity of the academic literacy practices to which students are exposed within the university (Cohen 1993; Ivanic 1998; Lea 1994; Lea & Street 1997; Lillis 1997; Pardoe 1997; Stierer 1997). They suggest therefore, a third model that of 'academic literacies' in which account is taken of the contested nature of academic writing in general and student writing in particular. This model takes account of the variety of literacy practices that students engage in as part of their studies and acknowledges the different positions and identities that participants in the writing process, both students and tutors, take up as academic writers and readers.

Earlier work by Charles Bazerman in the USA (1988), focusing more specifically upon published academic texts lays the foundation for much of the research on academic literacies now taking place in UK higher education. Bazerman (1988) outlines how written academic texts themselves serve to construct particular subject knowledge in individual and specific ways. He makes the crucial point that writing matters because the different choices around what we write result in different meanings; therefore the very act of writing constructs our academic knowledge in contrasting ways. Bazerman's analysis can be usefully adopted to help us when we are considering how adults bring their own knowledge to both their understanding — and the construction of — their own academic texts. In his analysis, Bazerman (1988) outlines four contexts for examining the ways in which meanings are constructed through the process of academic writing: the object under study; the literature of the field; the anticipated audience and the author's own self. Each time an adult student writes an assignment, she is constructing her own knowledge and adapting her own knowledge bases within that piece of writing, and negotiating the four contexts outlined by Bazerman. She is not merely replicating subject specific knowledge in a written form. The problem for many students is that merely reproducing academic knowledge can feel invalidating and constraining and can conflict with other more familiar 'ways of knowing'. Adults, with their own knowledge which may have led them to pursue certain areas of study, may find it difficult to negotiate the restrictions of the object under study, be confused when incorporating the literature of the field, find that anticipating the audience (the tutor) is not an easy task and, lastly, wrestle with the complexities of writing their own selves into their essay writing. Bazerman's analysis of academic knowledge gives us a way of conceptualising the complexities of writing academic knowledge for many students and highlights the ways in which the student has to interact with the construction of disciplinary knowledge from both an institutional and personal perspective.

More recently, Ivanic's research (1998) has looked more closely at the experience of mature adult student writers in a traditional university setting. She focuses on the notion of self and makes the distinction between the 'autobiographical self', the 'discoursal self' and the 'self as author' as ways of conceptualising the identity of a student writer when she writes. The autobiographical self refers to the identity that students bring with them to their writing. The discoursal self is more concerned with the impression of herself that the writer might wish to convey in her writing. The self as author is more related to the idea of authorial 'voice' and the opinions, beliefs and authority that the student feels she can lay claim to in her university writing. A fourth notion of writer identity relates more closely to the institutional context and the way in which student writers occupy different subject positions in relation to this context, in this case the traditional university setting within which Ivanic's participants were writing. Ivanic suggests that student writing is about more than conveying content but embeds conflicts of identity as students struggle with the dominant discourses and practices of the university and its different socio-cultural settings. This present research has also been concerned with issues of identity but the focus has been more specifically upon the construction of academic knowledge through the processes of reading and assignment writing and the relationship of this to assessment processes.

Research into the nature and processes of the construction of academic genres by Berkenkotter & Huckin (1995) is also relevant in debates around academic literacies. Although their work explores the construction of academic genres in different disciplinary settings it does not take the fixed view of genres and that an 'academic socialization' model might suggest. Instead they are concerned with emphasising the dynamic and fluid nature of genres in academic disciplines. They examine academic texts written by more experienced academic writers than undergraduate student writers, focusing on academics themselves and doctoral students. Written genres as manifest in journal articles are considered as evidence of socially situated processes which serve to both construct and represent membership and position within a disciplinary community, rather than merely written products appearing in refereed journals. Although their research is primarily concerned with established academic writers, as with Bazerman (1988), the approach that they take to the contested nature of academic genres can be usefully extended to address the difficulties that students may have in understanding the requirements of their written work within different courses throughout their studies. As with the work of Ivanic and Bazerman they are concerned with issues of writer identity. The case study outlined below illustrates the importance of this relationship between student writing, identity, and the construction of academic genres as the student explores her literacy practices and her own assessed writing. It is also concerned with the ways in which tutor feedback is implicated in students' perceptions of academic genres and what constitutes valid knowledge from the student point of view. Its major focus though is upon the way in which adopting different literacy practices can result in different approaches to learning and therefore ultimately result in different ways of making sense of the whole process of assessed writing in the learning process.

The research

Twenty four students Open University students participated in the research. They were all from one region in the UK and all had very little in the way of formal educational qualifications before embarking upon their studies with the Open University. The students were interviewed two or three times over a twenty two month period (February 1996-November 1998). In depth, semi-structured interviewing techniques were used and a check list was devised to make sure that all areas relevant to the research were covered. All the interviews were carried out in students' own homes and lasted between an hour and an hour and a half. The first interviews were used to provide a grounding for those that followed and to enable a progressive focusing of the research questions which were informed by the earlier interviews in the research. Some interviews were conducted immediately after students had finished their foundation level course and before they had embarked on the next level, whilst other students interviewed at a later date were well into a second level course. The initial interviews with students were in effect used to gauge the areas that needed most attention in order to address the initial research questions. As each interview was completed the research questions were revised and refined as necessary.

One of the major focuses of the research was to discover more about the ways in which students interacted with their distance learning texts and what reading and writing strategies they were bringing to their course units and tutor marked assignments (TMAs). A reflexive approach to the interviews was established in order for the participants to have the opportunity to consider their own understandings of their study strategies, both at foundation level and on the second level courses that they were currently studying or about to study. As the interviews progressed an increased focus was placed on the students' experiences of completing particular TMAs. Later interviews concentrated much more on individual student interpretations of actual Open University texts and course material, and students were asked if they would be willing to have available their TMAs for discussion. When these course documents became a central focus of the interview students were usually quite happy for me to take a copy of the text for further use in the research. Additionally, some students agreed to complete self-record audio-tapes, whereby they recorded their thoughts on completion of writing the TMA and, also, their initial reactions to the tutor feedback.

Adult Learning Domains

The research has focused on three adult learning domains and the relationship between them. Each domain is firmly embedded in the other two; in that sense no domain — no site of learning — can be clearly separated from any other, and an understanding of one domain of learning requires knowledge and understanding of the other domains. This model of three domains (Figure 1) puts the cultural and social contexts of individual adult student learning firmly at the centre of any understanding of the production of texts for assessment and illustrates the relationships that exist between all the identified domains: cultural and social contexts; academic literacy practices; learning texts.

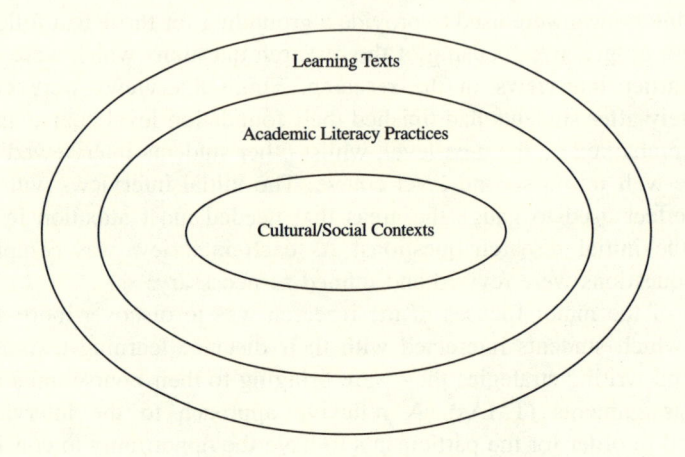

Figure 1

As a starting point, the cultural and social contexts of study situate the circumstances in which student learning is taking place. Literacy practices are at the heart of study and learning in higher education; these are the central ways in which students learn new subjects and develop their knowledge about new areas of study. They are the different practices of reading and writing which students engage in within a number of different contexts in order to make sense of their studies, and they are the ways through which students make meaning from the written texts that are part of their learning. With its focus on practices, the research has been able to look at the different meanings that are produced for students as they study and complete their written assignments. The learning texts domain is concerned with assessed pieces of writing, in this instance the tutor-marked assignments (TMAs), and the ways in which students construct their academic knowledge through the production of these texts. The learning texts (TMAs) are produced through, and therefore the result of, the interaction of particular ways of reading and writing within diverse contexts. As such, they are more than transparent reproductions of subject specific, course based knowledge arrived at through writing assignments. They are — in Berkenkotter and Huckin's terms — the result of socially situated processes rather than simple products of assessment.

A focus on social context, I believe, can enable a more complete understanding of what is involved in the acquisition of academic literacy for adult students, by looking at the different practices involved in reading and writing learning texts. Such practices are themselves embedded within a range of cultural and social contexts and researching these gives us more understanding of the relationship between the course texts and students' wider worlds. Students come to their studies with other more familiar practices of literacy and attempt to adapt these to their studies with varying degrees of success. They may be more used to reading novels or newspaper articles, or it may be more familiar for them to write work-based reports or personal letters. They may be used to writing collaboratively at work or reading documents for specific data. Additionally, they may not be used to receiving feedback and commentaries on their writing or may be used to working with very clear exemplars of written forms. Writing and reading may have previously taken place in communal office or home settings and not in individual private study sessions. At the same time, many students are drawing on their memories of literacy practices in other formal educational settings, such as school. Experiences of reading and writing for academic purposes may be connected to educational failure in the past; some students report difficult and unpleasant memories of school concerning essay writing and gaining formal qualifications through written examinations.

Academic literacy practices mediate the relationship between cultural and social contexts and the final production of the TMAs. The understandings and interpretations of reading the course materials and the meanings that are attached to these will be drawn on by students when writing their own TMAs, and therefore become embedded within the student's own text. The reason for examining the academic literacy domain is that this provides the opportunity to take a critical view of student learning and to examine some of the contradictions and constraints that are involved for adult learners, and therefore to find out more about the difficulties that students may encounter with their studies, which may ultimately lead to drop out or failure in higher education settings. In considering these three learning domains we are able to take account of different interpretations and understandings of text production and the ways in which these are embedded in cultural contexts. Focusing on students' understandings and interpretations of both writing TMAs and tutor feedback, we can examine how texts are given meaning by the social contexts within which language is being used and by the practices which surround their use.

Learning as the reformulation of texts

The research has highlighted how adult distance learners seem to display two distinct approaches to their learning; approaches which are integrally related to literacy practices. The approaches are not specific to particular students but reflect individual students' positions with regard to course material in any particular context. I use the terms 'reformulation' and 'challenge' to describe these approaches.

Some of the students interviewed for the research more readily adopted a reformulation approach to completing assignments. Having read the course materials, they interpreted the task in hand as reformulating the written material as closely as possible in their own writing:

> Mainly I think I've stuck to the course materials and examples from the course materials that we've been given.
> (Student: D103, Social Science Foundation Course)

With such an approach students resisted creating a dialogic relationship to the texts that they were reading. The primary purpose of assignment writing was seen as a reformulation of the course materials, to produce a text which was closely tied to the original texts but was still their own piece of written work. When students adopted this approach they appeared to be conceding to the authority of the course materials and were trying to replicate a particular academic perspective in their own writing. They read the course materials in a linear and detailed way and then attempted to reproduce as closely as possible — but using their own words — the gist of the course materials in their TMA. They often tried to adopt familiar reading strategies, for example reading from newspapers, magazines or novels, and therefore struggled with the sheer density of the texts as they moved through from section to section relating it to their chosen assignment title. Students' TMAs reflected the ways in which they had read and taken notes in a linear fashion and attempted to replicate this linearity in their assignments.

An important element of the reformulation approach is that, in an attempt to make sense of the text, students are attempting to replicate the text and the authority of the text:

> Well constantly, I am unpacking the question and re-reading the question and then re-reading the text until I have got the idea, the points tied up, and then thinking a lot about it and then putting it in my own words, which is often very different to the text itself. When I read it back often I think, 'Well is that what it really says?' and that is when you come to edit the thing, I suppose. I find that the textbooks are really beautifully written. You read something and think, 'Well I've got to express this in my answer but I couldn't put it any better', and there is difficulty there because you read something and think, 'Gosh that sums it up beautifully, you know'. You would like to be able to put it down in that way yourself and so putting it down in your own words becomes a bit lame. I feel it is a weaker exposition of what I am reading.
> (Student: DSE 202 Introduction to Psychology)

Subject specific and disciplinary terminology are seen as key elements of the reformulation approach. Students identify that it is important to say and write things in particular ways, but most importantly to use particular phrases and words in their assignments to convince the tutor that they have adequately engaged with the course content. The reformulation approach is fundamentally concerned with an attempt to learn the discourse or put another way to appear to have mastered the process of academic socialization, through replicating features of written genres. The focus for students themselves is often on terminology, and terminology is seen as a way into mastering a defined academic discourse. Tutor feedback can also emphasise the use of certain terminology and encourage students to rephrase their material in specific ways, using particular terminology to represent concepts that the student may have represented through other language forms. In this way feedback and therefore the very process of assessment actively encourages the reformulation approach:

In general this question calls for the application of the two liberal models to the article in the TMA booklet. To answer questions like this you must look for clues to the article by reading it out. Some of these are in paragraph one, line three, the word efficiency. In line two, bilateral monopoly and paragraph six bears reference to GP fund holders and paragraph eight GP fund holding again. To my mind the way to answer this question in the main body falls into three parts, an outline of the models, application of the models, application of the models to the article and the criticism.
(Tutor written feedback: D211 Social Problems and Social Welfare)

In this instance the tutor highlights the key words 'efficiency', 'bilateral monopoly' and 'fund holders' as vocabulary features of the particular written genre that the student is required to engage with as evidence of a grasp of the subject area and, therefore, presumably, successful learning. The tutor in this case also suggests a broader textual structure in relation to how to deal with discussion of the 'models'. It would appear then that encouraging the reformulation approach to writing for assessment is closely tied to textual content, rather than context; in a sense the texts are taken by students as reasonably transparent and are 'read off' for course content, which the student then tries to reformulate in other ways without interference from other texts or other knowledge.

Learning as challenging texts

In contrast to the reformulation approach, from the students position at least, the challenge approach seems to be related to the context of the texts that they are both reading and writing rather than merely course content. When students appeared to be adopting the challenge approach they were often very explicit about their desire to take a specific course and relate it to their own wider cultural context:

> My ideal job is something like a ranger in a wildlife reserve, or something like that but they are very few and far between, so something along those lines would be ideal...As I say the course is about the environment and the state of the environment and how man has affected it and I've always said my ideal would be living on a farm somewhere away from mankind and what I've got from the course so far hasn't changed that.
> (Student: U 206 Environment)

> A lot of the course I didn't agree with, because of my own experience and my life. It was not irrelevant that wasn't the right word. They were stating facts that from my own experience of say. living in the East End and being poor...

they were looking at it from a middle class point of view and OK, I now live
a middle class life. I've worked my way up. I have worked very hard and got
things in steps. But I still have my experiences and they invalidate some of the
information they give. I can't put it another way.
(Student: U205 Illness and Health)

They may have had a clearly defined personal trajectory which influenced the ways in which they approached learning the course materials; they brought other kinds of literacy practices to the course materials which mediated the kinds of understanding that they took from and brought to the written texts associated with the course: the course readers and the written assignments. This approach frequently challenged academic conventions, as students brought in their own personal perspectives and interpretations of the texts:

When you do challenge this right or wrong view you do meet with opposition
if your viewpoint doesn't necessarily fit in. This year you've got to try to give
her (the tutor) what she wants even if it's not necessarily what you believe in.
(Student: D211 Social Problems and Social Welfare)

Such students seemed to be actively engaging with the course in terms of their own personal needs and contexts and did not attempt to reformulate the original texts. As a consequence of this approach their writing often appeared incoherent and unstructured to the tutor. In addition, tutor feedback suggested that tutors were looking for evidence of understanding of the course materials in the particular way that they, as individual tutors, had read these. Such feedback could be quite confusing to students who adopted the challenge approach and believed that they had made an appropriate use of the course materials in writing their TMA; reading and writing against their own broader, cultural context. In consequence, since they had attempted to move away from the original text to their own textual interpretation, the feedback that they received on their work often seemed very tied to a specific TMA content and, therefore, not related to students' broader concerns in studying the course.

Making the links between personal commitments towards — and understandings of — course material and the academic study of what are often familiar issues proved difficult for these students. Instead of approaching their learning as if it were a separate sphere of their lives, learning, study and completing pieces of assessed work appeared to be integral to students' wider lives, and this was evident in the ways in which they approached the academic context. The course materials were regarded by them as texts which challenged their own interpretations and understandings, and were seen as a starting point for more reflexive engagement with learning. Interpretation of the course texts and the writing of the TMAs was firmly embedded within a personal framework of cultural and social contexts. Reading of course materials and the writing of the TMAs become part of a dialogic process. Students were concerned with issues such as: 'How does this relate to other knowledge and ways of interpreting the world? What is valid knowledge for this particular course? Can I use examples from my own experience? How far can I express my own ideas in my writing? Is it acceptable to use the first person in my writing?'

Challenge approaches are concerned with issues of epistemology and the construction of acceptable and valid forms of academic knowledge through student writing. This approach is particularly important for many adult learners because it is fundamentally concerned with issues of confidence, power and identity in academic settings and how these are embedded within academic texts (cf. Ivanic 1998). Central to our understanding of the challenge approach is an understanding of what adult students bring to their studies and the relationships between the production of their learning texts and the wider cultural social contexts within which they are learning. Adult learners in higher education are learning to construct their knowledge in ways which make it appropriate for assessment. Simultaneously, they are struggling to maintain a sense of themselves and the validity of other ways of knowing in their academic study (Ivanic 1998; Lea 1994).

Wendy — a case study

The case of Wendy illustrates some of the struggles over literacy practices that adult students experience during their studies, and the implications that these can have for the construction of academic knowledge. In this case, data is drawn from an interview transcript, Wendy's TMA and the feedback on her work. A research method which merges together the analysis of different types of texts, that is both interview data and evidence from students' own writing and tutor feedback on this, seems to be essential if we are trying to understand the complexity of the relationship between language and learning. The interview alone is a reflection on practice, the text alone cannot tell us what lay behind Wendy's thinking when she was writing. Considering both texts and practices may still only result in a partial representation of the writing process but at least takes us further towards an understanding of the relationship between the three adult learning domains: cultural/social contexts; academic literacy practices; learning texts.

Wendy was a middle aged women following course D211 Social Problems and Social Welfare. She had fairly recently been made redundant from a senior supervisory position in an administrative capacity and had begun working with disabled adults. Her decision to follow the course was influenced by the change of job and also by her own experiences of disability in her family. As she put it:

> I'd been tied up working with the same place for twenty odd years and suddenly woke up and said my goodness all this has been going on and I hadn't noticed, and I think the work that I'm doing you have to face issues everyday which I hadn't had to face. People's behaviour towards people with disabilities. I found that the social services had a language of its own. Before I was doing the course I found out that there was a certain amount of language difference and people were saying things and I didn't really know what they were talking about. I thought that well I've really got to find out more. I'm doing an NVQ (National Vocational Qualification) as well.

During her interview she talked extensively about the difficulties that she had in understanding the requirements of both the course that she was studying now and the social science foundation course that she had followed previously. In common with other students, she initially talked about this in terms of a notion of 'getting back to study':

> The biggest problem I have is over the essays, the TMAs.
> Last year it initially took over my life when I was doing the foundation course because I was new to study and the discipline of actually sitting down and getting through a certain amount of reading in a period and then writing an essay at the end of the time was very difficult and very time consuming.

She elaborated upon this and talked about the different reading practices that she had adopted to fit in with domestic and work commitments:

> The problem is that if it's been a hectic day then you just haven't got the concentration and you just sort of squeeze it in when I can, and then on my day off I'll devote a day of maybe extra time to sit and do the reading.
> If I'm at home during the day I'll do it down here if there's nobody about. If there's somebody about, and I've really got to catch up on some reading, I've got a spare room upstairs with a computer in and I'll disappear up there, but the family follow me. Sometimes it's easier to do it when you're in view and say, "Look I'm trying to do my reading, get down and do some homework". It's like social. If I disappear he becomes quite demanding. He seems to think he wants to help me and then when I just say I want a bit of peace and quiet he says, "Well you come and help me this way when I'm trying to write an essay". So it's really my son likes me to be about and that encourages him to do his studying.

In addition to negotiating her reading in relation to her family, Wendy also described how the time that she spent on reading was directly related to her engagement with the subject. She appeared to be adopting a challenge approach to her studies, attempting to relate her reading very centrally to her own experiences and motivations for following the course:

> I found the reading took a lot longer than it said, than they gave you, and you're thinking, 'I must be really dim and I don't understand this and it's taking me a long time.' This year maybe because it's more related to what I'm doing I found the reading easier. But the concepts are challenging and the way that I have to question things you know, I find that it takes up an awful lot of time and I'm thinking, 'Yes I never thought of it that way. Why hadn't I thought of it that way'. So I'm spending not so much of my time actually reading but more time actually sort of thinking things through and trying to come up with an answer.

Wendy had chosen the course because it dealt directly with many issues that seemed to her to be very pertinent to her own situation. She found that as she read the course materials she took a very personal position on what she read and felt that the knowledge that she brought to the course was continually challenged as she read. Following this course, for Wendy, was not accommodating to an 'academic way of knowing' but reconstructing her own ways of knowing and relating these directly to the course through her reading:

> Because of the issues, the agenda has got a lot of women's issues in it, which for our age group it is difficult to accept or even question some of these things. I'm finding it difficult sometimes. I found the last one, the last unit really quite difficult............ difficult because it was challenging things that I'd never thought of before and then having to look at it again and thinking why had I been accepting this instead of questioning it.

Her experiences of reading for, and writing, one particular TMA illustrate the relationship between the three learning domains: cultural and social contexts; academic literacy practices and the learning texts. The TMA concerned the relationship between women's' work in the home and paid employment: *'A woman's place is in the home.' Discuss with reference to the growth of women's paid employment.* The experience of writing this TMA for Wendy had been extremely important because she felt that it bore very directly upon her own personal experiences of working, and she wanted to explore these experiences through examining in more detail the subject matter of this particular piece of work:

> This TMA is about the women's place is in the home. I felt interested in it because obviously it affects me really and I'm thinking that's what I've been challenging ever since I was small. My mother worked and I hadn't really thought at that time that mothers didn't work. They had a grocery business and as I grew up the whole family were involved in this grocery shop. The

children used to weigh things up and put them for the shop. My sister used to work in the shop and I worked in the shop on Saturdays and holidays. and that was just our family and I hadn't really thought that mothers stayed at home. I really thought that was the norm. So when I got married I always assumed that I would work. We'd been married for thirteen years when my son turned up. It was a terrible shock and I didn't want to lose my identity as me. Within six weeks I was back at work. I sat at home thinking my identity is my work and yet I hadn't thought of it like that until I was doing the reading for 'a woman's place is in the home'. I hadn't thought. The way I had felt was actually explained in the reading why I was feeling that way and I hadn't thought about it and I hadn't thought about the previous reading, when I was in hospital giving birth and the things that happened to me then. So there was an awful lot in that essay that could relate to those feelings and I found it difficult to be objective about it. I was getting a lot of my own personal feelings involved in the essay when I first wrote it. Then I did some editing and I was taking out the wrong things.

As Wendy described, her reading of the text was determined by her own experiences of related issues. As a student, her description of reading for the TMA does not appear to support Laurillard's claim (1993) that academic knowledge is always a second order phenomenon. Wendy's experience of academic knowledge was directly through her own experiences; through reading the text in terms of her own knowledge, academic knowledge and other knowledge became conflated. Her reading of the course materials was mediated by understandings that she brought to the reading from her own familiar cultural contexts within which she was reading for and writing her TMA. Reading against this background of other/outsider knowledge, in contrast to academic/insider knowledge we can identify as a literacy practice. The course reader embedded an academic/insider perspective making assumptions about a body of knowledge concerned with 'Health and Social Welfare'. In contrast Wendy read the texts from her own perspective, her own contextualised experiences of the same body of knowledge but based on a different set of assumptions not necessarily shared with the authors of the course reader. The problem for Wendy arose when she became anxious about her interpretation of the course materials in terms of her perceptions of what constituted appropriate forms of knowledge for assessment purposes. She found it difficult to be objective in her essay. She had substantially changed her initial draft and finally submitted a revised version to her tutor. On receiving her feedback, she now felt that she had unknowingly removed, from her draft, elements of her written work which the tutor valued:

She said put in 'horizontal' and 'vertical'. I took out a whole paragraph and I only wished that I'd actually kept a copy of my essay unedited and this is what I've done this time. I've kept the unedited copy so that if it comes back, and if she says to me you should have done this, I can show her what I had originally done. It's obviously a problem with me identifying what she is looking for in the essay.

Wendy had taken out parts of her TMA which seemed less relevant for her in her own writing but were clearly important for the tutor. In fact Wendy's understanding of 'writing the course' and the tutor's understanding seemed to be at odds. Whereas for Wendy one of her starting points was reading and writing precisely to make sense of the other/outsider knowledge that she had already, the tutor feedback suggested that Wendy needed to pay most attention to a particular interpretation of insider/academic knowledge. In contrast to the student, the tutors' representation is akin to that of 'second order knowledge' (Laurillard 1993). Her feedback encourages Wendy to adopt specific literacy practices, presumably those that the tutor regards as evidence of understanding and representing academic knowledge within her own particular field of study, although I have no evidence of the tutor's disciplinary background:

> Dear Wendy,
> Good. This is generally clear and organised — although the long paragraph on page 3 is a little confused! You raise many important points but I felt that you could have improved your work by addressing more explicitly the links between familial ideology and women's experience of paid employment.
> You could have referred more specifically to the problem of vertical and horizontal segregation, and the difference between male and female levels of pay (i.e. expand your discussion in paragraph 2, page 3).
> You might have considered why policies aimed at improving women's working conditions have not always succeeded in doing so — a look at the Cuban and German studies could help here (Unit 9, pp. 87–90). Do you think that this shows the persistence of the ideology of women's place? You also needed to evaluate the claim in the light of your evidence and summarise the arguments in your conclusion. Generally though, your approach was good and your writing clear. I look forward to your comments.
> Best Wishes
> Mary

The tutor makes explicit reference to some surface features of the TMA, for example, paragraph length, and then goes on to introduce Wendy to what she — the tutor — appears to perceive as the important surface features of this particular written genre: 'horizontal and vertical segregation'. Feedback in the margin on Wendy's TMA relies heavily on introducing key terminology, for example, "perhaps you could explain patriarchal ideology in terms of women's work at this time, perhaps you could bring in familial ideology here". The tutor seems to be adopting what Lea & Street (1998) identify as an academic socialization model of student learning. For Wendy, engaging with key terms in what sometimes seemed to her quite decontextualised ways was indeed one element of her struggles with literacy:

> I still have trouble getting my head round 'ideology' and now they've brought in 'discourse'. You can read something and you can get hold of the wrong idea. If I talk to her face to face she'll be able to put it into language that I'd understand. What you actually mean by that and she could give me another way of doing it. When you're reading it you haven't got an opportunity to ask the question at the point you don't understand.

But it was not merely struggling with understanding terminology that Wendy found difficult. More importantly, she was unable to gauge what constituted appropriate written knowledge in her tutor's eyes. Wendy had taken large chunks out of her draft assignment; she expressed so much concern about her decision to edit these out that she had decided that next time she would keep these edits, to prove to her tutor if necessary that she knew what she was doing. Wendy does not describe the process of TMA writing in the same terms as the tutor who, in her feedback to Wendy, is concerned with 'using evidence and summarising arguments'. The tutor comments appear to construct the essay both 'as argument' and 'as arrangement', distinctions made by Hounsell (1997) in his research with student writers, but additionally focus on the use of correct terminology as the key to successful 'acculturation into the discourse'. In contrast, Wendy's view of a successful assignment seems to be one which, in some unidentified way, enables her to make links between her own interpretation of the course and 'what the tutor wants'. Choices made around literacy practices — how to make meaning from reading, what to leave in and what to leave out of writing — determine the final text which Wendy hands in for assessment. It is at the level of epistemology and the relationship of this to personal identity that learning seems to be taking place for Wendy.

In the feedback on the concluding paragraph of her work, Wendy is directed towards the tutors' position on the point that Wendy is making and inevitably away from her own interpretation. This paragraph reads:

> The statement '; A women's place is in the home' is being challenged by women today. The patriarchal order of British society is undergoing a significant transition with a new generation of women growing up in a world that expects them to work for a wage and pursue a career. The new technologies and work patterns evolving should make it more acceptable for women to work. Freedom from ideological and financial restraints together with the

sharing of child-care and housework would make equality with men an achievable goal benefiting today's ever changing society.

The tutor feedback immediately after the first sentence reads:
Yes — but in the light of your evidence how successful has this challenge been?
In contrast to Wendy's, the tutor has her own interpretations and expectations of how to write a successful TMA for this course, and her feedback reflects a particular set of implicit assumptions about writing academic knowledge which are not necessarily either obvious to, or shared by, Wendy. For the tutor, Wendy's position is not valid without reference to external evidence. Wendy's description of writing this TMA on the other hand was focused on making sense of her own struggles in constructing appropriate forms of knowledge in relation to the course materials. Although she never attempted explicitly to bring her other/outsider experiences into her own writing it was ever present as she read and wrote for the course.

Conclusion

This research has focused on the experiences of adult distance learners for whom structured course materials and extensive written tutor feedback is recognised as a major part of their learning experience. The changing nature of today's higher education means that increasing numbers of adult students are now relying on course dossiers, readers and standard written feedback sheets as major elements of their learning experience. I would argue that with the decline in face to face tutorial support in more traditional university settings many students now find themselves in learning environments which more closely resemble those of the distance learner. In this respect then, the experiences of students in this particular research project, of constructing academic knowledge through writing and reading for their courses, seems to be evidence for the importance of considering issues of literacy and language more centrally in student learning in higher education. Although tutors may have their own individual understandings of what constitutes academic knowledge these do not necessarily fit easily with the approaches that adult students are bringing to their learning which are influenced by a whole range of cultural contexts, far removed from academic knowledge bases. Students who more commonly adopt the reformulation approach may be engaging with their own attempts at 'academic socialization' and tutors may interpret this as a successful shift from engaging in everyday discourses to engaging with academic discourses. In reality, students may be doing little more than reformulating received academic knowledge with little real engagement with the epistemological issues underlying the courses being studied. They have however learnt to mask the influences that they bring to their studies from the broader cultural contexts within which they are studying. In contrast, the student who adopts the challenge approach, in attempting to create a dialogic reading of the set texts, therefore making more complex meanings from the course material, may find herself 'failing' in terms of the tutor's expectations. In other words, although learning the terms and using the right vocabulary may be evidence of one level of understanding of the course materials, they are only elements of complex academic literacy practices, concerning issues of both epistemology and personal identity, with which students need to engage in order to merge together their own experiences from broader social and cultural contexts with the university's requirements for assessment.

References

Barton, D. 1994. *Literacy: An Ecology of Written Language.* Oxford: Blackwell.

Bazerman, C. 1988. *Shaping Written Knowledge: The genre and activity of the experimental article in science.* Madison: The University of Wisconsin Press.

Berkenkotter, C. and Huckin, T. 1995. *Genre Knowledge in Disciplinary Communication.* Mahwah, NJ: Lawrence Erlbaum.

Cohen, M. 1993. "Listening to Students' Voices: What university students tell us about how they can learn." Paper to Annual Meeting of AERA: Atlanta, GA.

Gibbs, G. (ed.). 1994. *Improving Student Learning: Theory and practice.* Oxford: OCSD.

Hounsell, D. 1997. "Contrasting Conceptions of Essay-writing." In F. Marton et al. (eds). *The Experiences of Learning: Implications for teaching and studying in Higher Education.* Edinburgh: Scottish Academic Press.

Ivanic, R. 1998. *Writing and Identity: The discoursal construction of writer identity.* Amsterdam/Philadelphia: John Benjamins.

Laurillard, D. 1993. *Rethinking University Teaching: A framework for the effective use of educational technology.* London: Routledge.

Lave, J. and Wenger, E. 1991. *Situated Learning: Legitimate peripheral participation.* Cambridge: CUP.

Lea, M. 1994. "I Thought I Could Write Until I Came Here: Student writing in Higher Education." In G. Gibbs (ed.) *Improving Student Learning: Theory and Practice.* Oxford: OCSD.

Lea, M. and Street, B. V. 1997. *Perspectives on Academic Literacy: An institutional approach.* ESRC Final Report. Swindon: Economic and Social Research Council.

Lea, M. and Street, B. V. 1998. "Student Writing in Higher Education: An academic literacies approach. *Studies in Higher Education* 23(2).

Lillis, T. 1997. "New Voices in Academia? The regulative nature of academic writing conventions." *Language and Education* 11(3): 182–199.

Marton, F., Hounsell, D. and Entwistle, N. (eds). 1997. *The Experience of Learning*, Edinburgh: Scottish Academic Press.

Pardoe, S. 1997 Writing Professional Science: Genre, recontextualisation and empiricism in the learning of professional and scientific writing within an Msc course in environmental impact assessment. Unpublished Ph.D thesis, University of Lancaster.

Saljö, R. 1996. "Discursive Practices and the Constitution of Meaning." Paper to Annual AERA Conference April 1996. New York, USA.

Stierer, B. 1997. *Mastering Education: A preliminary analysis of academic literacy practices within master-level courses in education*. Milton Keynes: Centre for Language and Communications/Open University.

Street, B. V. 1984. *Literacy in Theory and Practice*. Cambridge: CUP.

SECTION B

Mystery and Transparency in Academic Literacies

The chapters in this section draw on a number of different theoretical perspectives and practical approaches to the exploration of perceptions of academic writing in the university.

Lillis in Chapter 7, explores the experience of 'non-traditional' students and their meaning making in academic writing. She takes a 'social literacies' perspective and draws on the Bakhtinian notions of 'addressivity' and 'monologic space' to elaborate the student writers' attempts to make sense of the conventions of essay-text literacy. Their confusion points to an 'institutional practice of mystery' which is enacted through the dominant addressivity of tutor-student relations and essay-text literacy conventions. The latter remain unexplicated and unquestioned by tutors, because for them it is academic 'common sense.'

The 'common sense' attitude towards academic literacy, is taken up by Turner (Chapter 8) and explored at the level of theories of language and related epistemological assumptions. She locates the source of the problem in a historically and culturally rooted 'discourse of transparency' whose values and assumptions continue to dominate the institutional understanding of academic writing. The assumptions of the discourse of transparency work to obscure the materiality of language and the operation of values in preferred rhetorical strategies, and so the 'visibility' of language means that something is wrong, and the issue becomes one of remediation.

A historical tack, this time outlining the teaching practices of academic writing is taken also by Davidson and Tomic in Chapter 9. They locate the current teaching of academic literacy in the United States and Britain on the path of a historical trajectory of shifting institutional status, beginning on a high as the teaching of rhetoric in the classical tradition at Harvard, flailing in the wake of the rise to status of English literature teaching, and currently more prominently in focus, as increasing demands are made for its services in different ways, but also in flux as institutions find different ways to resolution.

Scott (Chapter 10) focusses on the 'motivated sign' as a theoretical construct which rebuts the divisions between signifier and signified and language and thought and emphasises the fluidity of meaning making and individuals' re-making of meaning from their own social, and cultural knowledge and experience. Her concern is for a theoretical base which more firmly grounds the interrelationship between agency and subjectivity and she engages a range of theoretical perspectives in her discussion, including the literary critical perspectives of romanticism, new criticism, structuralism and post-structuralism, as well as the linguistic perspectives of critical discourse analysis and establishing identity in writing. Not unlike Lillis in spirit, she ends on a plea for greater attention to be paid, both in pedagogical and curricular terms, to the individual student as a re-maker of meanings.

In Chapter 11, Street rebuts the conventions of the traditional format and layout of the 'essay-text', by including the responses to a stimulus document on academic literacy, exactly as they were received. While discussing taken-for-granted assumptions, this particular 'literacy event' also disrupts them.

Certain themes recur in the work of these writers. One is the continuing predominance of the academic essay as a means of assessing student performance. The essay is the fulcrum on which a variety of issues turn, including staff feedback (Lillis, Scott, Turner); the demand for explicitness and the lack of clarity on what it means, (Lillis, Scott); the demand for argument or structure and what that implies, both for students and staff (Lillis, Scott, Turner); and the issue of its cultural power (Lillis, Turner, Davidson & Tomic). Another theme is the student's voice. Lillis is concerned with its absence in the monologic space reserved for the tutor, while Scott explores how it might best be given the freedom to speak and to make itself heard. A further issue relates to the intellectual space afforded by the institution to the area of working with students writing. Turner refers to its remedial role, which puts both the student and the work done with them on academic writing in a negative position, but Davidson & Tomic emphasise its fluctuation according to particular socio-political circumstances and are optimistic about current developments on both sides of the Atlantic. Street's interactive debate with colleagues in both places about 'academic literacies' likewise reinforces the positive value of making explicit the assumptions underlying student writing and its reception.

In sum, the cultural and epistemological backdrop of students writing in the university is diverse and multi-faceted. The long-term dominance of objectivity has continuing effects, while emerging epistemologies foregrounding agency and subjectivity require a re-working of pedagogical practices and a re-conceptualising of the process of writing or making meaning. As perceptions of writing, language, and knowledge change, writing in the university is also re-making the university.

CHAPTER 7

Whose 'Common Sense'?
Essayist literacy and the institutional practice of mystery

Theresa Lillis

1. Introduction

Access to UK higher education (HE) has historically been reserved for those privileged in British society. It is only in more recent times that access has been broadened to include students from social groups previously excluded. These include working class and Black students, and students older than eighteen at the start of their course.[1] In this paper I problematize the nature of this access, by focusing on one particular dimension of the experience of a group of 'non-traditional' students in HE: their attempts to make sense of the conventions surrounding student academic writing.

Whilst the view prevails that such conventions are unproblematic and simply 'common sense', I argue that confusion is so all pervasive a dimension of their experience as a group of 'non-traditional' students in higher education that it points to an *institutional practice of mystery*. This practice of mystery is ideologically inscribed in that it works against those least familiar with the conventions surrounding academic writing, thus limiting their participation in HE as currently configured.

I will illustrate how this practice of mystery works by using extracts from spoken and written texts to trace attempts by several student-writers to make sense of the 'essay question'. The examples show that the practice of mystery is not made up of a discrete list of actions but is enacted in different ways, at the levels of the contexts of situation and culture of higher education. A significant way in which this practice of mystery is enacted is through the dominant *addressivity* (Bakhtin: 1986) in tutor/student relations, where the denial of real participants works against the student-writers' learning of dominant conventions as well as their desire for a different kind of relationship around meaning making in academia.

2. Research background to the chapter

This chapter draws on a three year research project setting out to explore the experience of a group of 'non-traditional' students and their meaning making in academia. 'Non-traditional' is institutional discourse for referring to individuals from social groups previously largely excluded from HE in Britain (see for example HEFCE 1996; 'non-standard' is also used — see Scott & Smith 1995). The group of ten students who have been involved in the research project on which this paper is based, are 'non-traditional' in a number of interrelated ways. As a group they have in common the following: they are mature women students, aged between 20 and 50 years of age, and they all describe themselves as being from working class backgrounds. They differ, however, in terms of their ethnic and linguistic backgrounds, as is indicated in Figure 1 below. They have all been through the English state school system.

Writer	First generation at university?	Languages used on regular basis	Age	Qualifications on leaving school	Course/s studying at time of discussions
Amira	yes	Arabic, English	21	2 GCSEs – Maths, English	Language Studies (year 1 undergraduate)
Bridget	yes	English	47	3 O levels – English language, English Literature, Maths	Social work (year 1 undergraduate)
Diane	yes	English, Jamaican Creole	32	–	Communication Studies (year 1 undergraduate)
Kate	Father studied at university as mature student.	English	48	6 O levels – Maths, Geography, History, English language, French, Biology	Women's Studies (year 1 undergraduate).
Mary	Mother studied at university as mature student.	English, Jamaican Creole.	21	2 GCSEs – English language, Art	Language Studies (year 1 undergraduate) Combined Studies (year 1 undergraduate)

Nadia	yes	Arabic, English	20	–	Language Studies (year 1 undergraduate) Educational Studies (year 2 undergraduate)
Reba	yes	Sylheti-Bengali, English	20	5 GCSEs – Humanities, Science, Art, English, Bengali	Language Studies (year 1 undergraduate)
Sara	Both parents studied to degree level in Pakistan	Urdu, English	25	6 O levels – Chemistry, Biology, English language, Maths, Urdu, Art.	Language Studies (year 1 undergraduate)
Siria	yes	Sylheti/ Bengali, English	24	3 GCSEs – Science, Home economics, Bengali	Language Studies (year 1 undergraduate)
Tara	yes	English	36	–	Law (year 1 undergraduate)

Figure 1. The student-writers: a brief overview

I have been meeting with the above student-writers on an individual basis for between 1–3 years, to explore their experience of making meaning in 'essay-type' texts as part of their course work in HE. The scare quotes around 'essay-type' are to indicate that whilst their writing falls into one broadly recognisable category to those of us who are already familiar with academic writing, the conventions governing this type of writing often remained a mystery to the student-writers themselves (see similar discussions by English and Jones in this volume). Trying to work out *what they want* was a major theme in all the students' talk with me and is the focus of this chapter.

3. Problematising the gap between tutors' and student-writers' understanding of academic writing conventions

The distance between tutors' and students' understandings and interpretations of the conventions underlying student academic writing is a common theme across many studies seeking to explore the experience of students writing in academia. The criticism has repeatedly been made in recent years that the conventions student-writers are expected to write within remain implicit rather than explicit (see, for example, Hounsell 1984, 1987; Taylor 1988; Prosser & Webb 1994; Flower 1994; Lea 1995; Andrews 1995; Scott 1996). A significant pedagogical response to the 'gap' between tutors and students — particularly in relation to those students who have not entered higher education by the traditional A level route — has been to provide students with written guidelines on 'how to write an essay', as part of a study skills approach to the teaching of writing (for examples, see Northedge 1990; Race and Brown 1993). In these approaches, the distance between tutors' expectations and student-writers' understanding of such expectations is problematized as a mismatch which can be resolved, if tutors state clearly to student-writers in written or spoken words what is required. However, such an approach tends to reinforce the view that conventions are autonomous and discrete phenomena, rather than constituting and reflecting a particular literacy practice (for literacy practices, see Street 1995; see also Lea & Street 1998). This is clearly not the case, as can be illustrated by focusing on one tutor directive (spoken and written) which student-writers found problematic; 'be explicit'. In Figure 2 below, I point to specific instances of my attempts to clarify the directive to 'be explicit', in my talk with one student, Amira, over the writing of three texts. Figure 2 challenges any presumed straightforward notion of explicitness, pointing instead to a number of specific meanings within the context of student academic writing.

make clear link between claim and supporting evidence (a)	avoid vague wordings — *etc., lots of.* (b)	check that it is clear what *this, these* refer back/forward to (c)
make clear why a particular section was included (d)	**'BE EXPLICIT'**	say why using particular examples (e)
make links between sections (f)		say why particular punctuation used (g)
show that you understand key terms (I)	say how you are using contested terms (j)	link content with essay question (k)

Figure 2. Specific instances of exploring 'being explicit' with one student-writer, Amira

It is clear from this example that explicitness is not a unitary text phenomenon (see Nystrand and Wiemelt 1991: see also Gee 1990: 60). Each one of the above attempted clarifications of the directive, 'be explicit', raises further questions and demands further clarification. For example, (a) raises the questions of what is a claim and what is supporting evidence? These questions, in turn, raise further questions about what **count** as claim and evidence, in this context. The clarifications (i) and (j) raise questions about what are the key/contested terms in this context. The extent to which each one of the attempted clarifications above raises more questions, hence demanding further clarification, depends on the existing familiarity of the individual student-writer with academic conventions.

Being explicit in student academic writing involves learning how to construct meanings through a range of interrelated conventions, resulting from the particular socio-discursive context of higher education. In short, it involves engaging in a particular literacy practice, which I shall refer to, following Scollon and Scollon (1981) as *essayist literacy*.

4. The practice of essayist literacy

Gee draws on Scollon and Scollon's work on the literacies within the Athabaskan communities of Alaska, to further explicate their notion of *essayist literacy* within the context of schooling in North America (see Gee 1990, 1996). Gee outlines what he sees as the dominant features of this particular form of literacy as follows. Essayist writing (or talk based on similar practices) is **linear, values a particular type of explicitness, has one central point** — theme, character, event — at any one time, and is in **Standard (American) English**. It is a type of writing which aims to inform rather than entertain. Important relationships are not signalled between speakers or between sentence and speaker, but between sentence and sentence. The reader has to constantly monitor grammatical and lexical information and, as such, there is a need for the writer to be explicit about logical implications. There is a fictionalization of both writer and reader, the reader being an idealization *a rational mind formed by the rational body of knowledge of which the essay is a part*. The author is a fiction *since the process of writing and editing essayist texts leads to an effacement of individual and idiosyncratic identity* (Gee 1990: 63).[2]

What is important about the practice of essayist literacy, with its particular configuration of conventions, is that although it represents one way, rather than the only way of making meaning, it is the privileged practice within formal institutions of learning. That one literacy practice is privileged above others is of major significance when attempting to explore the meaning making experience of student-writers in HE. Numerous studies point to the ways in which the privileging of one literacy ensures continuity between home and formal institutions of learning for some learners, notably those from white middle class backgrounds, whilst significantly contributing to discontinuity for others — learners from working class and minority ethnic backgrounds.[3] Gee has argued that, on the whole, privileged practices are not taught to those who do not already know them, with the result that formal institutions continue to privilege those who are already privileged within society. In a similar vein, Delpitt (1988) has criticised progressive educators for failing to teach Black students how to successfully manage dominant conventions; and Flower (1994: 122–147) has critiqued so-called 'immersion' approaches to the teaching of writing, which supports 'insiders' most.

In order to begin to address such marginalization, we need to know more about how it happens. My aim in the rest of this paper is accordingly to trace how this process of marginalization and exclusion happens, by focusing on specific instances of confusion.

5. Example of the practice of mystery: the essay question

> Some of these rules are made up for no reason whatsoever..(laughs). That's why it's difficult to learn, you see, because sometimes there's no reason why.
> Mary

In this section, I want to illustrate the real confusion experienced by the student-writers in this project in their attempts to make sense of tutors' demands and the conventions therein, by focusing on one important and opaque aspect, the meaning and demands of the 'essay question'. With all ten, much of our talk centred on the meaning of the essay/assignment question.

I will begin by considering an example of advice on how to approach the essay question. I include it because I think it is not only typical of advice given in study skills manuals but also reflects notions about language and literacy which seem to underpin much tutor talk and action with student-writers:

Step 1 of 7 steps towards essay planning is presented as follows:

1. Interpret the question. This step overwhelmingly determines what follows; it is also likely to be the greatest source of difficulty. **Assuming that the question itself is clear, and reflects the instructor's intentions,** *the student needs to be satisfied as to* **the meaning of the question and any unclear words checked out.** (Biggs 1988: 194)

The wordings I've put in bold print illustrate the transparent and autonomous notions of language and literacy underpinning much advice (see Reddy 1979 and Wertsch 1991 for conduit metaphor of language: see Turner in this volume for discussion of *discourse of transparency* in academia). The advice in the extract above presupposes the following: that meaning resides in the wording of the question; that meaning is there for the student-writer to discover; that, should any difficulty arise, students will be able to consult with their tutors. The experience of the student-writers in this project challenges these assumptions, as I now explore, by focusing on four specific instances of confusion.

5.1 *'It turned out she liked it'*

The general sense of confusion about what a successful response to an essay question might look like, can be exemplified by Bridget's comments. For Bridget, a first year Social Work student, her confusion was a continuation of her experience at Access level. In our first meeting I asked her to bring along an essay from her Access course that she had considered to be successful, as a first step towards clarifying what she might want us to talk about. When I asked her why she considered it successful, she said she had got a better mark for it than for her other essays. However, she had little sense of what made it better:

> it was better in terms of marks. It was one of those essays I wrote and I didn't really know whether I was writing **what she wanted.** So I just sort of did it to the best of my ability. And it turned out **she liked it.** (My emphasis)

Bridget seems to suggest it was mostly a matter of the individual tutor's taste (indicated in the bold print) that the essay was successful and has little sense of the specific ways she has fulfilled criteria, and hence how she might do so in future. The mystery surrounding what 'they' really want is still with her in her first year at university where she focuses predominantly on the wording of the essay questions in her attempts to work out what *they're really asking*. Relying mainly on the essay question, however, is not illuminating for her:

> The more I read the question, the less sure I am.

5.2 *'She didn't like it one bit'*

The perception that success and failure depend greatly on individual tutors' quirks, can be further illustrated by Nadia's experience, where her misfortune contrasts with Bridget's unaccountable success above. Nadia was frustrated by her tutor's dismissal of part of the content of her essay. In her second year of HE, but her first year of Education Studies, she wrote on the following question:

> Essay question: Working class children are underachieving in schools. How much of this may be attributed to perceived language deficiencies?

When working on a draft for this essay Nadia talked of focusing on monolingual working class children but also thought she would focus on the experience of bilingual children. She was pleased that she would be able to draw on what she had learned from a previous course, Language Studies. However, the response from her tutor was not what she expected:

Opening section of Nadia's final draft.	Tutor written comment
Throughout this essay I will be focusing on the types of underachievers.	Your beginning section moves away from essay title.
Firstly the working class bilinguals and the misleading intelligence tests, of which bilingual children are expected to do.	Need to organise your thoughts more carefully and adhere to the essay title more clearly.
Secondly the working class monolinguals which are underachieving.	
Thirdly I will seek information on how much of this may be attributed to perceived language deficiencies.[4]	

Figure 3

Nadia sought verbal feedback in a seminar in order to clarify why the tutor felt she hadn't focused on the essay title:

> She didn't like it <u>one bit</u>... She said not all bilingual kids are working class. And I turned round and said not all bilingual kids are middle class. She said the question wasn't about bilingual kids.

Nadia sees this as an individual quirk of the tutor, rather than a dimension to meaning making within the context of culture of HE, where particular meanings are privileged. In this case, there is an expectation that she will take monolingual as the norm and focus on monolingual, rather than monolingual and bilingual, working class children. Nadia sees the tutor's comments simply as personal opinion, albeit with institutional power, as is indicated in her comment below:

> She's nice, but what she wants, she gets. You can't argue with her.

5.3 'Who do I advise?'

In some instances, as in Bridget's case above (5.1), the student-writer attempts to discover the expectations of the tutor in the wording of a question. On some occasions the student-writer identified a particular word as the source of her problems in trying to understand what was required. For example, Tara, a first year law student focused on the word *advise*, used in two essay questions and this became the main focus of our talk over the writing of these texts. Below are the two *advise* questions in full.

Question one
Justine Snook runs a small catering service from her home, providing hot lunches for the management of three firms in Sheffield. She has two employees-a driver and an assistant cook.
She would like to bid for catering contracts at more firms and possibly expand into catering for private dinner parties, but could not do all this from her home; and she is worried about how she would manage the operation. One of her worries is that she has no experience beyond institutional catering.

a) Advise Ms Snook about alternative forms of business organisation available to her explaining the legal implications and the advantages and disadvantages as they apply to her situation.
b) Ms Snooks anticipated expansion will necessitate considerable amounts of funding. Advise on possible sources of finance and examine whether particular forms of business organisations will act as a constraint on finance availability.
Which form of business would you advise her to accept? 2000 words
* As in original text.

> *Question 2*
> Shortly after 3 a.m. PC Williams is on foot patrol in a part of town where there are many pubs and clubs frequented by young people as part of Steelville's city council's policy of creating a '24 hour city for the 21st century'. He notices a young man, Jean-Claude, leave one such club. As he leaves Jean-Claude tosses a cigarette box into the street. PC Williams calls out the Jean-Claude to stop and pick up the litter. Jean-Claude makes a rude gesture to the officer and continues to walk away. Williams shouts to Jean-Claude again, telling him to stop and demanding his name and information about where he lives. Without stopping, Jean-Claude gives his name but says he is a temporary visitor from France with no local address.
> Williams catches up with Jean-Claude, takes hold of his arm, and tells him he is under arrest. Jean-Claude immediately struggles, and in an attempt to free himself, begins to strike at Williams. A passer-by, 'Big Frank' attempts to assist Williams. He aims a punch at Jean-Claude. He misses, and instead, his fist lands on William's nose. Williams loses his grip on Jean-Claude, who runs away. Williams takes 'Big Frank' to the police station, where he is charged with wilful obstruction. Jean-Claude, meanwhile has been gently recaptured and is gently taken to the police station.
> At the station Jean-Claude's pockets, and his bag, are searched and a substantial quantity of prohibited drugs are found. The custody officer, Howard, tells him that he is to be detained for questioning on suspicion that he is a dealer in such drugs and that he will be able to provide information as regards his suppliers. He is told that in the circumstances it is not appropriate to allow him to communicate with a lawyer; nor that his mum should be informed of the fact of his detention.
> Jean-Claude is questioned at length. On the following day, exhausted, he admits numerous offences in connection with prohibited drugs.
> Advise Jean-Claude and 'Big Frank'.

No specific guidelines were given in relation to these essay questions: they were not, for example, presented as part of an explicit role simulation within professional practice, but located only within the academic context of the course.[5]

The main obstacle Tara faced in trying to frame her essay was to decide who her text was meant to address: the *advise* directive seemed to suggest that her writing was meant to address the fictitious client, yet Tara knew the real addressee was the tutor. For the writing of her second essay, she pursued this with her tutor seeking explicit guidance. Here she recounts her attempts to clarify how she is to interpret *advise*:

> I've asked loads of questions but they said, 'you advise him' (Jean-Claude) and I said, 'yeah, but do I speak to him so I'm giving him the advice, or..?'
> .He said, 'Well, if you do that then you won't get all the acts done.' So..he just couldn't be bothered I assume.

She knew she had to show as much legal knowledge as she could for the benefit of the tutor-assessor, yet the directive to *advise* the client still worried her. This was particularly true of the second essay where she was concerned that the knowledge she knew she had to show the tutor, would not, in a real life situation, be shared with the client Jean-Claude. In our discussion she pointed to the dilemma she faced in attempting to follow the tutor's direction to *advise Jean-Claude*:

> If I was directing this to him personally, it'd be pointless me saying this and this and this..cause he wouldn't understand it. So I have to maybe, in the.. is it the third person maybe? Not to him directly, not advising him directly but pointing out <u>how</u> I would advise him. Not advising him personally. Should I put that maybe in the introduction?

In attempting to make sense of the essay questions, Tara pulls together both oral and written comments made about the essay question. In the first essay, for instance, as well as trying to make sense of the written directive *advise*, Tara was also trying to understand the tutor's oral instructions who had called for *not too many facts and to argue it*.

> I'm only there to advise her anyway. I'm not there to say anything else. I mean, there's a lot of information I could put down, but, like I said, when I look at it, I can't really <u>argue</u> it in any way.

There are significant problems surrounding the wordings *advise* and *argue* which in Tara's mind conflict. She knows she has to display all the relevant knowledge for the benefit of the tutor-addressee. But in trying to accommodate the client-addressee, Tara assumes she has to provide a range of perspectives in order to advise, rather than **tell** her one preferred option, which is what argue suggests to her. This is further complicated by the presumed need for Tara as writer to be absent from her text, as indicated in the written guidelines on writing for her course:

> Write in the impersonal third person. There are few things so irritating as the constant intrusion of the author *via* the (unnecessary) first person 'I think..'.

The function of the adjective *unnecessary* is ambiguous here — does it refer to all uses of 'I' or is it signalling that some uses are in fact justified? Tara, based on oral comments by tutors in seminars, understands it to mean that all uses of 'I' are prohibited. Yet such a prohibition seems to contradict the tutor's statement in the feedback comments on the final draft of Tara's second *advise* essay:

> Some good discussion of some of the issues involved. However, some evidence of what <u>you</u> thought the likely outcome would have been would have been useful.

This seems to contradict Tara's understanding of the directive not to use the first person, which she understands as not to include her opinion. Overall, the combination of directives, **advise-argue-write in the impersonal third person** and the directive, after completing the essay, **what you thought..would have been useful**, are confusing, to say the least, and make it difficult for Tara to respond in a coherent way to the essay question. She achieves passes in the low 50s for both essays.

5.4 *Trick Questions*

Trying to establish what tutors expect in response to essay questions was a central concern in discussions with all ten student-writers. In the second of the two essays Diane and I talked about, she moved beyond the wording of the essay question in her attempt to make sense of the question and focused on the teaching context: she waited for the relevant lecture, in order to help her make sense of the question. Yet it caused greater confusion as her comments below indicate.

2000 word essay for Communication Studies	**Diane's comments after lecture**
'It is not enough to show that stereotypes exist in the media; we need also to show their causes and effects.' Discuss with reference to media portrayal of ONE of the following; industrial relations, women, black people, deviance.	*D: Since we've had the lecture, he's just totally put me off.* *T: Why?* *D: Because they, like, give you these questions and they're like bloody trick questions.* *T: So what's trick about this one?* *D: He doesn't want..first of all he doesn't want to know that really stereotypes in the media exist. They already <u>know</u> that. What they want to know is the causes and effects.*

Figure 4

Although it seems that all the lecturer has done is to repeat the wording of the written question, his oral gloss actually changes the focus of the question. In the written question, the directive *discuss*, placed as it is outside the inverted commas, makes **both** of the preceding clauses its object, suggesting to Diane that she should discuss both. She had thus begun by discussing the first clause, by attempting to briefly define what is meant by stereotype and to provide examples from the media. However, when she heard the lecturer's comment, reported above, she became confused. In his oral gloss on the question, the lecturer tells the students that he only wants the second clause/proposition — *we need also to show their causes and effects* — to be discussed; the first — *it is not enough to show that stereotypes exist* — is not to be discussed but taken as given.

Diane points to the confusion she feels in the essay question and makes her new interpretation of what the question requires — based on the sense she has made after the lecturer's comment — clear to the seminar tutor:

> I even said to the woman in the seminar, and I said, you know when you give these questions out, it's like you're trying to trick students, like, that doesn't look how, it doesn't say, 'I don't mean talk about what stereotype is, just talk about the causes and effects.'

There is no further clarification from the seminar tutor so, throughout her writing of the essay, Diane continues to try to make sense of both the essay question as written and the lecturer's oral comments. In attempting to do so, she returns time and time again to the written text, but with the with the words spoken by the lecturer always in mind:

> (reads) 'We need also to show their causes'. It's this what gets me. Causes and effects.

In this context of a set essay question, the *we need* functions as an indirect command to the student to tell her what to write; here then if Diane focuses only on this clause and reads it as a command, her lecturer's comment to write about *causes and effects* is coherent. However, this understanding of the task continues to contradict what the written question indicates; that the student-writer should discuss both propositions within the question. So Diane is left with an overriding concern that whatever she does she cannot meet the expectations of the lecturer. In this instance, she decides to try to respond to the essay question as glossed by the lecturer and to focus on the causes and effects without considering in any detail notions of stereotypes and their existence in the media. At this point, it should be noted, Diane assumes that that it is the lecturer who will be marking her essay.

However, it is the seminar tutor who reads and marks her essay. From her written feedback on the essay Diane discovers that she might have been more successful, in terms of marks, had she worked with her original understanding.

Essay question	Tutor comment on final draft of essay (made by seminar tutor)
'It is not enough to show that stereotypes exist in the media; we need also to show their causes and effects'. Discuss with reference to media portrayal of ONE of the following: industrial relations, women, black people, deviance.	What I'd like you to consider further is the notion of stereotype. Can it (stereotype) adequately illustrate how and why unequal power relations are reproduced or does it merely demonstrate they exist? You need to address and critically evaluate the concept itself in order to fully answer the question.

Figure 5

There are several points to make here. Firstly, the two tutors involved in the teaching and assessing of the course — the lecturer and the seminar tutor — seem to either have different views about the nature of the task or, at the least, have significantly different ways of communicating their view as to the nature of the task. Whatever the nature of their difference, it is the student-writer who is left guessing. Diane felt that the lecturer had specifically emphasized that he did not want a discussion about whether stereotypes exist and had specifically requested that the students not spend time in defining stereotypes; the second tutor, the seminar tutor who in this case is the tutor-marker, disagrees.

Secondly, it is only from the second tutor's feedback on the completed essay that a key, but implicit, demand of the essay question becomes clear: *Can it (stereotype) adequately illustrate how and why unequal power relations are reproduced or does it merely demonstrate they exist?* These references to power relations and social reproduction are absent in the original question.

Diane receives a mark of 52%. What does Diane take away from this experience? Although she had been awarded a distinction for a previous essay, which was also a *discuss* essay question, she feels that this experience demonstrates that she does not know how to write such essays:

> And I'm not doing anything that says 'discuss'. I'm going to do things that say 'describe' next time.

Here she moves away from the necessary practice she was beginning to develop, that of making links between wordings, meanings and expectations in this sociodiscursive context and fixes her attention on the wording of the question, the assumption being that the wording/meaning will remain constant. But of course this is not the case. An obvious example is that even when the wording in an essay question at HE level directs the student-writer to describe, the expectation is that she will engage in some type of analysis rather than just description.

6. Student-writers' desire for dialogue

That the student-writers in this project want dialogue with their tutors is clear: this is reflected both in what they say and in their decision to spend time with me, as tutor-researcher, to talk about their writing. Their desire for dialogue contrasts with the frustration and disappointment they often feel with the type of relationship they have with tutors (see Hermerschmidt chapter 1 for students' desires around teaching and learning). An extreme example of the distance in communication between student and tutor is Tara's account of the abuse a lecturer had hurled at a lecture hall full of 100 students. She recounted how one lecturer had shouted at the students because, he said, one student had dared to leave an anonymous note under his door seeking clarification on the structure of the assignment. After berating the students for being cowards for not speaking to him directly about their questions — although, according to Tara, some had done — Tara said he gave them these guidelines:

> He goes on the board then and said..erm.. 'This is how you do it, introduction, main body, conclusion, that's it. Go off and do it now.' So we all said to ourselves 'thanks very much, like, you're a bloody big help'.

This is an extreme example of the assumption that the essay is an unproblematic form, that is, that the conventions surrounding student writing are 'common sense', and also of the lack of dialogic space between students and tutor.

More common examples of the type of monologic space that exists are those already discussed above, where student-writers not only found it difficult to make sense of the demands, but were frustrated by the little opportunity to explore such difficulties with the tutors. The encounter between Nadia and her tutor, reported below, illustrates the type of talking-learning relationship the student-writers feel they have with tutors, in contrast to what they would like (in bold):

> N: I'm not really taking them (the oral and written comments made by the tutor) into account.
> T: Ignoring her? Why?
> N: Ignoring her basically. **If I could go and talk to her about it** then maybe I'd take them into consideration, but I'm glad I actually changed from her to somebody else.
> (My emphasis).

In this instance, Nadia, having been given the essay question, attempts to make sense of it without ever re-negotiating her understanding with the tutor. She writes the essay and receives feedback, but sees such feedback as idiosyncratic, rather than helping her to learn more about the nature of the task and event in which she has engaged. So, although one obvious way for student-writers to make sense of what they are trying to do is to ask their tutors, the student-writers in this project generally felt this is often neither possible nor, if it does happen, useful. In general, they felt extremely frustrated by the type of talking space they encountered. This was even the case in an area of study where oppositional practices are encouraged. Thus Kate, even though she felt generally positive about the course she was studying, Women's Studies, she did not dare to ask for clarification of expectations or assessment criteria. The lack of communication was so extreme that she decided she could not study in such an environment and, although passing her course work with marks in the 60s, decided to leave at the end of her first year.[6]

7. Addressivity and meaning making within the context of culture of higher education

The confusion that all ten student-writers in this study expressed about the expectations surrounding essay writing, as exemplified in the specific instances in 5.1–5.5, was central to their experience of writing in HE. Moreover, such confusion was not confined to particular tutors, departments, institution or areas of study. I would therefore argue that it is important to view such confusion not as an individual student phenomenon but as reflecting a dominant practice in HE, which I am calling here, the *institutional practice of mystery*.

As can be seen from the examples discussed in the previous section, this practice is not made up of a discrete list of actions, but is enacted in different ways. In the first two examples (5.1, 5.2), student-writers do not understand why their essays are successful/unsuccessful and in both instances they perceive success and failure as the consequence of individual tutors' quirks. Thus through such an experience, Diane is no clearer as to the criteria for a successful essay and Nadia is no closer to understanding the conventions underlying such criteria; she does not know, when writing the essay or after tutor feedback, that she is not expected to bring 'minority' issues to the centre of her response to an essay question, unless explicitly told to do so. In the third example (5.3), it is the unproblematic use of the wording *advise*, resulting from the hybrid contexts of law as profession and as academic discipline, which causes the student-writer difficulties. In the fourth example, (5.4), problems are most obviously caused by one tutor's reading and interpretation of the underlying intention of the question being at odds with the interpretation of both the second tutor and the student-writer.

A central dimension to these different and specific experiences of the student-writers in the examples above is the dominant *addressivity* within which their meaning making takes place. I find it useful to draw on Bakhtin's notion of addressivity here (1986), rather than talking of student-tutor relationship or writer-reader relationship, because it goes beyond viewing the impact of such relationships as **important** to the meaning making process (as in, for example, Flower 1994) to seeing them as **central** to what the addressor can mean. In this framework, the real or potential addressee contributes to what can be meant as much as does the addressor. Addressivity is central to Bakhtin's understanding of language and meaning making, linking with his notion of the living utterance as one in which meaning comes into being between participants, rather than being transmitted from one to another (see Holquist 1981: 63). At a more abstract level, and beyond the scope of the discussion in this paper, addressivity refers to the way in which all meaning making involves drawing on the meaning making — the voices in terms of wordings, belief, knowledge — of others; thus, in any instance of meaning making, addressor and addressee are to be viewed as being involved in a *chain of speech*[7] *communication* (Bakhtin: 1986).

The socio-discursive space which is inhabited by student-writers and tutors as described in this paper is predominantly monologic: it is the tutor's voice which predominates, determining what the task is and how it should be carried out, without negotiating the nature of the expectations surrounding this task through dialogue with the student-writer. Within this monologic relationship, moreover, there is a denial of real participants, that is, actual tutors and student-writers with their particular understandings and interests, the elaboration and exploration of which might have a) enabled the student-writers in this project to negotiate some understanding of what was being demanded and, although beyond the scope of this paper, b) enabled a range of other meanings to be made.[8]

The dominant addressivity surrounding their learning generally, and specifically, around writing/reading stands in contrast to what the student-writers in this study desire and also to the demonstrated positive benefits of there being actual participants surrounding the production of written texts (for study pointing to importance of reciprocity see Nystrand 1990: see also Clark and Ivanic's emphasis on 'reading for real' 1997: 238).

Conclusion

In arguing in this chapter for an acknowledgement of an institutional practice of mystery, I am claiming the following: firstly, that the specific instances discussed here, whilst drawn from individual student-writer experience, reflect a dominant practice within HE; secondly, that this practice, which I have called *an institutional practice of mystery,* is of particular significance for those students least familiar with dominant conventions. What is at stake is the nature of their participation in HE.

My purpose in writing this paper was to foreground the experience of a group of 'non-traditional' student writers in HE, rather than to make specific recommendations for practice in HE (see Chapters 2, 3 and 4 for examples of practice which work towards the teaching and learning of essayist literacy). However, if access to HE is to mean more than physical access to institutions, then the experience of the student-writers in this study points towards the following general recommendations.

- Whilst the view prevails that essays/student academic texts are unproblematic forms, the construction of which should be part of students' 'common sense' knowledge, experience from this and other studies indicates that this is not the case. Tutors may know such conventions implicitly, having been socialised into them through years of formal schooling (and in many cases through sociodiscursive practices in their home and communities), but the student, particularly the student-outsider, does not. Institutions and the departments and tutors therein need to re-examine the notion of Access in order to consider ways in which they can actively provide access to the symbolic resources and demands of the institution.

- The dominant addressivity within HE works against facilitating such access. The student-writers desire a talking relationship around their learning and writing in HE. In practical terms, this means more face-to-face contact with tutors and the opportunity to do the following: negotiate and re-negotiate the specific nature of the task, for example, the expectations surrounding particular essay questions; explore the conventions the student-writers are expected to write within. Although this may be considered difficult, if not impossible, to organize within the constraints of current resources, it is a price that has to be paid if widening access to higher education is our aim.

Notes

1. For historical and continued under-representation of working class in HE see Halsey and others 1980, Blackburn & Jarman 1993, HEFCE 1996: for structural barriers to women's access, see Sperling 1991; for barriers to Black groups, see Rosen 1993; for expansion of higher education, see Wagner 1995. For discussion of relationships between success in higher education, language and social class, see Bourdieu 1994.

2. I do not think Gee's categories relating to an overarching literacy practice undermine the view

that there are also significant differences within this practice, as discussed in the main introduction.
3. For substantial work on links between social class and literacy practices within the home and school, see Wells 1985, 1986: see also Heath 1983 for continuity/discontinuity between home and school in literacy practices in working class and middle class communities in the US.
4. The wording in extracts from written texts — both of the student-writer and the tutor — are as in the original.
5. For discussion of the impact of such role simulation on academic writing, see Freedman, Adam & Smart 1994.
6. The material constraints acting on individuals, schools and disciplines obviously plays a major part in the specific communication possible: in this instance Women's Studies as an academic field was being squeezed out of this particular university at the time.
7. Bakhtin (1986) stresses throughout that in talking of **speech** genres, he is referring to both spoken and written utterances. For example, *Special emphasis should be placed on the extreme heterogeneity of speech genres (oral and written): 61* and *Everything we have said here also pertains to written and read speech*: 69.
8. The ways in which the dominant addressivity surrounding student academic writing constrains and enables meaning making is beyond the scope of this paper but I have begun to explore this elsewhere: see Lillis 1997. See Scott in this volume for discussion of agency, subjectivity and meaning making in student academic writing.

References

Andrews, R. 1995. *Teaching and Learning Argumen.* London: Cassell.
Bakhtin, M. M. 1986. "The Problem of Speech Genres." In C. Emerson and M. Holquist (eds) *Speech Genres and Other Late Essays.* Austin, Texas: University of Texas Press.
Biggs, J. 1988. "Approaches to Learning and Essay Writing." In R. R. Schmeck (ed.), *Learning Strategies and Learning Styles*, 185–228. New York: Plenum Press.
Blackburn, R., and Jarman, J. 1993. "Changing Inequalities in access to British universities", *Oxford Review of Education*, 19 (2): 197–214.
Bourdieu, P. 1994. *Academic Discourse: Linguistic misunderstanding and professorial power.* Polity Press.
Clark, R. and Ivanic, R. 1997. *The politics of writing*, London: Routledge.
Delpitt, L. 1988. "The Silenced Dialogue: Power and pedagogy in educating other people's children. *Harvard Educational Review* 58 (3): 280–298.
Flower, L. 1994. *The Construction of Negotiated Meaning. A social cognitive theory of writing.* Carbondale and Edwardsville: Southern Illinois Press.
Freedman, A., Adam, C. and Smart, G. 1994. "Wearing Suits to Classes. Simulating genres and simulations in genres." *Written communication* 11(2): 193–226.
Gee, J. 1990. *Social Linguistics and Literacies. Ideologies in discourse.* Basingstoke: Falmer Press. 2nd ed. 1996.

Halsey, A. H., Heath, A. F. and Ridge, J. M. 1980. *Origins and Destinations: Family, class and education in modern Britain.* Oxford: OUP.

Heath, S. B. 1983. *Ways With Words.* Cambridge: CUP.

HEFCE 1996. *Widening Access to Higher Education. A report by the HEFCE's advisory group on access and participation.* Bristol: HEFCE.

Holquist, M. 1981. "Answering as Authoring: Mikhail Bakhtin's Trans-linguistics." In G. S. Morson (ed.), *Bakhtin. Essays and dialogues on his work*: Chicago: University of Chicago Press.

Hounsell, D. 1984. "Learning and Essay Writing." In F. Marton, D. Hounsell and N. Entwistle (eds), *The Experience of Learning.* Edinburgh: Scottish Academic Press.

Hounsell, D. 1987. "Essay Writing and the Quality of Feedback." In J. T. E. Richardson, M. W. Eysenck and D. W. Piper (eds), *Student Learning. Research in education and cognitive psychology.* Milton Keynes: The society for research in higher education and OUP.

Lea, M. 1995. "I Thought I Could Write Till I Came Here." In *Language in a Changing Europe* BAAL/Multilingual Matters 9: 64–72.

Lea, M. and Street, B. 1998. "Student Writing in Higher Education: an Academic Literacies Approach" in *Studies in Higher Education* 23 (2): 157–172.

Lillis, T. 1997. "New Voices in Academia? The regulative nature of academic writing conventions" *Language and Education* 11(3): 182–199.

Northedge, A. 1990. *The Good Study Guide.* Oxford: OUP.

Nystrand, M. 1990. "Sharing Words. The effects of readers on developing writers." *Written communication* 7(1): 3–24.

Nystrand, M. and Wiemelt, J. 1991. "When is a Text Explicit? Formalist and dialogical conceptions." *Text* 11(1): 25–41.

Prosser, M. and Webb, C. 1994. "Relating the Process of Undergraduate Writing to the Finished Product." *Studies in Higher Education* 19(2): 125–138.

Race, P. and Brown, S. 1993. *500 tips for Tutors.* London: Kogan Page.

Reddy, M. J. 1979. "The Conduit Metaphor: A case of frame conflict in our language about language." In A. Ortony (ed.) *Metaphor and thought.* Cambridge: CUP.

Rosen, V. 1993. "Black students in higher education". In M. Thorpe, R. Edwards and A. Hansen (eds.) *Culture and processes of adult learning.* Oxford OUP.

Scollon, R. and Scollon, S. 1981. *Narrative, Literacy and Face in Interethnic Communication.* Norwood, NJ: Ablex.

Scott, M. 1996. "Context as Text: A course for student writers in higher education." In G. Rijlaarsdam, H. van den Berg and M. Couzijin (eds.), *Effective teaching and writing. Current trends in research on writing.* Amsterdam: Amsterdam University Press.

Scott, P. and Smith, D. 1995. *Access and Consolidation; The impact of reduced student intakes on opportunities for non-standard applicants: A second report.* Unpublished report to HEFCE, University of Leeds.

Sperling, L. 1991. "Can the barriers be breached? Mature women's access to higher education", *Gender and education* 3(2): 199–213.

Street, B. V. 1995. *Social Literacies. Critical approaches to literacy in development, ethnography and education.* London: Longman.

Taylor, G. 1988. "The Literacy of Knowing: Content and form in students' English." In G. Taylor, B. Ballard, V. Beasley, H. Bock, J. Clanchy and P. Nightingale (eds), *Literacy by Degrees.* Milton Keynes: The society for research into Higher Education and OUP.

Wagner, L. 1995. *The Changing University,* Milton Keynes The society for Research into Higher Education and the OUP.

Wells, G. 1985. *Language Development in the Pre-school years.* Cambridge: CUP.

Wells, G. 1986. *The Meaning Makers.* Portsmouth: NH: Heinemann.

Wertsch, J. 1991. *Voices of the Mind. A sociocultural approach to mediated action.* London: Harvester Wheatsheaf.

CHAPTER 8

Academic Literacy
and the Discourse of Transparency

Joan Turner

Introduction

In this paper, I view academic literacy as a critically, politically, and pedagogically focussed term. This richness of conceptualisation is the result of a number of different perspectives which can be brought to bear on the area. On the one hand, as a result of socio-economic forces and the demands of the quality assessment perspective which are changing the face of higher education, it is an increasingly important area of pedagogic practice. Both political demands to widen the intake of students into higher education and financial demands to increase the numbers of overseas students, most of whom have very different educational cultural and linguistic backgrounds, are shaping that practice. While 'academic literacy' and 'study skills' have come to the fore as pedagogic practices meeting the demands of the first constituency, EAP (English for Academic Purposes) has increased its provision in most institutions to meet the demands of the second. I suggest there should be closer collaboration between these different pedagogical traditions in the interests both of deepening awareness of what academic literacy entails for a wide variety of students, and of strengthening the impetus and standing of the work in institutional — political terms. Academic literacy needs to establish both its institutional place and its discursive space.

On the other hand, and this is the main focus of the paper, I see the marginalised status of the work as an effect of its suppression in the traditional understanding of academic discourse. I argue that academic literacy has always existed, but has been occluded in a 'discourse of transparency'. This discourse is an effect of the dominant conceptualisation of language in the western intellectual tradition. In construing language as 'transparent', it has effectively denied its workings. So in other words, when language is working well, it is invisible. Conversely, however, when language becomes 'visible', it is an object of censure, marking a deficiency in the individual using it. Additionally, the association of language use in academic discourse with rationality and logic can have the effect of marking out such a student with a deficiency in logic and rationality also.

Academic discourse as such is seldom critiqued and its imbrication in concepts such as logic and rationality which are virtually unassailable in the western intellectual tradition, tend to make it sacrosanct. In such a context, the notion of academic literacy as not so much a deficit but a revelatory mechanism of the workings and the value system behind such workings of academic discourse, becomes a powerful source of critique.

Academic Literacy in Different Pedagogical Traditions

The term academic literacy reveals its derivation from literacy studies and has already started to make its voice heard in that tradition as an area of literacy practice among others. For example, it is construed as a 'world of literacy' (Benson, Gurney, Harrison, & Rimmershaw) in a chapter of the book entitled *Worlds of Literacy* (Hamilton, Barton & Ivanic 1994). It shares with EAP in the Teaching English as a Foreign Language tradition, notions of 'study skills' and culturally preparing potential students for, or supporting existing students in, higher education. While the focus in the literacy tradition tends to be on the student's experience, the focus in the EAP tradition is more on the rhetorical structuring of texts and facilitating students reading and writing within such preferred structures. Jones (this volume), stressing the need for awareness building to facilitate students' understanding of what's expected of them in British academic culture, exemplifies this tradition.

Research documenting the student experience (e.g. Ivanic & Roach 1990; Ivanic 1992; Clark 1992; Lea, 1994; Hermerschmidt, and Lillis (this volume) has perhaps made the main contribution to date in fleshing out academic literacy as a research field. However, I suggest that work influencing the practice of EAP such as genre analyses in academic contexts (Swales 1993; Berkenkotter & Huckin 1995), contrastive cultural analyses of approaches to learning and writing, for example, Adams, Heaton & Howarth 1991, Purves 1988, and Connor 1996, as well as sociology of knowledge perspectives on academic disciplines [e.g. Bazerman (1988), Gilbert & Mulkay (1984)] can be seen as contributing to a wider understanding of the practices of academic literacy. In other words, such practical pursuits as the analysis of rhetorical structures along with an awareness of their cultural relativism and the fact that they might pose crises of identity for writers constrained to use them, might profitably be included as research practices within the field of academic literacy. In both theoretical and practical terms, such a widening of forces feeding into academic literacy would also play a political role in making it a more powerful force within the institutional discourse of academe. This is needed in order to redress its marginalisation.

Swales (1990: 11) encapsulates this marginalisation in a wonderful phrase, 'an ivory ghetto of remediation'. I want to co-opt his phrase here as the use of 'ivory' sets up a neat irony in that the 'ghetto' is created as the ivory towers of an elite education tumble in the face of the encroaching 'masses'. It also symbolises an abiding trace of the value system constructed by the institution of the university, which traditionally has served only an elite. My contention is that the value system of academic discourse as traditionally validated by the university continues to exercise sway.

The *Discourse* of Academic Discourse

In highlighting the term 'discourse' I wish to exploit its use in different academic traditions. On the one hand, in applied linguistics, it is conventionally glossed as language use beyond the level of the sentence (e.g. Brown 1980) while on the other hand its use in theoretical discourses in the social sciences is much broader and more abstract, where language use in as much as it is focussed on at all is seen as conditioned by rather than a condition of discourse. Gee (1990: 142), drawing on Foucault, glosses it as follows: 'Discourses are ways of being in the world, or forms of life which integrate words, acts, values, attitudes, social identities, as well as gestures, glances, body positions and clothes.' Hall (1992: 291) refers to 'a discourse' as, 'a group of statements which provide a language for talking about, a particular way of representing, a particular kind of knowledge about a topic.'

On the one hand then, academic discourse is a linguistic product whose rhetorical features can be analysed and taught, and on the other hand, it is a way of representing what is considered to be academic thinking. Academic thinking, tied up with notions of rationality and logic, assumes the possibility of absolute clarity of representation of knowledge. This 'representationalism' is associated with the universalist, intellectual tradition of the West, which has positioned itself at the centre of an objectivist epistemology on the one hand, and created a discourse of 'the West and the Rest' (see, Hall, op.cit.) on the other. Academic discourse then, in its linguistic manifestations, is also an effect of the *discourse of representationalism* or *epistemological objectivism*.

What Street (1984) has termed the autonomous model of literacy is also imbricated in this discourse. This model assumes that the acquisition of literacy enhances cognitive abilities, facilitating reasoning and abstract thought more generally. This means that the value system underlying what counts as academic literacy is tied up in the same discourse which has propounded the assumptions underlying the autonomous model of literacy. In this respect then, the notion of academic literacy and the autonomous notion of literacy are virtually synonymous.

However, my claim is that the notion of *academic* literacy puts a critical edge on these assumptions. On the one hand, the modification of literacy by 'academic' is itself indicative of the 'new literacy studies' approach to literacy practices, espoused among others by Street (1984, 1995), Gee (1990), and Barton (1994), in opposition to the autonomous model. When seen as a particular social literacy among others, the notion of *academic* literacy helps to break down the monolithic conception of *literacy*.

As with other social literacies, academic literacy is both the product and the process of perpetuation or change of a particular discourse, or sometimes intersecting discourses. As the product of assumptions generated most forcefully by the European Enlightenment's formation of rationality, academic literacy is in a good position both to expound what these assumptions mean in terms of preferred rhetorical structures and to act as a basis for critique of those assumptions. Also, somewhat paradoxically, the acknowledgement of academic literacy as a socio-cultural practice with its own historical formation loosens its ties with a taken-for-granted rationality despite the fact that the institutional positioning of academic literacy as a remedial pedagogic practice is in itself an effect of that taken-for-grantedness. While the notion of academic literacy focuses on the workings of language, the taken-for-grantedness of rationality acts as a denial of them. This denial is related to a conceptualisation of language as transparent.

Language and the Discourse of Transparency

"The desire for the perfectly 'transparent' language", as Crowley (1988: 64) puts it, "can properly be described as one of the metaphysical problems that emerges consistently in the history of western thought." Whether in terms of giving a true representation of reality, of words matching the world, or what philosophers call 'the correspondence theory of truth' (Rorty 1979) as was the more traditional philosophical concern, or giving a true representation of rationality, which was a major concern of the European enlightenment, what might be termed a discourse of transparency has prevailed. The first concern is revealed in the biblical 'In the beginning was the word' as well as in the Platonic dialogue 'Cratylus' where Socrates asserts 'the Gods must clearly be supposed to call things by their right and natural names' and also in the theological dogmatism of Archbishop Trench in the nineteenth century where etymology (from the ancient Greek, *etymon* meaning 'true') was seen as demonstrating the real meaning of words to which morally upstanding persons ought to return.

As well as an ontological role, language has been required to play an epistemological role. This was for example the case in Socrates' search for clear definitions of the virtues. Similarities were rejected and distinctions made because what could be *said* of one thing for example, could not be said of another. Tarnas (1991: 36) describes Socrates' arrival at his dialectical method as follows: 'After having investigated every current system of thought from the scientific philosophies of nature to the subtle arguments of the Sophists, Socrates had concluded that all of them lacked sound critical method. To clarify his own approach, he decided to concern himself not with facts but with *statements about facts*' (my emphasis).

From Reflecting Reality to Communicating Rationality

As with Adam, it seems that language was also born with 'original sin'. Baker & Hacker (1984: 1) refer to its being 'a wayward guide', 'pointing to a reality which underlies it and not always accurately reflecting what it thus represents'. The failure of language to live up to its role of 'transparency' was the stimulus to much conceptual and practical intervention in the seventeenth century. This was an opposing thrust to the Socratic use of language where language was used to gain insight into the true meanings which it represented. Now true meanings were the product of Enlightenment science and it was the role of language to convey them 'clearly and distinctly'.

The epistemological role of language had switched from that of revealing the intention of a divine logos to that of communicating clearly the knowledge of science, from being a palimpsest or trace, as it were, to being the vehicle of the rational or scientific mind. The importance of the communicational role is most sharply focussed in the ideal of a universal language. This was Leibniz's 'algebra of thought' which would 'synthesize into one system the merits of a deductive logic and those of a Cartesian logic of discovery' (Baker & Hacker, op.cit.). As Baker & Hacker state: 'Such a language would provide an exact and structurally perspicuous system of symbolization for the precise expression of all actual and possible scientific knowledge' (p. 23). They quote a letter from Descartes to Mersenne where he emphasises the benefits of such a language to the exercise of correct judgement.

> 'The greatest advantage of such a language would be the assistance it would give to men's judgment, representing matters so clearly that it would be almost impossible to go wrong.' (Letter to Mersenne, 20.11.1629 in Kenny, ed. 1970)

In England, Bishop Wilkins' *Essay Towards a Real Character and a Philosophical Language* (1688) was intended similarly to make signification unambiguous and pure. In the eighteenth century, Swift's *Proposal For Correcting, Improving and Ascertaining the English Tongue* (1964, [1712]) which was a plea for the stabilising of language, to make it a site of certainty, to 'make Words more durable than Brass' (p. 17) added the value of permanence in language forms to the desire for rational clarity.

While the model for a perfectly transparent language of rationality might shift, for example, from Leibniz's seventeenth century 'algebra of thought' to Russell's twentieth century 'logically perfect language' where 'there will be one word and no more for every simple object... '(Russell 1918: 58, quoted in Crowley 1988), the conceptualisation of transparency endures.

The Discourse of Transparency and The Value System of the Academic Essay

I would like to suggest that the values for language set up by the discourse of transparency continue to prevail in the assessment criteria for the academic essay. Despite the growing diversity of text types admitted to the arsenal of academic assessment in line with the range of courses of study, the essay remains a prominent assessment procedure in British higher education. It also epitomises what Nash (1990: 28) calls the 'western tradition of academic writing' which he characterises as combining 'precepts of rhetorical structure' with moral assumptions 'that the writer will scrupulously pursue truth in argument and narration, strict accuracy in ascertainable fact, lucidity in exposition.' The importance of lucidity in exposition, in particular reflects the domination of the discourse of transparency.

A useful source for the elaboration of what is expected in the academic essay is the comments that tutors habitually make on students' essays. In previous papers (Turner 1992, 1993) I have highlighted the conceptual consistency of many such comments around the value system of a demand for *clarity of focus* and *tightness of structure*. Adverse comments such as 'you do not focus your ideas

ACADEMIC LITERACY AND THE DISCOURSE OF TRANSPARENCY

clearly enough', 'this is all over the place', 'pay more attention to structure', 'your argument is too loosely drawn' are indicative of this value system, as are their positive counterparts, 'good concise analysis', or 'tightly structured'. While such comments index rhetorical preferences, they underspecify what is entailed by such preferences in the actual realisation of language. Injunctions to tighten the structure or express the argument more clearly are often a source of confusion to overseas students in particular who believe they have expressed themselves as clearly as they could. They do not know how to adjust their texts accordingly and often no detailed help is afforded in this respect by their subject tutors.

This problem of linguistically underspecified comments is neatly exemplified by the confusion Lillis (this volume) explicates around the injuction 'be explicit'. It seems that the emergence of paradoxes such as explicitness and confusion focussing the same issue is germane to the practice of academic literacy, where the assumption on the one hand that clarity of understanding and transparency of language use converge, and on the other hand, tutors' taken-for-granted assumption that students will demonstrate their understanding in the way that they (the tutors) unreflectingly expect, combine. A further issue, which lecturers often fail to acknowledge is that rhetorical preferences are culturally embedded. For example, English (this volume) shows how the taken-for-granted expectation of 'argument' can lead to the negative stereotyping of Japanese students, who 'never argue'.

In their research on lecturers' perspectives on what constitutes good academic writing, Lea & Street (1998) found that such lecturers foregrounded notions of 'argument' and 'structure' as key elements, but were unable to specify exactly what they meant by those terms. As it is unlikely that such lecturers would be unable to give more detail regarding an analytical term germane to their own discipline, their failure to do so with regard to 'argument' and 'structure' suggests that they are taken-for-granted terms in the value system constituting 'good' academic writing.

While the taken-for-grantedness of what 'argument' and 'structure' mean in academic writing may be seen as an example of what Polanyi (1966) has called 'tacit knowledge', i.e. acted upon by expert practitioners but not explicated, or possibly deemed inexplicable. The fact that little need is perceived to explicate something that plays an important role in the assessment procedures of higher education, demonstrates a general lack of critical awareness of the evolution of academic writing in a specific intellectual-cultural tradition. This is further evidence of the need to highlight academic literacy as an effect of an intellectual tradition which has shaped expectations of language use, and as the site where those uses of language are not only expounded but themselves critically assessed.

The *Territory* of Argument

A key concept in the academic literacy practice of the academic essay then, is argument. The term 'argument' relates both to the formulation of ideas, and their structural coherence. On the one hand, it refers to making a specific point or claim, where it is customarily rhetorically paired with a justification for the claim, and on the other hand, it refers to the end product of the essay as a whole. This latter usage may be seen as a metonymic extension from the specific to the general, where the rhetorical force of making a point extends to the forcefulness of the overall essay or 'argument'. The use of argument or structure as the basic metalanguage for commentary on the essay, while virtually synonymous may be seen as viewing it in terms of its rhetorical force and its shape respectively.

As with, and presumably because of the traditional western assumption of logic, the shape of argumentation is usually described as linear. Such linearity may be schematically described as follows. In the case of a cause and effect argument, if the premisses are clearly stated and the conclusions clearly derived from the premisses, then the argument is both logical in the tradition of the Aristotelian syllogism and linear. Alternatively, an equally linear route may be mapped out by a claim or an assertion, followed up by its justification. This 'backing' or 'following on' establishes the validity of an argument and this validity in turn works persuasively on the reader. The structure of an essay then should afford the reader consistency of gaze, as it were, and enable a steady walk through the argumentation. The 'consistency of gaze' of course is also an effect of the position the writer takes up in order to promote the argumentation. If the writer is clear on her/his position, then the gathering of ground (i.e. facts and justifications) around that position enables its identification within the wider landscape. Acknowledgement of that wider landscape works also in the interests of 'balance', another hallowed concept for the academic essay. The notion of balance, while in a horizontal rather than a vertical mode, also contributes to the conceptual dominance of linearity as the preferred shape of the essay.

Abstract linearity and concrete territoriality (albeit transferred metaphorically to the abstract domain) intermingle in the conceptual construction of rationality and knowledge acquisition. The *pursuit of truth* as it were, is linked with a territorial imperative to clear the ground, stake a claim, and construct a vantage point. As with colonisation, of which the discourse of 'the west and the rest' (op.cit.) is a reflection, so it is with knowledge production. Even in already established 'fields' of knowledge, there is an impulse to 'push back the frontiers' and for the practitioners within, to be 'at the cutting edge.' This general colonising mind-set might be seen to stem from the enlightenment mentality where scientific rationality is poised to conquer all.

Assessing the individual on the extent to which he/she is in control of the argument in an academic essay may be seen as a genealogical trace of this value system.

Academic Literacy or Academic Literacies

What the pervasiveness of structure and argument as criteria for assessment also indicates is the unifying force of argumentation in the genre of the academic essay. While there are obviously differences in the kinds and ordering of information, the kinds of analysis or interpretation, and the degree of personal involvement required for essays in different disciplines, in so far as argumentation is required there is an underlying demand for similar rhetorical functions.

In highlighting the dominance of argument in academic literacy, I'd like to take issue with the academic literacies approach of Ballard & Clanchy (1988), for example, when they demonstrate the disciplinary confusion apparent in the respective essays for anthropology and English of one student. While the essay title for each discipline highlights totally different issues:

> 'Compare and contrast the status of women in a patrilineal and a matrilineal society. Does the dominant descent principle have anything significant to do with women's status in the societies you have chosen?'

and

> 'Analyse the gravediggers scene (V,i), explaining both the internal structure of the piece and the dynamic function it serves within the total dramatic design of Hamlet.'

it serves the same function of 'signposting' the argumentative route the student must travel. The student they focus on is obviously transposing anthropological interests to the particular social setting of the gravedigger's scene rather than assessing its dramatic impact as Ballard & Clanchy point out, but this need not be seen as a contrasting 'literacy'. The analytical concerns of each discipline are different and therefore the positioning of the student 'arguer' will be determined by those concerns. If the student has not constructed a vantage point from which to adequately survey the appropriate analytical terrain, she/he will inevitably go astray. This is indeed the case with Ballard & Clanchy's student's initial attempt with the English essay.

Shattering the Mirror Image

The notion of academic literacy foregrounds the visibility of language, and thereby cuts through the transparency conceptualisation, as it were, shattering the mirror. This perspective situates academic literacy as a research and pedagogical practice within applied linguistics. Carter & Nash, in the punning title of their book, *Seeing Through Language* (1990) also draw attention to the visibility/ transparency dichotomy of language. Carter and Nash focus on the value of language analysis for deeper interpretive insight, but at the same time recognise the reluctance of related endeavours in the academic community to accept this. As they state, (Carter & Nash 1990: 24) 'in many courses in literature and communications in particular, there is a tendency to look *past* language at the more 'important' ideas or content that a text contains'. While their elaboration of language as 'the medium that is part of the message' focuses on interpretation, what this suggests also is that language is an inherently malleable substance. It *can*, for example, be made to appear transparent by moulding textual shapes so that they correspond to the intended reader's expectations of texture and shape.

The process of shaping language and of recognising shapes in language in academic discourse is what academic literacy draws attention to. For example, cohesive links in lexis and logical structure can be isolated to chart the development of a text, or to identify what is foregrounded and what is backgrounded. Furthermore, in the spirit of critical discourse analysis which may be seen as foregrounding the Foucauldian over the conventional applied linguistic notion of discourse, (see above) while applying the tools of the latter, the textually explicit foreground/background relationship helps to read in knowledge of the 'discourse' in which any particular text is situated. Such 'reading in' is itself a necessary condition of critical reading which requires locating omissions as much as understanding what is explicitly located in the text. Critical reading is a taken-for-granted aspect of academic literacy. The possibility of its explication, by reference to the interaction between textual structure and the background discursive formation in which the particular text can be located, both unpacks the procedure for initiates into academic culture and defamiliarises at another level, its taken-for-grantedness.

Such a process of analysis of academic literacy practices acts as a denial of the assumption that students learn a neutral, transparent medium in order to learn an epistemologically transparent message. This suggests that academic literacy should play a critical, rather than a remedial role in higher education.

References

Adams, P. Heaton, B and Howarth, P. 1991. *Socio-Cultural Issues in English for Academic Purposes.* London: Macmillan.
Baker, G. P. and Hacker, P. M. S. 1984. *Language, Sense and Nonsense.* Oxford: Basil Blackwell.
Ballard, B. and Clanchy, J. 1988. "Literacy in the University: An anthropological approach." In G. Taylor, B. Ballard, V. Beasley, H. Bock, J. Clanchy, and P. Nightingale (eds), *Literacy by Degrees.* Milton Keynes: Open University Press.
Barton, D. 1994. *Literacy: An introduction to the ecology of written language.* London: Routledge.
Bazerman, C. 1988. *Shaping Written Knowledge.* Madison: University of Wisconsin Press.
Benson, N. Gurney, S. Harrison, J. and Rimmershaw, R. 1994. "The Place of Academic Writing in Whole Life Writing." In M. Hamiliton, D. Barton amd R. Ivanic (eds), *Worlds of Literacy.* Clevedon: Multilingual Matters.
Berkenkotter, C. and Huckin, T. 1995. *Genre Knowledge in Disciplinary Communication.* Mahwah, NJ: Lawrence Erlbaum.
Brown, H. D. 1980. *Principles of Language Learning and Teaching.* Englewood Cliffs, NJ: Prentice Hall.
Carter, R. and Nash, W. 1990. *Seeing Through Language.* London: Basil Blackwell.
Clark, R. 1992. "Principles and Practice of CLA in the Classroom." In N. Fairclough (ed.) *Critical Language Awareness.* Harlow: Longman.
Connor, U. 1996. *Contrastive Rhetoric.* Cambridge: CUP.
Crowley, T. 1988. *The Politics of Discourse: The Standard Language Question in British Cultural Debates.* London: Macmillan.
Crowley, T. 1996. *Language in History.* London: Routledge.
Gee, J. P. 1990. *Social Linguistics and Literacies: Ideology in discourses.* London: Falmer Press.
Gilbert, G. N. and Mulkay, M. 1984. *Opening Pandora's Box: A sociological analysis of scientists' discourse.* Cambridge: CUP.
Hall, S. 1992. "The West and the Rest: Discourse and power." In S. Hall and B. Gieben (eds), *Formations of Modernity.* Polity Press in Association with the Open University.
Hamilton, M. Barton, D. and Ivanic, R. (eds). 1994. *Worlds of Literacy.* Clevedon: Multilingual Matters.
Ivanic, R. 1992. " 'I' is for Interpersonal: The discoursal construction of writer identities." Centre for Language in Social Life; Lancaster no. 42.
Ivanic, R. and Roach, D. 1990. Academic Writing, Power and Disguise. In *British Studies in Applied Linguistics* 5, 103–121. London: British Association for Applied Linguistics in association with Centre for Information on Language Teaching and Research
Kenny, A. J. P. (ed. & trans.) 1970. *Descartes: Philosophical letters.* Oxford: Clarendon Press.

Lea, M. 1994. "I Thought I Could Write Until I Came Here': Student writing in Higher Education." In G. Gibbs (ed.) *Improving Student Learning: Theory and Practice.* Oxford: OSCD.

Lea, M and Street, B. V. 1998 "Student Writing and Staff Feedback in Higher Education: An academic literacies approach." *Studies in Higher Education* 23(.2): 157–172.

Locke, J. 1975. *An Essay Concerning Human Understanding.* [1690] P. Nidditch, (ed.). Oxford: Clarendon Press.

McCarthy, M. and Carter, R. 1994. *Language as Discourse. Perspectives for Language Teaching.* Harlow: Longman

Nash, W. (ed.). 1990. *The Writing Scholar. Studies in academic discourse.* Newbury Park/London: Sage Publications.

Purves, A. C. (ed.) 1988. *Writing Across Languages and Cultures. Issues in contrastive rhetoric.* London: Sage.

Polanyi, M. 1966. *The Tacit Dimension.* New York: Doubleday.

Rorty, R. 1979. *Philosophy and the Mirror of Nature.* Cambridge: CUP.

Shapiro, M. (ed.).1984. *Language and Politics.* Oxford: Basil Blackwell.

Street, B. V.1984. *Literacy in Theory and Practice* Cambridge: CUP.

Street, B. V. 1995. *Social Literacies: Critical approaches to literacy in development, ethnography, and education.* London: Longman.

Swales, J. 1990. *Genre Analysis: English in academic and research settings.* Cambridge: CUP.

Swift, J. 1964. *Proposal for Correcting the English Tongue.* Polite Conversation, etc. [1712] (ed.) H. Davis with L. Landa. Oxford: Blackwell.

Tarnas, R. 1991. *The Passion of the Western Mind.* New York: Ballantine Books.

Taylor, G. Ballard, B. Beasley, V. Bock, H. Clanchy, J. and Nightingale, P. (eds). 1988. *Literacy by Degrees.* Milton Keynes: Open University Press.

Turner, J. 1992. "Focussing on Values and the Value of Focus in Academic Writing." In *IATEFL Annual Conference Report.*

Turner, J. 1993. "Falling into Place: Conceptual metaphor and western academic culture. *Intercultural Communication Studies* III(1): 49–62.

CHAPTER 9

Inventing Academic Literacy
An American perspective

Catherine Davidson and Alice Tomic

Introduction

"Every time a student sits down to write for us, he has to invent the university for the occasion."

This quote from David Bartholomae's well-known article, "Inventing the University" (1986: 4) refers to the sometimes difficult negotiations students undertake when writing within an academic discourse community. In order to write "successfully" students must enter into the secret life of the university — its ethos, values, expectations — all the elements that inform language but go beyond language. Yet it is important to remember that the university is invented not only with each act of writing, but with each act of teaching — what we ask our students to write and how we evaluate it. While the genesis of this collection reflects increasing interest in how academic discourse is shaped or invented culturally, socially and politically — the focus has perhaps been on a micro level — specific problems or institutions or practices. It might also be useful to examine the ways in which academic discourse is invented at a very broad level. This paper examines the development of academic literacy practices in the United States, how they were shaped by cultural and historical forces, how they reflect the role of the university in American society, and how that changed over time. Why should that be of any interest to colleagues in the United Kingdom, whose social and cultural imperatives are quite different? This is a moment when new debates are being engendered on the role of academic literacy in the university curriculum in the UK — a moment of possible invention or change. It is not the role of this paper to suggest how that might happen. However, comparing the development of one set of practices in a culture with common roots might be of interest to those who are critically examining their own practices. This overview is offered not as a template, but as a means of widening the debate.

Without drawing specific analogies between the US and the UK, there may be reasons why this comparison is particularly timely. Much has been written about how modern British universities are drawing closer to the US model — modular degrees, more flexible entrance requirements, broader intake. Whatever the impact on educational standards overall, such trends might provide a fruitful moment to reflect on the role of academic literacy in British universities. Up until now in the UK, most of the audible debates about academic literacy have been located with the broad rubric of "English for Academic Purposes" (EAP). In the American system, institutional responsibility for academic literacy has been located more centrally within the university, under the heading "Composition" or more recently, "Writing Across the Curriculum" (WAC). As concerns for standards in the UK spread beyond the borders of EAP, the role of academic literacy may widen — an opportune moment to examine both the successes and failures of a system which has had an historically broader brief.

There are other reasons why those working in the field of academic literacy in this country might find this comparison valuable. In this collection, Turner situates academic literacy firmly within the traditions of Western academic culture, a tradition that both Composition and EAP share. Indeed that cultural tradition belongs to British, American, Australian and Canadian higher education systems, among others, and has been negotiated differently in each. In order to unmask what Turner calls the "discourse of transparency" which informs so many of our assumptions about academic literacy, it is important to trace the imperatives which shape that negotiation. This is particularly true as we enter a period in which more and more "non-traditional" students are entering undergraduate degrees. (See, for example, Lillis, this volume) Without attempting to scrutinize UK practices, this chapter will attempt to examine how US practices were in fact mediated by social and historical forces. It will also analyze the dynamic relationship between US educational culture and literacy practices in that country.

How the University Invented Composition

In its early colonial foundations, the American university had no specific cultural identity to distinguish it from its British counterparts. As the nation developed, an educational ethos grew which allowed "Composition" to be invented. Several factors contributed to this invention: Composition's roots in Rhetoric and the influence of 18th and 19th century British rhetoricians at key historical moments; a rapidly growing immigrant population that saw higher education as the entry to the dominant culture; a cultural bias toward practical, transferable intellectual "skills". Over time, writing in higher education changed from the product of feathered quills pressed by the wealthy sons of the nation's young elite to mass-marketed pens wielded by both the daughters and sons of immigrants eager to push ahead. We can learn a great deal about the role of the university in American society by looking at the way it developed the teaching of writing for undergraduates.[1]

It is significant to note that the first "freshman writing" courses, designed to teach good writing practices to undergraduates, began in 1806, when Harvard established the first Boylston Professorship of Rhetoric and Oratory. (Bizzel & Herzberg 1991: 2) Far from being a "remedial" course, good writing practices were taught at the most elite American university, for the benefit of the young men being prepared to rule the nation. A direct line can be traced from early models of Rhetoric in classical education to contemporary "Expository Writing" courses still required of first year students at Harvard — the equivalent of having a mandatory writing course at Oxbridge. This early investment in good writing practices at the nation's most exclusive universities may have provided a model which allowed later, more wide-spread commitment to develop.

These elitist beginnings are reflected in the influence of Hugh Blair, a Scottish rhetorician whose *Lectures on Rhetoric and Belles-Lettres* became a standard text in the 19th century classroom. Blair's philosophy reflected the classical belief that good rhetoric was a sign of good character. Rhetoric as a means of both written and spoken oratory echoed the young democracy's attempts to root itself in classical democracy. The rising elite assumed that a university degree would fit them for leadership over others — what Lunsford has called cultural literacy as a key to both education and wealth (Lunsford 1993: 68).

Higher education in the US continued to grow but, in addition to training, the elite took on a new role — as a "practical tool to train an increasingly industrialised work force." (McQuade 1992: 487). This coincided with Alexander Bain's publication in 1866 of *English Composition and Rhetoric: A Manual*. Bain and the Edinburgh Philosophical Society's analysis of reading and writing as a pragmatic skill, which could be learned, fit well with the progressivist view (under the influence of John Dewey) of education as a way to equip students from increasingly diverse backgrounds with the social and rhetorical skills needed for adult citizenship. An example of this change can be seen in the founding of City College in New York in 1847, which Townsend Harris established as the nation's first specifically municipal higher education institution.

Although it took until later in the century for it to fulfil its role, it can be seen as a model for the way education developed in the US. City College flowered as the "Harvard of the proletariat" (Traub 1994: 76). Children of garment workers and dock hands passed through its gates to become the lawyers, doctors, leaders and intellectuals of the 20th century. Other public universities in other cities, founded along the same lines, echoed this role. Literacy in its broadest sense was seen as a key factor in this transformation.

A less positive development in the history of composition was the establishment in the 19th century of English as an academic subject. The university had always had a special role in the mythos of the nation, echoing Emerson's transcendentalist version of the Pilgrim vision of the new country as a "beacon on the hill" to others, a place where the human race could remake itself anew. The university was a place not merely of higher education and specialisation but of transformation, an ethos which is echoed to this day in the hundreds of prospectuses distributed to potential first year students. The role of the so-called Liberal Arts reflects the belief that an educated person, a university graduate, must have both a broad range of knowledge as well as a specialisation. So the university exists not only to educate experts, but to develop good citizens. McQuade (1992: 487–489) and Marius (1992: 471) have remarked on the fact that in the early years of higher education in the US, "composition" in the form of written and oral rhetoric played this role. Yet, with the development of English, the "soul-work" of liberal arts began to be done increasingly through the explication of literary texts. Meanwhile, "composition" began to be taught by the emerging English departments, as a strictly second order subject, given to graduate students or unpublished young professors, probably despised by teachers as much as pupils. McQuade and Marius both write of the rise of English studies as a disaster for composition. The loss of Rhetoric as a noble, classical precedent for good writing meant that, although writing continued to be taught, it was done so in an increasingly mechanistic and unimaginative fashion.

With few exceptions, this rather dreary view of the teaching of writing in higher education as a lowly but necessary and unsavoury task prevailed in composition studies until the second half of the 20th century. In the 1950's, a new professionalisation of composition was marked by the establishment of the National Council of Teachers of English's new Conference on Composition and Communication (CCC), and the Modern Language Association's Writing division. (Bizzel & Herzberg 1991: 4) Both lent respectability and, more importantly, helped develop a body of scholars/teachers who saw themselves as academics developing a field rather than as simply service workers. This trend, as well as the initiation of journals such as *College English* and *CCC*, meant that many in composition studies began to reconnect with their rhetorical roots, as well as to begin to try to break free of their second class citizenship by reflecting upon, researching and writing about their field.

This led to a renewal of interest in writing as an empowering force in education, what might be called by its supporters, "authentic voice pedagogy" and what has been called by critics, "expressivist" writing (Berkenkotter & Huckin 1995: 153). Although in recent years this trend has been criticised as leading composition in an excessively inward looking direction (Swales 1990: 5), it has to be seen in the context of what it was speaking out against. Ever since Alexander Bain, and in some places to this day, composition was taught through a tedious exposition of models and imitation. The 1966 Dartmouth Conference set the pace for the next two decades, focusing on writing as a process, with influential work being done by Peter Elbow, Linda Flower, Janet Emig and Nancy Sommers (Bizzel & Herzberg 1991: 5). These writers were often influenced by cognitive psychology, and composition as a field returned to some of its former glory by being able once again to link writing with thinking, composing words with the composing of the soul. (This emphasis on composition as a private, individual action has been balanced by a greater interest in composition as a social act. For a good overview of this development, see Nystrand et al. 1993.)

Composition's status was elevated further with the advent of Writing Across the Curriculum, another movement which was helped in its early development by a British thinker, James Britton. His 1975 book helped initiate writing to learn activities which invigorated so much of early WAC work, and gave composition a role in the university it had not had since the 19th century; writing program directors were hired, linked courses created. By 1988, half of all American universities had WAC programs (McLeod 1992: 1). At the same time, feminist and postcolonialist studies created another way of looking at composition — as part of the academic borderlands, in a privileged position to critique traditional patriarchal assumptions about education (see for example McQuade 1992; Lunsford 1993; Lu 1994) able to investigate not just the role of writing, but the meaning of academic discourse and the academic community.

Today, Composition, as well as WAC, has a firmly established academic role within the university — those who teach it have access to a long history reaching back to classical times through the discourse of rhetoric. With this stronger role, composition workers may be turning their attention not only to the meaning of education in the university, but the role of education in society, how it includes and excludes. For example, Flower's current work (1997) using computers and the internet to empower communities of students who have not previously been given opportunities to find their voices, links the most ancient traditions of rhetoric to the most futuristic potential of technology.

How Composition Invents the University

Having examined the ways in which composition developed during the history of American higher education, it might be useful to turn around and look at higher education through the lens of composition. To do this, it is necessary to try to generalise about the current role of composition, its position within the university, its weaknesses and some of its strengths.

One of the first things the current role of writing in the university reveals is that the fragmented nature of the liberal arts curriculum may have allowed it to pervade more extensively than its counterparts in other cultures. A system of combined degrees and one that is fundamentally "modular", the liberal arts has meant that composition could escape from under the wing of the English department and begin to establish an independent identity within the university. Under the guise of "Writing Across the Curriculum" composition theory and practice is increasingly seen as important in all subjects — including science.

Composition's diverse role is reflected in its almost magpie-like ability to draw on different theoretical traditions to enliven practice. In addition to rhetoric, composition has drawn increasingly on linguistics and literary studies. These two fields are its closest contemporary allies; although Raimes (1991: 408) identifies a foreshortened history for English as a Second Language Studies which reflects the movements in Composition from a focus on form, to a focus on the writer to one more concerned again with content, the influence has certainly been mutual. Theories about linguistics and discourse have had a powerful impact on Composition in recent years, judging by the presentations at the 1996 European Writing Conferences in Barcelona, as well as recent postings on the CCC Web site. The 1996 CCC Conference Website revealed a call for papers for a new sourcebook called *Theorising Composition* which lists sixty theories, including Cognitive Psychology and Cognitive Development and related theories, rhetorical theories like Classical Rhetoric, Communication Theory and Speech Modes, literary theories from Deconstruction to Poststructuralism, Genre Theory, both North American and Australian Schools, and theory coming out of identity politics, like Feminism and Queer Theory, as well as Freirean and Bakhtinian perspectives.

Another thing which Composition can teach us about American universities is the high value the culture places on practical, concrete results. This emphasis was first remarked upon by De Tocqueville — the way the culture valued action over contemplation, practical over theoretical science. This valorisation of "skills" over intellect has meant that American universities have always promoted themselves as providing what is becoming more acceptable in post-Dearing Britain (Leuner 1997) — transferable, intellectual skills — hence the liberal arts. Even the word "skill" has considerably different connotations in American and English — like the word "new" — used positively and enthusiastically on one side of the Atlantic and often regarded with suspicion on the other.[2]

The emphasis on practical skills has its downside. Some have described composition as the ultimate socialising agent in the university — the place where the middle class reinforces its sense of itself, or recruits new members. In "Freshman Composition as a Middle Class Enterprise," Bloom (1996: 655–656) points to the many aspects of composition practice that reflect fundamental middle class values. She traces principles such as writing from a thesis, persuasion, precision, "good grammar" to Benjamin Franklin's aphorisms to a rising nation — extolling the ideals of thrift, self-reliance, decorum, order and efficiency. It might be possible to mock the hundreds of self-help documents now being produced for the internet and available at websites such as the Purdue University Online Writing Lab — with titles such as *How to Take Notes; How to Write a Research Paper*. On the other hand, they do offer an increasing resource base which is available to any English speaking student with access to the internet.

It is also the case that composition's rise in status has taken place as part of an often precarious, continuing struggle. While many administrators support the notion that staff can and should help students by helping them to write, composition still has no natural constituency — and universities are ultimately economic institutions. Unlike EAP programmes which can draw on funding from fee-paying second language students, few students choose to take "Comp" — and those who are forced to have to be convinced, semester after semester, that it can be useful to them. The academic maturity projected by the wide range of theories available to the field does not necessarily filter down into better practices, as Marius (1992: 466–468) has pointed out. Many first year writing courses are still taught by graduate students on stipends, who see themselves as "doing time" in composition, and, unless they are part of a well-structured program, like that at the University of Southern California, they may be equipped only with one of the hundreds of textbooks that try to distil theory into practice, without receiving any other grounding. While Harvard may have an excellent "Expository Writing" program as mentioned earlier, Marius (1992: 475) could still write as its director:

> What miracles they expect of us! How patronising are those faculty members in our institutions when they tell us firmly they support our labours, even as

they let our adjuncts toil twice as hard as assistant professors for thousands of dollars less money.

Where institutions have no graduate pool to call on, as in community colleges, they may hire professional writing staff. These professionals have often written beautifully about their field, but many are simply far too busy with far too little support to theorise or advance practice.

In conclusion, looking at the university and American culture through the lens of composition provides a mixed picture. At its worst, education can be prescriptive and rule-bound — part of a quick-fix solution in a quick-fix culture. At its best, it represents positive and democratic ideals — a place where debate is encouraged, the individual voice is nurtured and the relationship of the individual to the community is developed and encouraged. Despite a sometimes stubborn lack of support in real terms from within the university and the culture at large for writing as an intellectually creative task, at times composition returns to the role earlier rhetoricians would have recognised: not only promoting competency but investigating, questioning and even shaping the discourse of the university. So the composition which the American liberal arts curriculum invented may find itself playing a part as the university continues to reinvent itself.

Notes

1. For an overview of some of the key rhetorical texts discussed, see Bizzell & Herzberg's (1990) *The Rhetorical Tradition*.
2. We are indebted to Theresa Lillis for pointing out that even within the US composition community, the term "skills" is highly contentious. See for example, Patricia Bizzell's 1997 speech on the CCC website. Compositionists continue to debate and define their roles, and a sweeping overview such as this one is bound to contain some questionable generalisations.
3. Peter Abbs in his book, *The Polemics of Imagination*, gives a strong rationale for using autobiography with postgraduate students as a launching pad for academic writing, a way of putting them in "engaged and critical contact with their cultural history." He also contributes to the "skills" debate (1996: 111–113).

References

Abbs, P. 1996. *The Polemics of Imagination*. London: Skoob Books.
Bartholomae, D. 1986. "Inventing the University." *Journal of Basic Writing* 5, No.1) 4–22.
Berkenkotter, C. and Huckin, T. 1995. *Genre Knowledge in Disciplinary Communication: Cognition/culture/power.* Mahwah, N J: Lawrence Erlbaum.

Bizzell, P. and Herzberg, B. 1991. *The Bedford Bibliography for Teachers of Writing*. New York: St. Martin's Press.
Bizzell, P. March 1997. "Rhetoric and Social Change." Available: http://www.hu.mtu.edu/cccc/97/bizzell.html.
Bizzel, P and B. Herzberg (eds). 1990. *The Rhetorical Tradition*. Boston: Bedford Books.
Bloom, L 1986 "Freshman Composition as a Middle-Class Enterprise." *College English* 58(6): 654–675.
Britton et al. 1975. *The Development of Writing Abilities (11–18)*. London: Macmillan Education.
De Tocqueville, A. 1956. *Democracy in America* (R. Heffner (ed.). New York: New American Library.
European Writing Conferences 1996. *Abstracts*. Barcelona: University of Barcelona.
Leuner, P. 1997 "Waiting for Dearing." *World Education News and Reviews* 10(4).
Lunsford, A. 1993. "Intellectual Property, Concepts of Selfhood, and the Teaching of Writing." *The Writing Instructor* Winter: 67–78.
Lu, M. 1997. "Professing Multiculturalism: The politics of style in the contact zone." *College Composition and Communication* 45: 443–458.
Marius, R. 1992. "Composition Studies." In S. Greenblatt. and G. Gunn (eds), *Redrawing the Boundaries: The transformation of British and American literary studies*, 466–490. New York: Modern Language Association.
McLeod, S.1992. "Writing Across the Curriculum: An introduction." In S. McLeod, S. and M. Soven (eds), *Writing Across the Curriculum: A guide to developing programs*, 1–11. London: Sage.
McQuade, D. 1992. "Composition and Literary Studies." In S. Greenblatt. and G. Gunn (eds), *Redrawing the Boundaries: The transformation of British and American literary studies*, 482–519. New York: Modern Language Association.
Nystrand et al. 1993. "Where did Composition Studies Come From?" *Written Communication*, 10(3): 267–333. Purdue University. Online Writing Lab. Available: http://owl.english.purdue.edu/writing.html.
Raimes, A. 1991 "Out of the Woods: Emerging traditions in the teaching of writing." *TESOL Quarterly* 25(3): 410–419.
Swales, J. 1990. *Genre Analysis, English in academic and research settings*. Cambridge: CUP.
Traub, J. 1994. "Class Struggle." *The New Yorker* September 19: 76–90.
Woolvard, B. 1996. "The Future of WAC." *College English* 58(1): 58–79.

CHAPTER 10

Agency and Subjectivity in Student Writing

Mary Scott

Introduction

When I was four years old I was given a kaleidoscope. It quickly became my favourite toy. I delighted in seeing the pieces of its mosaic shiver and fall into new patterns with every rotation — patterns in which the individual pieces each acquired a new semblance. The object which fascinated me as a child now provides me with a metaphoric means of indicating the significance of the title of this paper. In other words, when perceived within the context of kaleidoscope-as-metaphor, "agency" and "subjectivity" represent new configurations within the multifaceted field of theory and research relating to student writing.

It is the failure of existing configurations to accommodate complexities facing me as a tutor which has prompted my re-ordering of the currently available patterns. The complexities I refer to derive from the fact that the students I teach represent a wide range of academic, linguistic, and socio-cultural backgrounds and so bring to their written assignments considerable individual diversity. It is, however, a diversity which is not given serious attention in the array of pedagogic approaches and theoretical perspectives which a growing body of literature makes available to the tutor. In other words, the individual writer tends not to be a central focus in the theory and research relating to student writing. Nevertheless, as I shall show below, it is paradoxically by virtue of its very exclusion or neglect that the individual writer shapes the currently dominant theoretical landscapes; in short, it is a factor which is always present either openly or off-stage. The initial purpose of this paper can thus be metaphorically described as a redrawing of the theoretical map of "student writing" — a redrawing in which "agency" provides new contours which make visible currently excluded or unnoticed features.

What will emerge is the extent to which "agency" is entangled in conflicting sets of meanings around conceptions of the writer. In contemporary literary criticism these meanings turn mainly, and in often subtle ways, on three competing points of reference, viz., the writer, the text, and the social context. The writer reached its apotheosis in the Romantic emphasis on the unique sensibility as the sole source of meaning — a view which is now largely discredited; the text is dominant not only in new criticism but also, in a very different way, in structuralism and those forms of poststructuralism which claim the irrelevance of the writer, while the social context is emphasized primarily in the many kinds of criticism which are indebted, even if only indirectly, to Marxism. Though this outline is crude, it serves to highlight the fact that what tends to be missing is a conception of the writer as a social-individual, that is — to put it very generally at this point — a view of the individual as in society, and of society as in the individual. Such a view would locate the writer in time and place. In other words the writer would be seen to have a history and a context but a naive subjectivism on the one hand, and objectivism on the other, would be avoided. Although this view of the writer as a social-individual may seem to offer little that is new when presented in such broad outline, it is in fact largely absent from the literature about student writing, including, ironically, from that in which adherence to the principles of critical discourse analysis results in the explicitly stated goal of avoiding the binary opposition of the individual and the social. Furthermore, the absence of the social-individual is a lacuna which can be made visible by attention to "agency" but which also embroils "agency" in paradox and contradiction.

At this point, however, I am confronted with a problem relating to terminology. In order not to pre-empt discussion I need to replace "individual writer", which tends to evoke the discourses of Romanticism, with a more neutral term. I have chosen "the subject" since it offers the advantage of a relative openness of meaning deriving initially from the duality whereby "the subject" can signify both an actor and a recipient. Furthermore, "the subject" can undo the fixity and strong demarcations of "identity", replacing them with the complexities of "subjectivity".

I have borrowed "agency" mainly from sociology. Its meaning in its usual sociological contexts is, of course, not fixed. However, this paper does not wander down the side paths of that sociological debate but takes from it the question that is central to my attempt to find new routes within the field of theory and research relating to student writing — routes, that is, which do not by-pass the individual student writer. The question I have devised to aid this attempt is: what kinds of agency are being attributed to the subject? It is a question which derives from my observation that in the literature I am examining, agency cloaks itself in several forms which are explicitly or implicitly presented as the primary goal of higher education. To be more specific, my perception is that "agency" shapes and is shaped by the many different, and often widely divergent, discourses which cluster around power, freedom, and action but which nonetheless converge in their overt rejection of the objectivist view of the individual as the mere puppet or reflection of external forces. In brief, from that perspective, "agency" is a concept which holds together markedly different versions of the western ideal of education for democracy.

Student writing in higher education in the UK

To give substance to the generalizations above, I now turn to higher education in the UK. Here tutors are currently expected to provide their students with explicit guidelines and criteria relating to the written assignment which still constitutes the most important form of assessment on most academic courses. The call for explicitness co-exists, however, with a view of agency which draws its meaning from a loose constellation of theoretical fragments, but especially from the importance attached to reflection on practice as both the means and the sign of independence in learning ("We are all reflective practitioners now", Barnett 1992). In other words, the kind of agency that is valued in higher education is generally held to manifest itself in an interpretive focus which results in the individual making of meaning. In the specific context of student writing this general emphasis on interpretive meaning-making is translated into the importance of adopting a distinctive individual stance and gives that core of meaning to terms such as "creativity" and "critical thinking", and especially to "argument" which research at a UK university reveals as the primary and most widely applied criterion relating to student writing (Riddle 1994).

In my experience students now arrive at university with a general awareness that an individual focus will be required in their writing. I quote

> We will have to express our own ideas and not just copy what is in the books
> I know I will need to be critical in what I write; that means I must consider possible positions and argue for mine
> It will be important to be creative and not just to imitate
> Originality will be important

However, my experience has also shown me that such apparently knowledgeable statements disguise much confusion and anxiety — as is, in fact, suggested in the quotations above by the use of the future tense with its implication of a break with the familiar. The uncertainty and confusion are hardly surprising, though, since terms such as "critical" or "argument" become conceptually problematic when an attempt is made to unpack them (Barnett 1997), and, according to Pennycook (1996), denote, even at the most apparently general level, culture-specific values and practices (see also Lea & Street 1998). My concern with agency in this paper does not evade these thorny issues. It does, however, recontextualise them in an attempt to highlight their day-to-day pedagogic relevance. I consequently begin with the contradiction between the particular view of the subject's agency, which I have identified above in referring to expectations of students in higher education, and the fate of that agency in the attempts at explicitness. To put it another way, my immediate purpose is to show that agency in the sense of individual meaning making is edited out of the very descriptions of academic writing which are intended to contribute to its enhancement.

Descriptions of academic writing: theory and pedagogic practice

I focus first on descriptions which demonstrate similarity within apparent difference. I find the source of that similarity in an overt concern with the methodological. Riddle (1994; 1997) and Mitchell (1994), for example, draw on Toulmin (1958) and refer to claims, warrants and grounds as strategies or techniques, while Swales (1990) writes of moves. However, such accounts of academic writing which could accommodate the individual making of meaning, tend to be transformed in pedagogic contexts in ways that implicitly exclude the view of agency which I have identified above. Although phrases such as "establishing the field", "making a claim" and "arguing not argument" project a dynamic view of academic writing as a process of individual meaning-making, in pedagogic practice that view tends to be converted into the treatment of texts as assemblages of mechanically linked features which students need to incorporate in their written assignments. In my experience, this conversion is evident in tutor feedback such as: "where is your claim?"; "point out your argument"; "you have omitted an important move". In other words, procedures become structural components. Thus the focus on strategies, moves or techniques in the production of academic writing loses its fundamental distinctiveness from those apparently different approaches which explicitly emphasize the formal architecture of the academic text; for example, overtly formalist EAP approaches which concern themselves with structure within the hierarchy of lexis, syntax and discourse (e.g. Laird 1977) and also those more recent descriptions of text which have a much broader focus and explicitly include the individual subject as agent but which are also finally concerned with structures of one kind or another when pedagogic practice is the focus.

An example of such descriptions is to be found in Mitchell (1994). In reporting her research on argument she provides a useful theoretical discussion of key words and phrases in which she indicates the complexities and competing definitions around "argument". Drawing on Harre and Bakhtin, she allows a place for individual meaning-making, and, in referring to "genre", tempers the suggestion of text types conforming to rules by emphasizing the dialogic nature of all texts — an emphasis in which "dialogue" denotes an "agent of change rather than replication" (1994: 18). However, when she turns to the teaching of argument her concern is with patterns and rhetorical or linguistic devices, with the dialogic, for example, becoming a form which can be taught by means of questions or split texts relevant to the particular disciplinary discourse. This reductiveness is hardly surprising since there is a substantive problem at the core of attempts to make argument the central focus of attention. The problem lies in the fact that a concern with teaching and learning argument inevitably tends to obliterate difference; in other words "argument" becomes a matter of text type or discipline-specific features and so cannot fully accommodate the notion of particularities of individual meaning-making — particularities which, as I shall attempt to demonstrate later, inevitably bear witness to students' past learnings in different academic contexts as well as to their response to their current situation.

Thus it can be said that approaches which are intended to assist the individual making of meaning do not actually enhance such a view of agency. In fact, their particular meanings and applications derive from its absence. This carries a number of pedagogic consequences. Within the immediate context of day-to-day teaching, giving students feedback about their essays becomes primarily a matter of pointing out missing elements in the matching of essay to abstract paradigm. A wider educational perspective reveals a view of student writing as a mode of enculturation; an emphasis which is reflected in the literature of the field in references to students as apprentice members of a discourse community (e.g. Swales 1990). Yet another shift of focus, together with the use of a sociological lens, foregrounds a concern with the collective in the shape of conventions which, at their most tightly circumscribed and circumscribing, become formulaic rules — a situation which again allows little if any space for agency (Giddens 1987).

This is not to imply that student writers should not be introduced to the conventions of academic writing. It is rather to suggest that the place and role of the conventions in the teaching and learning of academic writing are currently located in parameters which foreclose discussion and edit out individual meaning-making. A primary example of such parameters is to be found in the contrast between explicit teaching and induction (e.g. Reid 1988) — an antithesis which simply channels debate in ways which concentrate on the what and how of learning and tend thus to exclude detailed consideration of the subject's agency.

Problematizing agency in its relation to pedagogic practice

At this point it might be argued that I have tended to present agency as itself unproblematic in its relation to pedagogy. In an effort to remedy that uncritical focus I now turn to Bernstein's (1995) discussion of pedagogic discourse, which I shall selectively plunder. This may seem an unwise move since Bernstein is principally concerned not with higher education but with primary and pre-school pedagogic practice. Furthermore, he places pedagogy within detailed and logically interlocking paradigms. To take up only parts of his theoretical framework is to risk their distortion and misrepresentation; it is, however, a risk I feel justified in running since a selective borrowing can make visible problems and pedagogic consequences which might attach themselves to the concept of agency as individual meaning-making. Of particular usefulness in this regard are central aspects of Bernstein's "performance" and "competence" models of pedagogy. "Performance" relates to "specialized outputs" and the explicit rules for realizing them. The attempts to provide student writers in higher education with explicit guidelines or descriptions of academic writing clearly correspond to this characterization of performance. Within this discourse the subject emerges as the exponent of detailed pre-determined criteria. In Bernstein's description of the pedagogic discourse relating to competence, on the other hand, the subject's agency is emphasized and seen to reside in the active and creative construction of a world of valid meanings and practices. This is a view of agency which matches the importance attached in higher education to individual meaning making. However, key aspects of the competence model enable us to add detail to that emphasis — detail which can reveal problematic possibilities clustered around conceptions of individual meaning-making. The problems derive from the fact that, in the competence model, meaning making is associated with a "self-regulating subject" and an emancipatory view of pedagogy as liberating competences that the subject is seen to possess already. Bernstein was writing of primary and pre-school education, but the self regulating subject whose progress is viewed as the freeing of inner capacity is present, too, in the everyday discourses of higher education which emphasize learner autonomy and inner attributes. For example:

> Students should be independent learners
> He has not done himself justice. He is really very intelligent
> In time she will settle down and be able to express her academic gifts

Such discourses can be said to mark a continuity from the days when university students were seen to need not study skills but the use of a library and other facilities so that they might engage in their principal task which was thought to be largely that of educating themselves. Thus the competence model implicitly reiterates the opposition between agency and explicit teaching, which has already been referred to in relation to theory and practice regarding student writing. It also enables us, by virtue of its more detailed perspective, to see the current discourses in higher education as a contradictory mix of past and present. Confronted with these antitheses I am led to conclude that in criticizing the call for explicitness in pedagogic practice in higher education I should not simply assert the importance of individual meaning making. However, that conclusion is not only, or mainly, based on a wish to avoid an exclusive either-or. It derives primarily from the problematic view of the subject which emerges from the competence model of pedagogy. Although it eschews the Romantic emphasis on unique sensibility, the model is not dissimilar in that it also places the subject centre stage. Furthermore it would rearrange the social context around the liberation of the subject's inner competences. Thus, even in those instances where the competences within the indivdual are viewed not as universal human characteristics but as the products of earlier socialization, pedagogy is based on an idealization of the subject. In short, the social is located deeply within the subject but the subject is then abstracted from the particularities of the immediate social context. To put it another way, what the competence model of agency lacks as a basis for pedagogic practice is a view of the subject as located within time and place — or, as I expressed it earlier — of the individual in society and society in the individual.

Problematizing the meaning of agency in critical discourse analysis

Before developing the perspective which I have suggested above, I need, however, to address a set of ideas developed in relation to critical discourse analysis which makes agency a central concept within its rationale. This will also bring us closer to the issue of language which any discussion of writing needs to consider. In the UK Critical Discourse Analysis is strongly associated with the work of Norman Fairclough and his colleagues at Lancaster University, who concentrate in one way or another on the relation between language and power. In referring to language education, Fairclough (1989: 239) writes that its purpose is the development of students' capabilities as "producers and interpreters of discourse". However, at the core of the importance thus attached to agency in critical discourse analysis there is a conception of a creative subject which, in some instances at least, is paradoxically indistinguishable from the Romantic self. This may seem a perverse point of view since the discourse used is very different from that associated with Romanticism: in place of views of the self typical of liberal humanism there is an explicit, Foucault-derived, emphasis on the workings of power in societies and on the construction of the subject by discourse. However, a contradiction appears when, as in the writings of Fairclough (1989), for example, the concept of the subject's creativity is retained and is implicitly treated as the necessary condition for the deconstruction of dominant discourses. We are thus confronted with incompatibles: a deterministic view of the subject as a discursive construct on the one hand, and on the other the concept of a critical, creative subject which escapes determinism and actively engages in its own construction by deconstructing dominant discourses. Furthermore, while Fairclough may regard the subject's creativity from what Bernstein (1995) defines as a radical perspective (i.e. as inseparable from the liberation of the internalized values of a dominated group) Ivanic's (1993) concept of the "committed-I" offers a view of the student writer which is virtually indistinguishable from the unique self of the Romantic tradition in that it represents the victory of the student's personhood over the oppressive conventions of academic writing.

Contradictions such as those described above do not in themselves invalidate the questioning of the notion of an essential self, which is at the centre of critical discourse analysis. However, in mounting that challenge critical discourse analysis introduces a further problem of particular relevance in a discussion of writing. It emphasizes modes of signification — or to put it another way — the linguistic code — and gives too little attention to the signified. This has been pointed out by Van Leeuwen (1996), who argues that critical discourse analysis focuses on syntax at the expense of the semantic. Referring to the ambiguity of signifiers, he offers a mode of textual analysis which sets out to avoid the danger of implying an inevitable link between particular linguistic forms (e.g. passive voice, nominalization) and issues of agency. However, in developing this line of argument, van Leeuwen produces binary categories which might be the basis of a semantic grammar. In other words, van Leeuwen's primary focus is on deep semantic structures within the text, a focus which gives more significance to how the text means than to the writer's agency as a maker of meaning.

Looking back and looking ahead

At the beginning of this paper I referred to three competing points of reference in literary theory, viz., the writer, the text and the social context. What has emerged in the discussion so far is how these points of reference form different, usually contradictory, patterns of co-existence, dominance or opposition in relation to the conception of agency as individual meaning-making — the view of agency which typifies discourse about student writing in higher education. Thus the Romantic view of the unique, creative individual as the source of meaning still lurks within critical discourse analysis — an approach which explicitly rejects it — while the current call for explicit and detailed rules of realization for student writers edits out the idea of the subject as an individual maker of meaning. Agency tends to disappear, too, from the radical emphasis on agency as resistance to the social conventions of the university when it becomes converted to a textual concern with grammar — either linguistic or semantic. An excursion into Bernstein's theories indicated another kind of problem — the tendency in some pedagogic discourse to idealize the subject and to ignore the immediate social context. What thus emerges as my necessary next step is an attempt to bring together writer, text and social context. In other words, as I have already indicated, I am in search of a way of thinking about student writing which places the writer in society and society in the writer — a view which locates the writer in time and place. Fortunately, when I turn to Kress (1995; 1996(a); 1996(b)), I find a view of writing which does that.

Agency as individual meaning-making: the motivated sign

On the basis of his early work (e.g. 1989) Kress might be unequivocally described as a critical discourse analyst and in some respects his recent publications (1995; 1996a; 1996b) continue to echo emphases within critical discourse analysis. For example, Kress still presents writing as a social practice which occurs in particular social contexts involving particular social relationships. It seems to me, however, that there are now subtle differences between Kress and, for example, Fairclough and his colleagues — differences which might be said to be largely a matter of emphasis but which are very significant in the context of student writing. The primary difference which I see lies in Kress' central emphasis on the transformative action of the subject who is now presented as the producer of motivated signs (words, texts or images). From this perspective the writer is seen to be engaged in the remaking of her available resources (which are of many different kinds — linguistic, social, cultural) out of her "interest", a term which denotes the focussing (both intuitively and consciously) of a complex of factors; for example, social and cultural histories; present social contexts. This means that the texts produced are "saturated with the meanings of their makers in every aspect of their form" (Kress 1996b). Viewed in this way "resources" denotes the complex of knowledge, understandings and experience which comprise the individual's subjectivity — a subjectivity which is, however, always a remaking of what has been socially made. In setting out to make the individual's creativity central Kress avoids both Fairclough's tendency to determinism and the excesses of Romanticism. He also moves beyond the view of the writer as using language as a tool or mediational means — a separation of the individual and her resources which is how Vygotsky's theory is being interpreted by some (e.g. Wertsch 1991). Agency in writing now connotes a social-individual engaged in remaking what is socially made (i.e. forms and meanings) — a remaking which is inevitably a transforming (even if only in small ways) of the writer's subjectivity. A quotation from Bakhtin helps me to amplify this focus on agency in writing. Declaring that the word cannot be entirely abstracted from the contexts in which it is, and has been, used, Bakhtin (1981: 293–94) wrote:

> The life of the word is contained in its transfer from one mouth to another; from one context to another context, from one social collective to another, from one generation to another generation. In this process the word does not forget its own path and completely free itself from the power of those concrete contexts into which it has entered.

This quotation elaborates Bakhtin's key concept of the "dialogic" text: "there are no voiceless words". Thus every text cannot but speak to, hear, and understand other meanings deriving from the word's past contexts. This means that in writing (or speaking) one has to take the word from others' mouths in a sense and "make it one's own".

Text as motivated sign: theoretical and pedagogic implications

The concept of the motivated sign, as elaborated above, together with the correlative image of the writer actively remaking her subjectivity, seems to me to be of primary theoretical and pedagogic significance. It enables us to avoid some of the current but unhelpful concerns of writing theory and debate in order to concentrate on neglected but important issues. I begin with the theoretical entanglements we can avoid. First and foremost among these is the concept of intention. Having been expelled from academic discussion in the sixties by Wimsatt and Beardsley's (1954) insistence on the intentional fallacy, intention has, however, crept back onto the scene in, for example, some feminist criticism and as a reaction against structuralism (Eagleton 1983). However, within the context of empirical writing research, references to intention tend to set up a false antithesis — in other words to form part of a binary opposition comprising text at one pole and the actual writer at the other. Consequently there is a tendency to find the "real" meanings of a text in the intentions the students can articulate. The concept of the motivated sign, on the other hand, foregrounds the text, not as an autonomous object but as a hypothesis on the part of the writer — and, of course, reader — a hypothesis which represents the remaking of knowledge, understandings and experience in what is partly at least an intuitive process. Thus the reading of a student essay should become an imaginative attempt to identify what each student is doing, and where it might come from, and should not represent an exclusive concern with what the student has not done or with how the essay does or does not conform to the paradigms of argument favoured in the particular discipline or field.

Another of the problem areas which the motivated sign enables us to refocus relates to "critical" (or "analytical") thinking. Taking her cue from Pennycook (1996), Lee, a Korean student, points out in an unpublished MA dissertation, that the western idea of critical thinking is actually culture specific but presented in the literature of the field as the universal norm; a practice which she summarizes as resulting in an "ongoing struggle... that international students including myself have to confront in themselves". However, although there are welcome signs that western universities are increasingly recognizing their ethnocentricity with regard to "critical" thinking, I am unhappy about the "positive" reactions which I have encountered as a practitioner. These take several forms as illustrated in the quotations below:

> All students are capable of critical thinking. They just need to learn how to do it (This matches Bernstein's description of the liberal/progressive mode of the competence model)
> They can think critically in their own language. They need to learn how to do it in English
> They can quickly learn how to think critically; it is the language they find difficult

All these statements illustrate the same problem, viz., the separation of signifier and signified. It is a separation which substitutes procedures and codes for the individual making of meaning. In other words the quotations above actually empty "critical thinking" of the very meaning I identified earlier in discussing the synonyms of agency which appear in the discourses of higher education in the UK. The motivated sign, on the other hand, avoids this danger by virtue of the fact that it does not divorce signifier from signified, form from meaning, or language from thought. At the same time it invites attention to difference of various kinds — linguistic, socio-cultural, gendered..., and thus to the students' contexts, past and present.

The final problem which the concept of the motivated sign makes visible concerns "identity". Critical discourse analysis tends to make identity central in its concern with power, so linking it to the positioning of the writer — and reader — within a text. From a different perspective, which nonetheless partly derives from critical discourse analysis, Ivanic (1993) considers the identities the student writer adopts in a text and how academic discourse threatens students' sense of identity. Valuable though such an approach can be, it suggests a firmness of persona or a movement from one clearly defined persona to another, which is inevitably at odds with the fluidity suggested by agency as the individual making of meaning. For that reason" subjectivity" becomes the more appropriate concept — subjectivity freed that is from both its Romantic and its explicitly power-related connotations and representing instead the escape from tight categorization, which is a necessary condition for any remaking.

Reading student essays as motivated signs

While Kress (1995) has offered a very useful theoretical orientation, he has not as yet demonstrated its application in relation to individual texts except briefly and in very general terms. For example, in emphasizing that the individual who is engaged in remaking her resources is a social individual he devotes only a paragraph to pointing out how uncertainty about the nature of the social interaction affected the way in which parent-writers' resources were remade in the set of swimming club rules which they drafted for their fellow parents whose children were members of the club. In this paper I attempt to take Kress' ideas further in a discussion of particular motivated signs, viz., excerpts from student essays. In other words, I read the texts as hypotheses on the part of the student writers. I recognize that my readings of the texts are also motivated signs — probably in far more ways than I am aware of. But that is in fact inevitable, though it is an inevitability which tutor-student interactions do not always accommodate. I was not able to interview the students whose essays I shall be discussing. They were undergraduates at another UK university. Asking students to tell us how they view what they have written, can, of course, be helpful, but in this paper I am concerned to tease out the kinds of meaning which inexperienced undergraduate writers would almost certainly not be able to articulate. Had I been the students' tutor my readings — seen as hypotheses — would, however, not have excluded, and should have enhanced, the type of tutor-student dialogue which Hounsell (1987) recommends when he states that feedback should be:

> an attempt to articulate and explore premises — on the student's as well as the tutor's terms (1987, p. 118)

Such discussions around what a student writer has in fact done would represent the lending of consciousness on the part of the tutor. However, although I think that dialogue with the individual student should be seen as indispensible, I would argue that the need to rethink the curriculum is as important — particularly in the case of English studies in higher education, where, paradoxically, in spite of the shift from literature to writing in the seventies, little attention is given to the examination and discussion of writing about literature — either students' or critics'. An interesting move in that direction is taken by Geslin (1997) in a recent, as yet unpublished, conference paper in which she contrasts examples of new and poststructuralist criticism within a Hallidayan framework. Peck MacDonald (1995) has also turned her attention to literary criticism remarking on the irony of the fact that literary critics study all manner of texts but not those from their own field. However, neither Peck MacDonald nor Geslin treats her sample texts as motivated signs, each approaching the texts from the perspective of her conception of textuality. Furthermore, both are concerned only with "professional" academic writing.

Yet students' writing about literature probably offers the novice undergraduate a greater diversity of approaches, and thus of possible sources of difficulty, than does, say, scientific writing. Furthermore, a literary text which refers to characters and events evokes the everyday world to an extent that is unusual in academic discourse apart from the narratives which may occur in history or in case studies. For those reasons, and also because students arrive in higher education with views of literature acquired mainly at school, or from the writing and talk about books which takes place outside educational institutions, it seems particularly valuable pedagogically to study students' writing about literature in relation to the concept of the motivated sign with its emphasis on the bringing together and transforming of the individual's resources. I have thus chosen to discuss excerpts from essays written about fiction by first-year undergraduates in the first term of a degree course in English.

Elaborating my perspective: the need for a new discourse

In approaching the students' texts as motivated signs I have not excluded from my focus the academic conventions regarding structure and choice of language. I have, however, needed to recontextualize those aspects in order to emphasize the individual making of meaning within the context of a course in higher education. I derive my approach to the essays from several sources. Firstly from Olson's (1994) discussion of the literate mind in which he rethinks his earlier controversial views which turned difference into cognitive deficit. Olson now points out that schooled literacy is an induction into ways of taking meaning from the page. This insight enables me to ask of the student essays: what kinds of meaning are the student writers taking from the fictional texts and, also, of course, from the essay title, and where might those particular meanings be coming from? This question indicates that the taking of meaning is actually a making, and not an extraction, of meaning. The phrase thus comes to avoid the narrow and narrowing focus on text as text which is represented by the distinctions which Scholes (1985) draws between reading, interpretation and criticism — distinctions in which reading represents the construction of texts within texts, while interpretation produces texts upon texts, and criticism sets texts against texts. In other words, from my perspective, such distinctions if relevant are only so because they represent resources of knowledge and understanding which the students are realizing in their essays as part of the process of meaning-making. Bartholomae (1985: 145) has also contributed to my perspective; by placing students in their contexts in the university he has helped me to see that the student writer's mode is that of as if:

> I don't expect my students to be literary critics when they write about Bleak House. If a literary critic is a person who wins publication in a professional journal (or if he or she is one who could) the students students aren't critics. I do, however, expect my students to be, themselves, invented as literary critics by approximating the language of a literary critic writing about Bleak House

Bartholomae can be validly accused of oversimplification in that he implies a unitary literary critical discourse. Nevertheless, I find that the notion of "as ifness" can illuminate the Janus-faced aspect of student essays, that is, the fact that such essays inevitably reflect assumptions regarding both the field of study and the kinds of writing expected of students of that field — assumptions which include the question of authoritativeness which is Bartholomae's central concern. This doubleness of focus leads to duality in students' essays — a duality of which the students may, however, be unaware and which may represent uncertainty or ambivalence on their part. In the case of the essays to which I shall be referring it is a duality which is located in the fact that features of the essays can be read as reflecting both an idea of fictional literature and an idea of the university. "Idea" is not, however, intended to indicate a primary concern with a high level of abstraction since that would convert the many strands of subjectivity to static paradigms. My quest is for metaphors which can represent the students' texts as meaning in the making while retaining the distancing which derives from the fact that "every form of practice including the literary critical kind, presupposes a form of theory" (Jameson 1981). Thus I have come to adapt to my own purposes a metaphor from Iser (1978: 127) who referred to the reading of fiction as a process which involves a tension between "total entanglement" and "latent detachment". The essays to which I shall be referring differ in the extent to which the detachment is actualized. That difference depends largely on the different idea of fiction which each student is developing and on the chains of association around that idea.

Meaning-making in the essay title

It is not only student essays, however, which involve meaning-making; the essay titles provided by tutors do so too. The full title in the case of the students whose essays I will be discussing was: "Concentrate on one early crime fiction text and give an account of its social and/or psychological meaning, including in your analysis some close analysis of both form and meaning".

This essay title strikes me as highly problematic in several ways. Firstly it can match more than one set of discourses about literature. For example, the reference to form and meaning could be based on a conception of a literary text as the autonomous and unified integration of form and meaning. On the other hand, it could suggest the deconstructionists' decentred text in which the possibility of a unifying meaning is disrupted by the marginal and the absent. Furthermore, the phrase, "social and/or psychological meaning" can encompass a number of conflicting perspectives regarding the relation between literature and society or literature and the individual, or collective, psyche. However, co-existent with, and in contrast to, this openness to different interpretations, are strong indicators of what the students should do. These indicators mainly take the form of instructions: "concentrate on"; "give an account"; "including... analysis", but also include the insertion of "both" before "form and meaning", and the repetition of "analysis". There is thus an in-built contradiction: on the one hand the essay title suggests an ideal student who would hold a sophisticated knowledge of literary theory while on the other it implies that the students need explicit guidance. In brief the essay title is problematic in that explicitness is conjoined with a multiplicity of possibilities which can only be visible to someone in possession of certain kinds of knowledge. As will be demonstrated the students drew on the knowledge they had but in neither case was it considered sufficient.

The students' essays

Student X chose to analyse the social meaning of Wilkie Collins' novel, *The Woman in White* while Student Y elected to write about the social and psychological meaning of Conan Doyle's Sherlock Holmes stories. I have selected particular passages from each essay in order to highlight two contrasting ways of making meaning. My comments are by no means exhaustive or uncontentious; they are simply intended as a brief demonstration of an approach which is based on a view of students' writings as motivated signs.

Student X's opening sentences carefully match the instructions in the essay title, thus implying the student's idea of the university as an institution which expects students to take pains to conform to its requirements:

> This essay will concentrate on the Wilkie Collins' novel, The Women (sic) in White analysing its social meaning for the reader. The essay will demonstrate that Collins has incorporated three main social themes in the text...

The sentences above are, however, also an illustration of the duality to which I referred earlier since they suggest conceptions of literature which occur in professional literary criticism, viz., the fiction of a universal reader and the view of a text as containing themes. The reference to Collins in conjunction with the metaphorical "incorporated" also reflects a particular view of a literary text in that it suggests an authorial function rather than the "real" author.

Student Y's first paragraph directly addresses the essay title, too, but, in her case, her idea of the university resides uneasily within her idea of literature. The paragraph initially presents a confident and sophisticated view of the Sherlock Holmes stories as symbolic representations. Metatextual terms of differing degrees of abstraction — "world", "paradox", "creation" — subsume details of character and event. However, when the student's focus shifts and she concentrates on responding to the essay title she loses control of the syntax (or perhaps the punctuation) at "because of", and, more significantly, disrupts the particular register of literary criticism which typifies her paragraph as a whole, so moving towards a mimetic view of the stories. In other words, "because of" suggests a manner of speaking which is more common in everyday "real life" discussions of individual motivations than in professional literary criticism:

> The world of Sherlock Holmes, 'the greatest of great detectives', is something

> of a paradox. Conan Doyle's creation is essentially superhuman, flouting conventional Victorian forms but embroiled, by his work, in every level of society from the opium den of east London to the company of Bohemian royalty. By concentrating on Doyle's earliest stories such as 'A Study in Scarlet', useful as it is as an introduction to Holmes and in giving the reader a rounded insight into the man and his methods, and the later stories published in the Strand magazine, one can come to understand the social and psychological meaning of the text because of Holmes' preoccupation with his detective work and the apparent lack of activity outside of this, loathing 'every form of society with his whole bohemian soul', his social world and psychological inner sanctum that his companion, Watson, struggles to understand, are inextricably linked.

This paragraph points towards the principal difference between the two essays — a difference which relates mainly to the mode and extent of the detachment from the view of literature as mimesis which each essay demonstrates. By mimesis I mean not only represented behaviours and events but also the reader's entanglement in them. In other words, as I shall try to show below, the essays reflect different conceptions of "form and meaning" which in their turn derive from different views of the nature of a literary text.

Student X's second paragraph mostly comprises particularities of character and action offered as illustrations of one general theme — the lack of power women have over their own destiny.

> A primary theme within the novel is the gender theme. The novel is critical of women's legal and economic inequality in Victorian Britain. Tamar Heller believes that "The Woman in White is an extraordinary feminist work". Throughout the novel the lack of power women have over their own destiny is constantly conveyed to the reader. Laura has no legal power over her marriage to Sir Perceval. She must submit herself to him in order to obey another male, her father, who the reader discovers has committed his daughter on his deathbed to the marriage with Sir Perceval. Thus Laura must dismiss her true love for another man, Walter Hartright...

In the paragraph above Student X's closeness to the text as mimesis is evident in her representation of the women characters' plight. The irony in her reference to Laura's only possession as no possession ("has no legal power"), and the repetition of "must" serve to suggest that for Student X the text is a lived series of events and situations. This focus together with her choice of "theme", with its implications of a unifying thread and a singleness of meaning, actually prevents her from perceiving the paradoxes and ambiguities in the form of the novel. Nowhere in the essay does she comment on the ironies surrounding the fact that though the central character is ostensibly Anne Catherick, the woman in white, it is Walter Hartright who controls the novel's many narratives. As her tutor rightly commented at the end of the essay she has not "opened up the issues".

Student Y, on the other hand, writes from within a different conception of "form and meaning". In short she is at a greater distance from a mimetic view of literature than is Student X. She approaches character and event as constructs which serve as vehicles of meaning, and it is the meaning which is emphasized. Furthermore, in referring to Conan Doyle's actual Victorian context she presents particular events (e.g. crimes) as representative of general unifying meanings. In other words, she briefly approaches, though no doubt unconsciously, the theoretical perspective (e.g. Barthes 1973) from which the "real" world is seen as a set of signs.

> The world in which Holmes operates professionally is predominantly bourgeois, with occasional 'threats to the middle class order' (3). The threats come from within the victims' own circles, very often from either family or past acquaintances that had been wronged and often as a result of greed. Sherlock Holmes was an almost paternalistic figure, one who protected the established order from potential disturbance, he was 'society's agent' (4). Indeed it was Holmes who 'saved' Watson from his 'comfortless meaningless existence' (5) and introduced him to the world of crime and mystery. However, to his clients Holmes was a normalising force who re-established the balance of society. The Victorian values of the era, the laissez faire attitude towards the economy and the doctrine of self help did little to decrease the population's greed. Many people adopted the self help ideal to its fullest extent, even being prepared to betray their own family as in 'A Case of Identity'. The crimes committed in Holmes' stories are an integral part of Victorian society.

Neither essay received a high mark though Student Y's was considered better than Student X's. The primary weakness ascribed to Student X's was, as I have already stated, that she did not "open up the issues". Student Y was also judged as presenting too unified a text in that she lost sight in the body of the essay of the paradoxes she mentioned in her introductory paragraph. These seem to be just criticisms in themselves. However, a question which might be asked is: to what extent was the students' tendency to unify the fictional texts prompted by the phrase "give an account of" which appears in the essay title? In other words, to what extent did that phrase trigger memories of the kinds of writing practised at school where telling and showing is still a dominant requirement? Student X's essay bears obvious traces of conventional school essays about literature in which the emphasis is on identifying themes and showing a detailed knowledge of the particularities of plot and character. Student Y's approach is reminiscent in many ways of conscientious A-level work in which the opinions and statements of the critics are carefully, and, as in Y's case, often skilfully woven into statements about a literary text.

What has emerged for me from this attempt at reading the excerpts from student essays as motivated signs is the extent of the students' entanglement in past learnings and present assumptions as they bring their individual resources to the task of meaning-making. This has implications not only for feedback from tutor to student but also for the content of curricula. The student essays suggest that in undergraduate English courses, for example, more attention could well be given to the discussion of the theories informing writing about literature — writing not only by published critics but also by students.

Finally, it is a metaphor taken from a work of fiction which serves to sum up for me the new awareness which the students' essays have led me to. In Doris Lessing's novel, *The Golden Notebook* (1962), the central character, Anna, is a writer. She is, however, caught up in conflicts of different kinds which confront her with two extreme possibilities — slavish conformity to the conventions of writing as represented by the outer novel, Free Women, or going mad as in the inner golden notebook in which all the forms are rejected and Anna is "sunken in subjectivity". Anna finally escapes both these extremes. She writes *The Golden Notebook*, a text which can be said to represent the agency of a writer who is a social-individual. For me the question now is: how can I help my students in any field of study to write their own golden notebooks?

References

Bakhtin, M. 1981. "Discourse in the Novel." In M. Holquist (ed.), *The Dialogic Imagination*, 257–422. Austin: University of Texas Press. (Original work published 1934–1935).
Barnett, R. 1992. *Improving Higher Education: Total quality care*. Buckingham/Bristol: The Society for Research into Higher Education & Open University Press.
Barnett, R. 1997. *Higher Education: A critical business*. Buckingham/Bristol: The Society for Research into Higher Education & Open University Press.
Barthes, R. 1973. *Mythologies*. London: Granada.
Bartholomae, D. 1985. Inventing the University. In M. Rose (ed.), *When A Writer Can't Write*, 134–165. New York: Guilford Press.
Bernstein, B. 1996. *Pedagogy, Symbolic Control and Identity: Theory, research, critique*. London: Taylor & Francis.
Eagleton, T. 1983. *Literary Theory: An introduction*. Oxford: Blackwell.
Fairclough, N. 1989. *Language and Power*. London: Longman.

Geslin, N. 1997. Writing Literary Criticism. Paper given at 24th International Systemic Functional Congress (ISFC 24), July, 21–25, York University, Canada.

Giddens, A. 1987. *Social Theory and Modern Sociology.* Cambridge: Polity Press.

Hounsell, D. 1987. "Essay Writing and the Quality of Feedback. In J. T. E. Richardson, M. W. Eysenck and D. W. Piper (eds), *Student Learning: Research in education and cognitive psychology.* Milton Keynes: Society for Research into Higher Education & Open University Press.

Ivanic, R. 1993. "Who's Who in Academic Writing." In N. Fairclough (ed.), *Critical Language Awareness,* 141–173. London: Longman.

Jameson, F. 1981. *The Political Unconscious: Narrative as a socially symbolic act.* London: Routledge.

Iser, W. 1978. *The act of reading: A theory of aesthetic response.* London and Henley: Routledge and Kegan Paul.

Kress, G. 1989. *Linguistic Processes in Sociocultural Practice.* Oxford: Oxford University Press.

Kress, G. 1995. *Making Signs, Making Subjects: The English curriculum and social futures* An Inaugural Lecture. London: Institute of Education University of London.

Kress, G. 1996a *Before Writing: Rethinking paths to literacy.* London: Routledge.

Kress, G. 1996b. "Discourse semiotics." In T. van Dijk (ed.), *Handbook of Discourse Analysis.* London: Sage.

Laird, E. 1977. *English in Education.* Oxford: OUP.

Lea, M. and Street, B. 1998. "Student Writing in Higher Education: an Academic Literacies Approach." In *Studies in Higher Education* 23 (2): 157–172.

Lessing. 1962. *The Golden Notebook.* London: Paladin.

MacDonald, Peck, S. 1994. *Professional Academic Writing in the Humanities and Social Sciences.* Carbondale and Edwardsville: Southern Illinois University Press.

Mitchell, S. 1994. *The Teaching and Learning of Argument in Sixth Forms and Higher Education.* A project funded by the Leverhulme Trust. Final report. Hull: The University of Hull.

Olson, D. R. 1994. *The World on Paper.* Cambridge: CUP.

Pennycook, A. 1996. "Borrowing Others' Words: Text, ownership, memory, and plagiarism." TESOL Quarterly 30(2).

Reid, I. (ed.). 1988. *The Place of Genre in Learning: Current debates.* Geelong, Australia: Deakin University Press.

Riddle, M. 1994. *Report of an Enquiry into Staff Practice in Setting and Marking Coursework Essays.* Working Paper One. London: Middlesex University.

Riddle, M. 1997. *The Quality of Argument.* London: Middlesex University School of Education.

Scholes, R. 1985. *Textual Power: Literary Theory and the Teaching of English.* New Haven: Yale University Press.

Swales, J. 1990. *Genre Analysis: English in academic and research settings.* Cambridge: CUP.

Toulmin, S. 1958. *The Uses of Argument*. Cambridge: CUP.
van Leeuwen, T. 1996. "The representation of social actors." In C. R. Caldas-Coulthard and M. Coulthard (eds.), *Texts and Practices. Readings in Critical Discourse Analysis*. London: Routledge.
Wertsch, J. 1991. *Voices of the Mind: A sociocultural approach to mediated action*. London: Harvester Wheatsheaf.
Wimsatt, W. K. 1954. *The Verbal Icon: Studies in the Meaning of Poetry*. With two preliminary essays in collaboration with Monroe C. Beardsley. Kentucky: University of Kentucky Press.

CHAPTER 11

Academic Literacies

Brian V. Street

Preface

This is an unusual 'paper' for an academic book — it does not follow the rules of the academic 'essay' that have come to dominate academic discourse in the west. Where the 'proper' essay consists of an argument, supported by theory and (usually) data, written by a single person or a group adopting a single authorial voice, this contribution consists of a series of disparate comments linked by their reference to a common stimulus — a short piece by me on 'Academic Literacy'. This short piece was originally written as a result of my own experience of trying to make explicit to students my own assumptions about 'academic literacy'; it was circulated amongst groups of colleagues and at some workshops on the subject, and a number of people then responded in writing. I asked if they objected to their responses being treated as part of a conference paper I was planning and received general agreement. It would have been more conventional to refer to these response pieces within quotations or through reported speech, in my piece. That I have not done so was deliberately in order to draw attention to the genre and to force myself as well as the reader to re-consider what we take for granted there — in proper anthropological fashion 'to make the familiar strange'. Those who find the attempt irritating, perhaps factitious — or just plain lazy — are asked to consider the source of such sentiments and to treat themselves as ethnographic evidence for the contemporary academic 'reader'; are we so imbued with the principles of the classic essay-text that we cannot lend credence to other forms, at least within a larger text already inscribed with the signs of that genre — the academic imprint, title page and cover, contents page, referencing paraphernalia etc.

At the symposium itself, there were responses from a different direction, particularly from feminists more accustomed to such challenging of conventions and critical that I was being dishonest about my own power position and processes: it is disingenuous, for instance, to cite my own academic background as 'Oxford' just in passing without indicating the power that such an institution gives — in the UK, even in the 1990's, the term 'Oxford' is itself not innocent in any discussion of academic literacies. Moroever, my own right to pronounce, both to students and readers, and to try to challenge the canon, comes from a position at a prestigious university and from having already produced some publications that do conform to the norm. I have tried, therefore, to make more explicit the conditions of production of my own text — a theme that did run powerfully, I believe, through the whole symposium — and to be more reflexive in the concluding section.

Ultimately, however, the test of this experiment seems to me to rest on two criteria: firstly, does the argument within the piece as whole come across as clearly and as fully as it would in a single composition; and secondly, does it really help us to reflect usefully on the genre as a whole ? In my view, if the answer to both questions is positive, then the exercise will have been worthwhile. I shall address these issues in a postscript after the reader has had an opportunity to read my initial piece and the various responses to it.

Academic literacies: a case study

There is a growing literature (Taylor 1988; Lea 1994; Lea and Street 1998) on the gap between faculty expectations and student interpretations of what is expected in student writing. Lea, for instance, notes that faculty frequently put comments on essays such as 'make explicit', 'this needs expanding', 'elaborate', 'put more structure' etc. without making clear to student writers what is involved in doing this. As a faculty member myself, I think faculty assume that these ideas will be learned over the years through constant interactions between tutors and students so that we can make these comments without having to make explicit the underlying assumptions. Recent accounts of students' own perspectives (Cohen 1993; Ivanic 1998) have brought it home that this is not necessarily the case. This may happen at all levels, from first year students to doctoral candidates: in a recent doctoral hearing that I was involved in it became apparent that the candidate did not share the meanings of key phrases being used by the examiners, when we asked her to 'tease out' the meanings of her statements in the thesis; to 'elaborate'; to 'analyse'; to 'follow through' an argument. We were also at cross purposes regarding the notion of 'making generalisations', 'pitching it at a more abstract and analytic level'; of 'making themes more explicit' and 'pulling them out from the embedded text'; as the examiners struggled to communicate our meanings the student felt we were either asking for 'repetition' and 'redundancy' or that she had already done everything we were referring to.

I thought it might be helpful, therefore, to provide an example, from another text that is not so close to home, of what I think we mean by the expectations above; to make explicit my own conception of 'academic literacy' as an anthropology lecturer. To do this I analyse a passage from a book by Godfrey Lienhardt called *Social Anthropology* (see attached). I use this passage with students applying to do anthropology at Sussex, to give them an idea of the kinds of things we are trying to do in seminars and that we expect in essays and also as an example of the kind of analysis of text, its authority and its relationship to the reader, now current in much research literature — which is why my title is 'Academic literacies' and not just 'academic writing' (Street 1993).

The passage from Lienhardt begins with a number of general abstract statements on which the subsequent concrete examples hang: viz. **positive social functions of customs** and the **interdependence of social institutions**. I would argue that the rest of the text is an attempt to explicate these abstract claims about the nature of social life and, conversely, that the detailed descriptions of exchange, gift giving etc. are made sense of through relation to these abstractions. On their own, the descriptions that follow are interesting, but do not provide a basis for comparison from one culture to another: we could just list such examples forever without gaining any great insight into their significance. By relating them to the abstract claims of the two sentences at the beginning, Lienhardt gives us a basis for making generalisations, for seeing the more general significance of these local activities. Once we have seen the principle, we can begin to apply it in other circumstances. I find that students with whom I use the text quickly begin to make comparisons with gift giving in their own experience, such as Christmas cards, parties etc. They are aware that the concrete details and social contexts of Indian potlatches and of British Christmas card giving are very different; and yet there are principles they may have in common and that we can test off by further exploration. They also see ways in which the original analysis could be extended — by noting that in Britain, for instance, it is often women who do the work of managing card distribution. Is this part of a wider analysis of gender roles — eg. that women manage family relations; could Lienhardt have brought out the gender implications in his own examples? And so comparison and analysis proceed...

What we mean by such terms as 'analysis' and 'tease out the meanings', then, is what is going on here. 'Analysis' here means 'link the immediate concrete examples to more general, abstract claims'; 'tease out' means 'show

how the particular example does or does not link to the generalisations', perhaps by also bringing in further examples; what 'follow through' means in this context, is 'consider whether the general principles discovered in one case could be applied to another' (such as the gender example above).

It is helpful to notice the ways in which Lienhardt does this in his text. Having set out his general, abstract principles, he then provides detailed concrete descriptions of gift giving, but he keeps making reference back to the initial points: eg. (p. 80) "... was the basis of a complex social organisation that could not be maintained without it", e.g. (p. 81) 'The patterns of social interdependence which the Indians had created ..."; "modern industrial society [is] in some way comparable to that found among the Indians".

This is the sort of writing we are frequently asking students to do. We ask them, firstly, to set out, as Lienhardt does, one or two basic claims of an abstract kind and then to provide ethnographic examples that illustrate, elaborate or chellenge these claims. To take an example from a thesis I recently examined; the abstract propositon was 'that there are different models of literacy — professional workplace/schooled/community that may come into conflict'; Then in the text, as the writer is describing particular literacy practices eg. parents' concern with grammatical correctness, she could make reference back to these abstract principles (as Lienhardt does) and briefly remind us how the specific case is an illustration of the general principle (or not). A comparison with concrete examples of teachers' views of learning literacy could then provide a way in to a more general, comparative point in which the author draws attention to the underlying principles and to differences — at the level of conceptions or models — between this case and others. The relationship of concrete examples to abstract propositions, then, provides both deeper insight into this particular situation and a broader basis for comparison with others. As these points of abstraction weave their way through the text, they will add texture and depth to what otherwise would be simply a list of events and comments. The writer can then go back over the thesis or essay and pick out the passages where these more abstract points are made, then pull them all together and write a conclusion that outlines her current position in the light of all the conflicting evidence and argument. Finally, that conclusion goes to the beginning of the thesis/essay and becomes an initial assertion: "this thesis argues that x, on the basis of y, and I will take you through how my data and my analysis of it (from particular research perspectives) led me to those conclusions". The reader can then make up their own mind and make their own comparisons and the writer will have added to the ongoing conversation.

I am acutely conscious that this is my own interpretation of 'academic literacy' as a Social Anthropology tutor who had been teaching at Sussex for the past 20 years and also as a researcher in literacy looking for these issues in texts. Also, that I have used examples from doctoral theses as though they could be applied directly to first year essays: the differences obviously need exploring more closely, but my point is that the same principles and problems occur across the range and the same general expectations — of abstraction, structure, analysis — are being used to define 'academic writing'. At a recent workshop on this material colleagues pointed out some of the problems with my over-positive approach to Lienhardt's text. The opening sentences, for instance, which I revere as a model of good academic writing, could be seen as simply a means of establishing his authority viz a viz the reader/student by opening with a complex and unfamiliar set of abstractions. Throughout the text he provides proof of his own wide reading and knowledge, again establishing authority. More interesting from a 'literacy' perspective, his distancing strategies — use of noun phrases, impersonal style — serve to hide the (real) social relationship being established between him as writer and the student as reader: that relationship is the dominant social feature of the interaction, and yet it is disguised here, the author hides behind the text. This becomes apparent when we reach the long quotation from an 'Indian chief' where he addresses the listener directly: "And now, if you are come to forbiid us to dance, *begone*, if not you will be welcome to us". It might be objected that this is spoekn language whereas Lienhardt's text is written, but the point is that both are sociallty constructed according to specific, culturally-embedded assumptions — the medium itself does not determine the discourse. What the example points up for me, through the directness of address in the imperative '*begone*', is that Lienhardt does not give us such explicit clues to his own character and relationship (although a further reading suggests that he does implicitly present himself as a 'goody' up against either less radical anthropologists or against 'developers', who would 'abolish' the potlatch through lack of the kind of understanding he is advocating). The lack of explicitness about the author/reader relationship in texts such as this is a feature of 'Academic literacies' that many students — especially mature students — find hard to accept. As Lea (1993) points out from her study of mature students, many were already skilled in writing before they came to university, but the demands of 'academic literacy' seem to deskill them — 'I thought I could write until I came here'. As Ivanic points out (1993), many students see this academic literacy as a 'game' in which they are being asked to take on an identity that is 'not me', that is not true to their image of their 'true' self. It is at this level — identity, self-hood, personality — rather than simply at the level of writing technique, skills, grammar etc. that the conflict and miscommunication around academic writing often occurs between students and tutors (Lea and Street 1999).

It has been argued that students are simply being exposed to a new 'genre' (Franklin 1993; Cope & Kalatnzis 1993) — one that has considerable power in society at large and in the institution to which they have chosen to come, and they can learn to use it just as they have developed other genres in other contexts (business letters, personal writing, school tests etc.). Indeed, being conscious of the styles required in different genres is an important part of reading any text. Lienhardt's, for instance, involves a number of 'voices' — his own authorial authority as academic and writer; that of the Indian chief; the phraseology adopted from Veblen as a secondary source. Such mingling of texts and voices — often referred to as 'intertextuality' following Bakhtin (1981) — is a key part of how we communicate in both oral and written mode and university should be a prime site for the elaboration of such skills and the analysis of them. However, students have argued that this process mostly remains hidden (Taylor 1988); few tutors make explicit that this is what is happening and is expected of them, and they are seldom given the basis for analysing genres and voices for themselves. In the absence of explicitness, variety becomes a problem rather than a resource, especially when different voices are not just a 'game' to the student but a central aspect of their identity and personhood. This is an arguemt. then, for more than just 'study skills' as a kind of technicist solution to problems students encounter in doing academic writing: the issues involved are those of epistemology (who controls knowledge and how; who has the right to give voice) and of identity (what version of self is being expressed in different forms of writing — cf. Street 1994). This represents a different challenge to tutors than simply sending students with 'difficulties' to a 'study skills' Unit, whilst they get on with the job of 'teaching' academic knowledge.

References

Bakhtin, M. 1981. *The Dialogical Imagination*, ed. M. Holquist. Austin: Univ. of Texas Press.
Cohen, M. 1993. "Listening to Students' Voices: What university students tell us about how they can learn", Paper to Annual Meeting of AERA: Atlanta, GA.
Cope, B. and Kalantzis, M. 1993 *The Powers of Literacy: A genre approach to teaching writing*. London: Falmer Press.
Franklin, S. 1994. "Sounding the Right Words." *Special Children* 72 Feb.
Ivanic, R. 1998. *The Discoursal Construction of Identity in academic writing*. Benjamin's, Amsterdam.
Lea, M 1994. "I Thought I Could Write Until I Came Here: Student writing in Higher Education." In Gibbs, G. (ed.), *Improving Student Learning: Theory and practice*. Oxford: OSCD.

Lea, M. and Street, B. 1998. "Student Writing in Higher Education: an Academic Literacies Approach." In *Studies in Higher Education* 23 (2): 157–172.
Lea, M. and Street, B. 1999. "Writing as academic literacies: understanding textual practices in higher education." In Candlin, C. and Hyland, K. (eds.) *Writing: Texts, processes and Practices.* Longman: London pp. 62–81.
Lienhardt, R. G. 1964. *Social Anthropology.* Oxford: OUP. Street, B. V. (ed.) 1993. "The New Literacy Studies." *Journal of Research in Reading* 16(2). London: Blackwell/ UKRA.
Street, B. V. 1994. "Struggles over the Meaning(s) of Literacy." In M. Hamilton, D. Barton and R. Ivanic (eds), *Worlds of Literacy.* Clevedon: Multlingual Matters.
Taylor, G., Ballard, B., Beasley, V., Hanne, B., Clanchy, J., Nightingale, P. 1988. *Literacy by Degrees.* Milton Keynes: Society for Research in Higher Education/Open University.

Academic Literacies

Social Anthropology

Godfrey Lienhardt

Brian V. Street

In the very nature of their material, social anthropologists have been forced to draw attention to the positive social function of customs which, if looked at from a purely economic point of view, appear irrational and sometimes ruinously wasteful. This approach does not, as is sometimes supposed, spring from any anthropological desire to conserve exotic customs, but from experience of the interdependence of social institutions. As those who have official responsibility for directing social change have sometimes found out to their cost, institutions of which they approve are often inseparably connected with customs which they would prefer to abolish, and an ill-considered measure which appears to be for the good may produce effects quite other than those intended.

One of the most familiar anthropological examples of the non-economical use of wealth was to be found among the Indians of the coasts of British Columbia in an institution called *potlatch*. These Indians, immensely rich by the standards of even the wealthiest subsistence economies, had a most elaborate system of rank and status. This was largely maintained by display and competition in gargantuan feasting and entertainments, where from time to time persons of distinction would *potlatch*—that is, give away or even destroy vast quantities of their possessions. Of these the most highly regarded were plaques or sheets of copper, of no intrinsic utilitarian value, but counted worth great numbers of blankets and other useful goods. Though blankets, cloth, fish oil, and other commodities dispensed on a wildly extravagant scale in *potlatch* were, unlike the 'coppers', potentially useful, they were accumulated by the rich in such quantities that their owners had little use for them outside the *potlatch* situation.

The purpose of this entertainment and distribution of gifts was to assert relative social standing and compete for higher and higher prestige. The recipients at a *potlatch* 'party' were required by custom to accept the gifts; and in order not to lose face they 'fought' to outdo their previous host when, after perhaps a year, their turn to *potlatch* came round. A good indication of the scale of this obligatory gift-exchange is to be found in Helen Codere's monograph *Fighting with Property* (1950), where *potlatches* are recorded in which thousands and tens of thousands of blankets, as well as many other commodities, have been given away. The Indians' enthusiasm for the non-utilitarian copper plaques is conveyed by a traditional account of a very large copper, which had come to represent, in terms of exchange, more or less limitless riches:

... there was nothing that was not paid for it. It made the house empty. Twenty canoes was its price; and twenty slaves was its price; and also ten coppers tied to the end was its price, and twenty lynx skins, and twenty marmot skins, and twenty sewed blankets was its price; and twenty mink blankets was its price; and one hundred boards was its price; and forty wide planks was its price; and twenty boxes of dried berries added to it and twenty boxes of clover....

and the list continues, giving a very direct impression of the nature of the wealth of that Indian culture.

The Administration made strong efforts to forbid and discourage *potlatch* on economic and other grounds, and in some cases indeed it reached such a pitch of wastefulness, in manic competitions by the actual destruction of property—breaking coppers or throwing them into the sea, and burning blankets and oil—that it is easy to see the administrative point of view. Yet the Indians clung to their custom, as when one Indian chief said to Boas:

We will dance when our laws command us to dance, we will feast when our hearts desire to feast. Do we ask the white man, 'Do as the Indian does'? No, we do not. Why then do you ask us 'Do as the white man does'? It is a strict law that bids us dance. It is a strict law that bids us distribute our property among our friends and neighbours. It is a good law. Let the white man observe his law, we shall observe ours. And now, if you are come to forbid us to dance, begone, if not, you will be welcome to us.

Helen Codere has shown that the *potlatch*, from the European point of view a form of madness, was the basis of a complex social organization which could not be maintained without it. The heavy expenditure it made necessary could not have been undertaken without an intricate system of loans, credit, and interest. Indebtedness, as anthropologists have often pointed out, is a form of relationship with many integrating social functions. To abolish *potlatch* then was not merely to abolish an

Brian V. Street

ECONOMICS AND SOCIAL RELATIONS

isolated wasteful custom, but to destroy the system of ranking in the society, the relations between tribes and their chiefs, even the relations between friends and kinsmen. The pattern of social interdependence which the Indians had created and valued would have been radically altered. Further, as some of the people themselves recognized, the destructive *potlatch* was a substitute for warfare, proscribed by the Administration, and certainly even less acceptable to those responsible for government than the *potlatch* itself. An Indian said: 'When I was young I have seen streams of blood shed in war. But since that time the white man came and stopped up that stream of blood with wealth. Now we are fighting with our wealth.' He might well have understood some of the international loans and gifts made by the Great Powers in our own time as they bid for influence.

Extravagance and display in the use of wealth in modern industrial society, and competition for power and prestige there in some ways comparable to that found among the Indians, engaged the interest of the nineteenth-century American sociologist and economist Thorstein Veblen. Veblen introduced the expression 'conspicuous consumption' for the competitive use of wealth to establish and validate social status. His *The Theory of a Leisure Class* (1899) is a wider-ranging survey and analysis of the relation between wealth, labour, social prestige, and power, based upon his observation that activities economically and practically unproductive—fox-hunting might be an example—often carried high social prestige, while productive labour was often a mark of lower social status. So in his own American society useless objects (comparable to the coppers of the North-West Coast Indians) were frequently accorded higher value, and conferred greater prestige on their owners, than merely utilitarian articles. With much attention to details of social behaviour in the America and Europe of his time, Veblen argued that the highest social prestige was accorded to those who did not need to work in order to live. In the economic competition for power (which he attributed to a surviving predatory instinct) those were most likely to succeed who had the marks of inherited wealth and leisure.

Academic Literacies

Comments on Academic Literacy: a case study. Brian Street.

It seems to me that there is a problematic concerning academic texts, or more specifically, with the practices surrounding the uses of academic texts, which makes it impossible to separate the relationships of power and authority, created through interpreting the text, from the organisation of knowledge and ultimately the validity of "ways of knowing". I think this is why the "genre" approach is an incomplete model for learning academic disciplines. I had an interesting conversation at a workshop at Lancaster last week with Andy Northedge, from the OU —the author of the Good Study Guide, on this same issue. He believes that if you introduce the discourse— as he described it to me— to students, then you enable them to understand the discipline and ultimately academically accepted ways of presenting the discipline. I would argue that this approach has some benefit but one must also consider the constraints of learning a discourse: "genre" and "discourse" are being used interchangeably here as I understand them. The constraints are a result of the ways in which texts are read, understood and replicated at different level in the academic institutions.

When you refer to the doctoral candidate who did not appear to share the same meanings as the examiners, there seems to be an expectation that these meanings could be created through shared ways of knowing. Academic texts are not shared ways of knowing but are read or heard in contrasting ways by students and staff at different levels within the university hierarchy. The author/reader relationship is problematised for students because they are frequently exposed to texts which are addressed to academic staff. I would suggest three problematic relationships within the text and your example of Lienhardt's text could be used to illustrate this. Firstly, the relationship between the author and the student could be read as " I am an authority on this subject and I intend to set out, within the conventions of anthropology, an interpretation of this event which can be abstracted and used to understand other phenomena which are traditionally understood to fall within my discipline." Secondly, the relationship between the author and other anthropologists: "I believe that this is a useful and valid interpretation of knowledge within our disciplinary boundaries and this publication is intended to maintain my standing as a recognised academic authority." The third relationship exists with readers of other disciplines:"This is the way in which knowledge is organised within anthropology to enable us as anthropologists to make abstract claims about the nature of social life."

Academic texts —spoken and written— cannot be understood as impartial bearers of specific ways of organising knowledge. If students are replicating a genre then which relationships within the text are they replicating? Embedded within a first year undergraduate essay, a doctoral thesis, a paper for publication, an academic book are —as you elaborate —different relationships of authority between the author and the reader. Yet all these authors may have drawn on the same texts for the creation of their own texts. I think that it is impossible to separate the multi-faceted power relationships embedded within the text from the organisation of knowledge. If students attempt to replicate

Brian V. Street

features of disciplinary texts within a different set of power relationships i.e. within their own texts, then their interpretation and organisation of knowledge may appear inappropriate and incomplete. Additionally, for many students their own more familiar ways of representing knowledge feels invalid within academic settings.

I think your own article is a good example of what I am suggesting. Early in the paper you introduce a description of the problems encountered by a doctoral student. You use this to elaborate on your own theoretical position. I wonder how many undergraduates would feel comfortable using personal anecdotal material e.g. about a personal incident of card giving. Those students who have little experience of reading academic articles may find it difficult to use anecdotal experience within the academic model. They are constrained by the relationships of authority which exist within their own texts: the tutor as the reader; can I do this in anthropology? The illustration of an abstract concept through descriptive or anecdotal material may not appear to follow in the logical order that you suggest. How can a novice student understand the relationship between abstractions and a particular personal incident? This way of organising knowledge is for recognised authorities. The recognised authority does as you suggest" hide behind the text", but the student has no authority with which to do that.

Traditional study skills approaches are not designed, or equipped, to address the dialectic between the relationships which are surfaced by different individuals processing and producing academic texts, and the "ways of knowing": the organisation, presentation and interpretation of knowledge. I hope this adds a little more to your debate on genres and voices.

MARY LEA
23/2/94

Academic Literacies

Goldsmiths UNIVERSITY OF LONDON

GOLDSMITHS COLLEGE
New Cross London SE14 6NW
Telephone 081 692 7171

DEPARTMENT OF ENGLISH
Head of Department Professor Chris Baldick
Direct fax 081 694 8911

ENGLISH LANGUAGE UNIT
Co-ordinator Joan Turner MA

10th May 1994

Brian Street,
School of Social Sciences,
Arts Building,
University of Sussex,
Falmer,
BRIGHTON,   BN1 9QN.

Dear Brian,

I was very interested to read your article on Academic Literacy which was sent to me by Roz Ivanic. I am particularly interested in what you have to say about underlying assumptions because a lot of my own work is taken up with finding ways of making such assumptions explicit to students from other cultures. I am currently doing some research on cross-cultural pragmatics with a Japanese colleague, Masako Hiraga, and one area which we have highlighted particularly is "elaboration". We are looking particularly at elaboration in spoken interaction between Japanese students and British tutors and hoping to make comparisons with British/British interaction and Japanese/Japanese.

We have found that what are formally produced as yes/no questions are treated as simply that and not expanded upon whereas the implicit expectation on the part of the British tutor is for greater elaboration. For example, a tutor asking a Fine Art student "Are you particularly interested in the work of X?" might just receive the answer yes. Other question types which seem to embody the implicit demand for exploration or elaboration are hypothetical questions and these too tend not to meet with appropriate responses. This seemed to me to tie in with what you described as "at cross purposes" in doctoral hearings.

I feel that both spoken interaction in academic contexts and academic writing are subject to a specific value system underlying academic culture which needs to be made more explicit. My own work is primarily with international students but I have in the past worked with mature students returning to study and feel that the problems in terms of getting to grips with academic culture are similar.

Best wishes.

Yours sincerely,

Joan Turner.

GOLDSMITHS IS A COLLEGE OF THE UNIVERSITY OF LONDON INCORPORATED BY ROYAL CHARTER

Brian V. Street

A RESPONSE TO "ACADEMIC LITERACY: A CASE STUDY".
David Howes.

Brian Street's paper, "Academic Literacy: a case study" (1994), raises the questions produced by the study of all and any literacies: what constitutes this literacy?; why is it so constituted?; and how is it acquired? Some answers to the first two of these questions have been suggested to me by recent personal experience.

Last year, in Melbourne, I carried out a quantitative study into the effectiveness of a particular teaching methodology. It was an unusual study in that it brought together two previously distinct fields: the teaching of writing (from the domain of the teaching of English) and the question of individual differences in cognitive style (from the domain of psychology).

When I initially designed the study, I discussed my ideas with an academic friend. She was enthusiastic but pointed out that the study involved many contested areas: marker reliability, trait scoring and the subjects of the study were just some she listed. Her advice, later reiterated by my supervisor, was, "Make sure you have a reference to support every decision you make".

The study progressed well but my supervisor, whose academic background is psychology, was horrified when I presented my first write-up. I had blithely written in the manner to which I am accustomed - for an audience of those within the "English" domain. Phrases such as, "I think", or, "This, to me, is a clear indication ..." littered the text. Red circles filled the pages: "All this has to be de-personalised!" was the emphatic response.

This year in London I happened to mention this experience to an academic and writer. She responded in something like these words:
"I write as a feminist on feminist themes for a feminist audience. I have to use the 'I' form if I am to have any hope of communicating with my audience. I have to be very careful not to be seen as taking too authoritarian a stance as a writer."

What do these three responses say about academic literacy?

The most obvious is that, contrary to the position implicit in Street's paper, they reveal there is no such thing as a generic "Academic Literacy". Rather, there are different academic literacies for different academic audiences. Writing for an audience of psychologists, for example, requires the personal element in the presentation to be excluded in order to maintain the status of scientific inquiry as an objective process that can be conducted uninfluenced by a researcher's individual history. Writing for a feminist audience, on the other hand, requires the authorial self to be foregrounded to reduce the notion of authorial status and authority, to present the writer as just one voice among many. There is, however, a certain element of sleight-of-hand in this technique. The writer uses a strategy such as foregrounding herself in order to apparently reduce her authority as author, which in fact is the most effective way to establish her authority in the particular context in which she writes.

The common pursuit in each of these strategies is, of course, the search for textual power. My anecdotes suggest one way to achieve such power is by the promotion or diminution of the authorial voice, while another is the use of references.

The injunction I mentioned earlier, "Make sure you have a reference ..." is particularly revealing. Note the injunction is not, "Make sure you present a rational reason supported by evidence". The use of references in academic literacy has become a system of self-evident proof of an argument and hence of power. The dangers of this are obvious, as exemplified by the self-referential nature of much of the writing produced by early genre literacy theorists in Australia. Propositions supported by earlier work (published, unpublished or even "work in progress"!) assume an authority derived without any examination of the actual arguments that led to the conclusions of such work. Those who construct academic literacy now rely on their reader sharing this assumption that reference = proof. This shared assumption now constitutes a prime source of textual power in all academic literacies and therefore the rules of the game that students are asked to play, as the students cited in Street's paper so accurately perceived. Should the game continue to be played according to these rules?

A broad answer to the third of my questions ("How is academic literacy acquired?") is hinted at in Street's paper. Street cites two studies that show that at least some students do not understand what it is that constitutes academic literacy. He then discusses an example of academic literacy he uses with his own students to "make explicit" his own understanding of academic literacy. The conclusion the reader seems to be asked to draw is that this will help his students acquire academic literacy.

But what does "make explicit" actually mean? In the conclusion to his paper Street rejects any interpretation of this phrase that would lead to a search for a "technicist solution". By this he presumably means the kind of strategy that would focus on

Brian V. Street

explicitly teaching students how to write "academically". Street goes on to identify what it is that constitutes academic literacy (the ability to discern "who controls knowledge and how") but does not propose a method for making this knowledge knowable.

This is characteristic of the discipline of "literacy" as presently practised. The arguments on which so much current thinking about literacy is based, that is, that "form is meaning" and its corollary "process is indistinguishable from product", have led to the assumption that a statement of what literacy is includes a statement about how it should be taught. The process of teaching and learning is presented as implicit in the identification of the product. For example, when Street writes that the issues in helping students overcome problems encountered in "doing academic writing" are those of epistemology and identity, he has presented an implicit answer to the question, "How do you overcome these problems?", which is: "By helping students learn how to work out who controls knowledge in a social situation and what 'version of self' an author presents in a text". But this has not answered the unfashionable question, "*How* do we best help students learn how to work out etc. etc."

It is not surprising that it is unfashionable given the unproductive nature of so much of the literature that has been generated in response to this question. These responses have generally fallen into two categories: those who propose what Street terms a "technicist" approach, and those who have proposed what might be termed the osmosis approach.

Street is right to reject the "technicist" approach. It is an approach which posits the answer to the question of what constitutes literacy as determined rather than constructed. It is, in any case, as my own study I referred to earlier eventually showed, ineffective. It is, I think, also time for the necessary rejection of the romantic vision that universities or schools can reproduce the learning environment of a literate home which is the argument central to the osmosis approach. Leaving aside the question of whether all students do learn by osmosis, the economic order under which we presently live and which we will continue to suffer for the foreseeable future has ensured the destruction of that vision.

Instead, we need to propose and trial new ways of helping students learn. It is no longer sufficient to identify what we mean when we speak of academic literacies or any other kinds of literacies. What is needed is a clear understanding of how all students can be helped to share this understanding. This may emerge from a renewed interest in the ways students represent knowledge and therefore how they can best be helped to

Academic Literacies

acquire knowledge. It is likely that the answer will be not be found in any of the traditional academic disciplines alone but will require a synthesis of the study of semiotics, language, culture, linguistics and psychology.

What is certain, as the experience of the students cited in Street's paper makes clear, is that in a time of ever-increasing education the task is an urgent one.

Brian V. Street

Notes on your "Academic Literacy: A Case Study"

One of my current projects is to collect and analyse case studies of academic literacy in American higher education. Because of the Writing-across-the-curriculum movement in US higher education and because the field of composition studies has gained some academic respectability (and research funding) in the last decade, there are quite a few of these studies. I've found over 100 so far.

Yours takes us to some common themes in these studies: that "academic writing" is not a single thing but a aggregation of literacy practices that make and are made by the epistemologies and practices (including the use of power) of specific disciplines and other institutional formations; that it mediates identity struggles; that it is largely transparent to instructors socialised in a discipline, assumed; that technical solutions such as "study skills" do not get at the problem.

But what interests me the most is your relating these issues to wider literacy concerns. Academic literacy is not "autonomous," to use your term. Thus, it cannot be studied as a ding an sich, whether in composition courses, as in the US, or in "study skills" courses as in Australia and England. One must go to those involved in the activities that give rise to textual practices a group of students wants to learn to participate in and ask to spend time learning what is involved.

For example, I would like to know what Lienhardt (and his "core set," as the sociologists of science call those researchers who acknowledge each other as participants in the research dialogue) thinks those textual practices you refer to are doing. From his (their) perspective, the "author/reader relationship" might be quite "explicit": one member of the core set to another.

As sociologists of science have found out to their pain, it's quite difficult to become an ethnographic observer in academic contexts because of the potential threat to the work of the "culture." I wonder if social anthropologists would be amenable to having a social anthropological study done of their practices!

David R. Russell
English Department
Iowa State University
Ames, IA 50010   E-mail: drrussell@iastate.edu

Academic Literacies

Response to "Academic Literacy: a Case Study" by Brian V. Street

Shirley Franklin (M.Phil. student at Institute of Education, University of London).

I enjoyed reading your interpretation of "Academic Literacy", because you have are addressing the issue of Genre, but particularly, because, in so doing, you are using the work of our late teacher and drinking companion, Godfrey Lienhardt. However, I am not in agreeement with your interpretation of my viewpoint on Genre.

I like your idea of using Godfrey's method of writing about the *potlatch* as useful in establishing for students a model for writing anthropologically. But this example could only be used for specific academic writing. Does all academic writing necessarily follow this structure, incorporating this empathetic approach? Does empathy have a role to play in Scientific Report writing? Surley not. Godfrey's writing is a model for anthroplogists and perhaps historians writing about people's practices in other cultures or other times within a particular, perhaps academic, setting.

I do not think there is one Genre called "Academic Literacy". Life as an academic reader or writer would be quite simple, and perhaps boring, if this were true. A multiplicity of social factors affect the genres we use. Genres reflect the purpose for writing. Thus the staging which Godfrey used in this text, starting with his position of the importance of understanding the importance of the social function of customs, rather than interpreting them through Western economic perspectives. His purpose, then, is to explain how the *potlatch* is integral to social relationships amongst the Indians. .

The problem of difference, which you pose, between the interpretations of the student writer and the academic faculty. is true of most student/teacher literacy experiences across the educational strata. Students of all ages come to education ewith their own literacy experiences (Street 1984,1992, Cole and

Brian V. Street

Scribner 1981, Heath 1983) and therefore have to be taught the genres used for the varying academic purposes they meet. In schools, the "S"treet literacy experiences of students are insufficiently extended to meet the demands of cross-curricular genres. Writing appropriately to reflect understanding, to put forward an argument, or to write a scientific investigation requires a familiarity with styles of writing appropriate to these textual tasks.

These styles or genres have been shaped socially mainly by those in power: those academics in the particular field of study who have an effect on shaping appropriate genres to their field, those who mark examination or test papers, teachers, and of course increasingly the Government through their dictates on Standard English or "correct" forms of writing.

Thus the somewhat inpersonal or "not-me-ness" (Ivanic,1993) of writing in academic genres is not about identity, beyond the identity of being an academic "anthropologist" or a "Sociolinguistic PH.D. student". Students do not have to be "exposed" to the academic genre, but to succeed in their acdemic writing, to be taken seriously, they need to be able to understand and to use the appropriate genres.

Once empowered by an ability to be able to write in the "acceptable" form, to be able to express new understandings in ways that are acceptable within the disciplinary area, students and academics are closer to a position from which they can reconstruct and create their own generic structures.

References

COLE,M and SCRIBNER,S. 1981, *The Psychology of Literacy*. Harvard University Press.

HEATH, S.B. 1983, *Ways With Words*. Cambridge University Press.

Academic Literacies

IVANIC,R. 1993, *The Discoursal Construction of Writer Identity: an Investigation with Eight Mature Students*. Unpublished Ph.D. University of Lancaster.

STREET,B. 1984. *Literacy in Theory and Practice*. Cambridge University Press.

STREET,B. (ed.) 1992. *Cross-Cultural Approaches to Literacy*. Cambridge University Press

(Please correct this draft for appropriate genre/linguistic usage!)

Brian V. Street

To Brian Street
Some Thoughts in Response to 'Academic Literacy: a case study'

It seems to me that identifying mismatches between teachers and students in the way academic writing is used and interpreted is an important first step in overturning a deeply engrained, rather circular, assumption in higher education; put crudely, that good students do well because they are good and that less good students do less well precisely because they are less good. Putting the assumption like this may sound extreme, as if denying the influence of teaching on an individual's success. Yet assumptions such as this do influence the way students are enculturated more or less successfully into academic disciplines. What they do is to naturalise the process of academic learning and sustain the emphasis in teaching on content and the coverage of topic areas rather than on the literacy practices/discourses through which that content is given disciplinary specific meaning. The emphasis is identifiable also in the way teaching is described in, for example, promotional material and course handbooks, where it is plainly the *what* rather than the *ways* that are presented as substantial. One consequence of regarding disciplines as receptacles rather than practices is the creation of study skills or induction programmes, which are conducted as additional extras to the main business of learning. In my experience the instrumental – what you call technicist – aims of these programmes fall short of allowing students greater access to 'knowing in' their discipline (since they are not based on authentic experience within that discipline) and also shy away from 'knowing about' – in the sense of having a critical perspective on – the discipline.[*]

Overturning assumptions and changing emphases is not simple and does not lead to easy solutions, but it seems to me that effective (itself a debatable term in this context) approaches need to incorporate an understanding of teaching and learning which is based on discourse rather than knowledge and which breaks down such unhelpful dichotomies as form and content, knowledge and argument and replaces them with more rhetorical notions such as authority, persuasive purpose, use or strategic value. These are aspects of literacy which are very much dependent on understanding of and orientation (whether positive or negative) towards specific contexts.

There are difficulties and dilemmas with this approach however – as I think your case study illustrates. It is discourse, not knowledge, that is powerful in academic contexts and a condition of power is invisibility. The implications of making discourse visible and exposing the means by which it configures the world are not straightforward. If those who are seeking to acquire the discourse are simultaneously in the process of undermining it, how does this affect their access to the position of power that it embodies? Is the power they gain, as one teacher put it to me, simply that of the cynic? There is something of a chicken and egg situation here, for if discourse remains hidden behind

---

[*] 'knowing in' and 'knowing about' are distinctions made by James Gee (1989) who describes discourses as 'ways of being in the world', '*saying-(writing)-doing-being-valuing-believing combinations*' (p.6-7)

the visibility of content, then belief in the naturally selected 'good' student is upheld and for many access to transactions of power remains elusive.

In that it signals the discourse of the discipline as something which can be discoursed about, I would consider your use of the anthropology text with students to be an example of the approach I am suggesting. Equally your case study illustrates the more radical ground to which such an approach might tend. As you acknowledge, your 'meta-discourse' on the text operates in accordance with a specific agenda, that of the teacher who exposes to his students (whether through discussion or instruction is not clear) exemplary modes of argumentation within his discipline. The mechanism of the text (as a manifestation of the discipline) is apparently laid bare, but, as your conversations with colleagues suggest, this mechanism is constructed as much by the hidden assumptions of the reader as it is inherent within the text itself. Another type of meta-discourse, another set of interpretative tools produces a very different set of meanings for the text – ones which challenge rather than endorse the conventions of academic literacy. By selecting these alternative tools the investigation is moved beyond 'successful' practice towards reflexivity and critique; tipping from the positive to the negative mode of interpretation (Ricoeur, 1970 p.27).

This is where those unsettling questions start. What are the aims of making discourse visible? Where do the parameters lie? How does the balance of power shift in the process? How is it distributed between teachers and students? Are they equally empowered to endorse or critique what they read and how they write? What are the actual consequences of critique in terms of the assessment and examination systems by which institutions operate? What would be at issue, for instance, if students brought the charge against the academic thesis (as you describe it) that it excludes or subsumes dissident voices and alternative interpretations, that its expressions of certainty enact a kind of violence – and what if they, as a consequence, refused to write in this way?

In the research I have recently completed on argument in post-sixteen academic education (Mitchell 1994), the objective of finding ways in which students could become better arguers was continually hedged by questions of this kind. The research's focus on *argument* caused me to think inevitably beyond the delivery of content and in terms of process, ways of organising and operating upon given material (through reading, writing and in speech) as well as in terms of authority, legitimacy, spaces and boundaries, ways of showing deference and orientation towards others and ways of creating identity for oneself. It seemed to me that not only was argument used within the relatively closed world of a discipline to make new knowledge in certain conventionally sanctioned ways but that it frequently also had the potential to cross the boundaries of these worlds, to critique them and to make possible new connections (such as with personal identity or experience). This transgressive tendency seemed altogether a more risky business, but one to which I was drawn sensing that it might ultimately enrich the disciplinary worlds or (which is perhaps not the same thing) help students to find their way more meaningfully within them.

Below I give two examples of how students might both be given access to what Sheeran and Barnes (1991) call the 'ground rules' of academic literacy and at the same time how they might be given space to reflect on these. What I hope these exercises create is some kind of tension between reproducing the given and reforming it, between consolidation and change.

The first example is based on an extract from the writing of a first year undergraduate Sociology student in which she reflects on her experiences of taking on the 'role' of student. The aim of the writing task was to move the students from their personal experience towards sociological explanations: a goal which is only marginally realised in Kate's writing. When I read the piece I started thinking how it might have been more successful; what, that is, it lacked 'sociologically'. From this I developed an approach similar in some respects to yours.

The exercise consists in taking one text and, in trying to 'spell out' what it is saying using particular criteria, developing a new and different text. The activity is neither 'translation' nor 'paraphrase' – though it may involve attempting to rewrite in other words – rather it is a kind of 'transformation'. The aim is not to preserve original meaning but to extend and develop it to create new significances.

This is the extract from Kate's writing:

> Certain aspects of behaviour were spelled out quite literally – how to not appear as a freshman. For example, freshmen women tend to want to carry purses – college students just don't do that. Also, only freshmen would be seen wearing high school jackets, sweatshirts or other paraphernalia - within a few weeks these signs were completely gone as the new students adapted to their new environment.
>
> I remember not knowing the procedure for getting course syllabi and buying books. By observing and asking, I acted as if I knew what I was doing, but I was merely going through the motions. In subsequent semesters, I did indeed know exactly what I had to do. This is when I became the student.

And these, my reflections upon it:

> Kate's writing is largely descriptive, though she registers the change from conscious adoption of the role to living the role. What does writing like this need in order to become sociological? Is it a degree of abstraction higher; a systematic way of characterising the observations; an interpretation of rules which are implicit, so that what is now description becomes illustration? Would a sentence such as 'The student conforms to certain dress codes which are picked up within the first few weeks of term' be sufficient? This is a general statement which introduces sociological categories. It might be improved by an indication that groups achieve identity also by being different from others: so 'The student conforms to certain dress codes which are picked up within the first few weeks of term and which differentiate him or her from other roles.' This seems to me to be a level of description which is sociological. I could strengthen my comment by

introducing some parallel examples to show that I am talking more widely about role adoption.

From here, it might be possible to formulate a hypothesis: 'Becoming a college student involves putting aside certain other identities and the outward appearance that signals them. Specifically the student puts aside both the signs of belonging to an earlier group (high school) and the signs of impending adulthood (purses?). These rejections suggest an identity which has side-stepped conventional paths of development.' To make this hypothesis I have looked at the particular illustrations as evidence from which to infer and then with which to support a broader statement. I have had to ask myself why the purses and the high school jackets were unacceptable, rather than simply to register that they were. Beyond this I've begun to wonder whether I want to differentiate student role adoption from other kinds of role adoption?

My text very obviously contains two elements or voices; the actual rewriting of Kate's text and a kind of meta-commentary on the tentative process of rewriting. These two voices could quite easily be prized apart and worked into separate texts and, for the purposes of the discipline, the sociological text would most likely represent the final outcome.

My second example is related to the first. It utilises the difference between texts as a discursive space in which the reader/writer's voice might come to be heard in a more reflective and critical mode than closed and monologic forms tend to allow. In this example two texts are configured side by side on a single page, so that the self-containedness of each is disrupted to create in the interplay a third dialogic text. The example is given by Meyer (1993) as an exercise for students whose thinking was, she felt, stifled by the 'illusion of mastery' demanded by academic convention.

ASSIGNMENT: Double Trouble

Fold a piece of paper in half. On one side, tell me what you think the sentences say. Be declarative, stating your reading as though you're sure of yourself and the author's intentions. Begin your writing with a description of the text and what it "means" or represents.
Now on the other side, begin your statements with, "But something bothers me". On this side be hesitant, questioning your assertions and certainties of the "right" side. Think about contradictions, about "what ifs", about what the sentences don't say directly. Explore double meanings and alternative conclusions. Relate what is said to personal experience and to subjective responses. Don't censor the outrageous or the improbable.

>Higgins: Pickering! Nonsense: she's going to marry Freddy. Ha ha! Freddy! Freddy! Ha ha ha ha ha!!!! [He roars with laughter as the play ends]. (Pygmalion 100)

Brian V. Street

SAMPLE RESPONSE

I know that Higgins is laughing at Eliza and Freddy. Shaw shows that Higgins has not changed at all and is still scornful of others. The tone expresses his continued sense of superiority and Shaw's in relation to other human beings. He is laughing at their weaknesses, compared to his own strength.	But what if the joke is on Henry? Perhaps his laughter has a slight edge of hysteria to it. Maybe Shaw is suggesting that Henry is not the Superman he thinks he is but is vulnerable to the same emotions such as jealousy as everyone else. I'd like to believe in a more sympathetic Higgins, one who is not fully in control. But then, maybe Shaw has the "last laugh", showing me how much I want a different ending.
(Meyer, 1993, p.60)	

I don't consider the voice of one side to be more 'authentic' than the other, nor that one side of the page has the greater claim to truth about the literary text. One side may indeed be more authoritative, but this authority is thrown into relief by the other, questioned by the context in which it finds itself. The split text creates spaces in which to discover not a true self so much as to create different roles and voices and through these to explore opportunities both to acknowledge and critique authority and discourse.

Both of the exercises I've described use difference to make discourse visible and therefore the object of discussion and reflection: what kind of writing is this? who and how does it seek to persuade? what claims to authority is it making and how? By basing such questions around more than one text dialogue is created. The dialogic principle in the Bakhtinian sense operates on sameness and difference and this is how the identity of the reader/writer is conceived of here, opening spaces in which she can both place herself within the dominant discourse and outside it.

These texts offer, then, rather different roles for writers and readers than those inferred from the text you used. This is not to say that your text could not play a useful part in such a multi-vocal process. It might form the initial text an a three (or more) columned page, the subsequent columns containing alternative interpretations of the academic literacy it exemplifies and forming the basis for further dialogue and reflection.

References

Gee, J. P. (1989) 'Literacy, Discourse and Linguistics: introduction' in *Journal of Education*, Vol. 171 No. 1 pp. 5-17.

Meyer, S. L. (1993) 'Refusing to Play the Confidence Game: the illusion of mastery in the reading/writing of texts' in *College English* Vol. 55 No. 1 (January 1991).

Mitchell, S. (1994) *The Teaching and Learning of Argument in Sixth Forms and Higher Education: Final Report* Hull: University of Hull, Centre for Studies in Rhetoric.

Sheeran, Y. and Barnes, D. (1991) *School Writing*, Buckingham: Open University Press.

Sally Mitchell, July 1994

Postscript

In the Preface to this 'article' I set out two criteria by which to assess the value of adopting the unusual format represented here: firstly, does the argument within the piece as whole come across as clearly and as fully as it would in a single composition; and secondly, does it really help us to reflect usefully on the genre as a whole ? I argued that, if the answer to both questions is positive, then the exercise will have been worthwhile. I shall address these issues in this postscript now that the reader has had an opportunity to read my initial piece and the various responses to it.

The initial piece on 'Academic literacies with which this 'article' began, was an attempt to reflect upon my own experience as a university lecturer encountering students' difficulties in mastering academic discourse. In particular, I was concerned with their encounter with academic writing and reading in which many quite able people appeared to experience debilitating and identity-shattering problems. I used a case study of an essay-text by my own former tutor in Oxford, Godfrey Lienhardt, in order to make explicit my own assumptions about what is 'good writing'. Based on these assumptions, I help students to read such texts both as a means of learning anthropology and also as a model for learning to write their own anthropological essays. My faith in Lienhardt's writing was already called into question by colleagues who read early drafts of my piece and pointed out that he could be interpreted in a more critical way that would help explain why students have difficulty with such discourse. For instance, the text embeds statements about his own authority which may deter students coming with different experience and resistant to the academic claims. Already there is a tension around the text, but already also there are power relations at play: in Lienhardt's relationship to his readers; in my relationship to Lienhardt's text and my uses of it; and in the power of colleagues to question my approach in ways that students might find more difficult. In this case, I incorporated those comments into my own text, reporting them at second hand and responding to them in my own voice so that they are encapsulated. This is more in keeping with the traditional academic genre and I could have continued to do this as responses came in from other colleagues. However, by keeping the other responses separate, in the sense of reproducing them in terms of their own conditions of production — letter heads, full text, signatures and address conventions — I believe that I have made more apparent the nature of the different voices, their own writing styles and conventions, and the subtleties of their argument, which were my first criterion for the value of this mode of presentation. If I now respond to them I must do so in the full glare, as it were, of the reader's acquaintance with them and the possibility that my reading will differ from theirs. This will fulfil, I would argue, both the first condition I set out in the Preface — and also the second one — by drawing attention to the genre itself.

What do I think the commentators have said and what do they add to the original piece? If I go through each in turn with my own commentary I will be making explicit what, in much academic discourse, remains implicit. The dialogic nature of reading and of writing is frequently disguised in the essay-text genre; by the separation of texts in time and space; by the incorporation and re-presentation of secondary commentary into an author's account so that it can serve his or her purpose rather than those of the original commentator; by the detachment of the authorial voice from personal responsibility (it was the experiment or the theory that 'spoke'); by the homogenisation of text production (a source's comments appear in the same type face and text type as those of the author who cites them). Students may well find it bewildering — but lack the confidence to point out that it is contradictory — that they are being asked to comment critically on texts and yet to disguise the conditions of difference between those texts and their own, to reduce the whole discourse to a common genre, to take themselves out when it is themselves that are the source of critical commentary. By going through each of the commentators on my text in turn I hope to make explicit the implicit debates and interpretations that occur in any reading and yet that many students feel disempowered from admitting to or representing in their own writing. This, then, may be a source of many of the 'writing blocks' that apprentice academics experience and that tend to be dealt with as though they were technical issues to be resolved by mechanistic training procedures.

Mary Lea extends my comments on this mechanistic view to the use of 'genre' approaches to teaching literacy. Writing herself in a direct and personal voice — 'I had an interesting conversation at a workshop at Lancaster last week with Andy Northedge' — she immediately sets up a dialogue, with both the reader and with Northedge — as she describes his view. She then addresses me directly — 'when you refer to a doctoral candidate' — and seems to criticise an implication of my argument that I had not made explicit. This is that shared ways of knowing would enable examiners and students to overcome their miscommunication. Academic texts, she argues, are 'not shared ways of knowing', at least not as far as students are concerned: writers frequently address other writers, or academics and the student is simply listening in. These relationships could, she believes, be made explicit by deconstruction of Lienhardt's text, bringing out more explicitly the power relationships involved. She lays out her own theoretical proposition in abstract form, though with some personal mitigation: "I think it is impossible to separate the multi-faceted power relationships embedded within the text from the organisation of knowledge". It is this that often makes student writing seem inappropriate — if they adopt the 'wrong' or unexpected power relationship, use the conventions of a different discipline, present themselves in unacceptable ways, then their texts are invalid. That could also be happening to this text, as readers from different disciplines approach it with different expectations and challenge my attempt, indeed right, to present discourse in this manner. But Lea is not just agreeing with me — she also uses my text to bring out the hidden nature of my own power position. I use anecdotal material in ways that students are disallowed by their authority relations with their tutor. Lienhardt may do this (he uses anecdotes too); I may (attempt to) do this; but may a student writing a term essay? She is not, I think, arguing against the convention that students should avoid anecdote in such essays, so much as arguing that the right to do so or not is hidden in the text. When students learn to write as academics they are learning about authority — and about disguising it — not simply about abstraction and what counts as evidence as might appear on the surface and as their tutors might claim. I, as author of this text, cannot claim to stand on a separate platform from the subject of my inquiry: if I am right about the hidden power relationships in text, then they are there in my text too — but, as Lea points out, I seemed to find it easier to notice them in others than in myself.

Joan Turner addresses the point about tutor expectations in terms of different cultural views of 'elaboration'. Where I had commented that students do not always understand what a tutor means when he or she asks them to 'elaborate' a point, she points out that such expectations are sometimes implicit rather than explicit — embedded in apparently simple questions such as 'Are you particularly interested in the work of X?' to which Japanese students might just answer 'yes', whilst British ones may have learned that fuller accounts are expected. This may also help explain the nature of certain examinations, such as the Oxbridge Entrance exam where questions like 'Art is in the Eye of the Beholder' may appear bland to the non-initiate, whilst those trained to the convention will recognise that they are expected to write for perhaps three hours on the basis of an elaborate structure of rules. Similarly, a French professor once set as a 'question' in the International Baccalaureate 'La Nature', on which he expected a lengthy disquisition, whilst English students and tutors did not even recognise that it was a question. The hidden structures are carried by cultural and class groups, whose ability to satisfy examiners rests as much on knowledge of conventions as on cognitive skills and abilities. Hill & Parry (1994) have recently argued that the test is a prime example of the claims for 'autonomous text embedded in the 'autonomous' model of literacy: they elaborate the model to demonstrate that it applies not only to autonomy of text but also to autonomy of institutions and individuals and autonomy of skills; the person taking the test is expected to provide only information elicited from the text provided and any reference to knowledge derived from their real life experience is likely to disadvantage them. Those who know this convention can play the game of test taking successfully whilst those who do not may inadvertently bring in background knowledge or personal reference that rules out their answers as invalid. Again academic literacy represents a barrier, and the reasons for failure may not be apparent to those many able people who fall at the gate. Turner seems to believe, in contrast to Howes and in keeping with my own initial argument, that making the 'underlying academic culture more explicit' can help overcome many of these problems. I am now less certain of this and wonder what its implications are for her own work, both cross-culturally and also with mature students.

David Howes similarly calls upon personal experience to elaborate the questions raised in my text. He provides an intellectual biography of a project he designed (a convention becoming more acceptable now that process as well as product are on the agenda, partly perhaps as a result of the more critical and social view of literacy represented here). As Lea pointed out, his supervisor would not be happy with anecdote. More precisely, a supervisor from a different discipline — psychology — was resistant to the conventions now emerging in literary studies and required depersonalisation of the text. The contrast between this and the equally dogmatic conventions of personalisation in some contemporary feminist discourse, leads him to criticise my implicit assumption that there is a single genre 'Academic Literacy'. There are, he argues, as did Lea (cf. also Chiseri-Strater 1991) 'academic literacies for different academic audiences'. Both the use of references and the use of personal voice may be ways of pursuing — if not always achieving — textual power. Such power can be acquired partly through shared assumptions. The assumption that reference equals proof, for instance, may operate as kind of privileged inter-textuality that includes those who know these texts and excludes others. But whereas he claims, I had argued that students could be helped to learn these processes by focussing on their form, Howes argues that simply making explicit who controls knowledge etc. does not tell us *how* to help them. I think he is suggesting here a similar argument to that used by radical black educators in the US, such as Delpit (1988), who argued that the process approach to learning privileges those from middle class and academic-style homes where such discourse is already taken for granted. Black children, she argues, may be disadvantaged by this learning style if they arrive at school unfamiliar with it: some of the product-oriented, rote learning and fact-based styles critiqued by radical educators as uncritical, may actually be more empowering for such children, she claims, than the supposedly radical writing process, whole language approaches advocated by liberals. This is what I take Howes to mean by his critique of the 'osmosis' approach: there is a gap in my account at the level of pedagogy. My project of identifying academic literacies and their underlying assumptions and then making them explicit will not in itself, he argues, achieve the pedagogic aim of helping students to learn.

David Russell also looked at work on the 'writing-across-the curriculum' movement in the US and implies that it is culturally specific and may hide the underlying epistemologies and identities on which it is premised. Applying this argument back to my original anthropological text, that by Lienhardt, he notes like Howes that the way in which researchers 'acknowledge each other as participants in the research dialogue' is central to the issue of academic literacy and the barriers it creates. Like Howes, too, he sees the members of the 'core' believing they are perfectly explicit — to each other. Again those outside the circle are not being addressed: they may either try to listen and understand from outside the dialogue, or spend years in apprenticeship in order to enter it: how they learn to do so remains problematic since the text only encodes its shared conventions, not the methods for acquiring them. Russell seems to go further and argue that insiders have a vested interest in restricting access: indeed, that anthropologists might be resistant to having anthropology done on them because that would represent a 'threat'. In this somewhat conspiratorial view, it would appear not to matter what the particular conventions are since those in power may simply alter them if too many outsiders learn the rules.

This indeed is the argument being put forward by Gee in criticising the 'genre' approach to literacy learning currently popular in Australia. Some there would argue that children cannot learn to question the power structures of the society they inhabit until *after* they have learned these genres. The teacher's task, then, is to impart knowledge of the traditional forms of reading and writing — the dominant literary forms, the genres of expository prose and essay-text writing, the ways of composing letters to business organisations — in order to empower their students. Only then can those students be in a position to question whether these forms are biased against their particular backgrounds — in gender or ethnic terms for instance — and work to change them. Gee (1990) points out a number of problems with this "wait for critique" approach. Much of the linguistic triviality that goes to make up such genres and to mark social groups as separate (phonology, spelling, surface grammar, punctuation etc.) is learnt in "socially situated practices" (p. 149) not in the classroom: hence "they cannot be 'picked up' later, outside the full context of an early apprenticeship (at home and at school)". This is the problem with J.D. Hirsch's much-publicised notion of "cultural literacy", which is strikingly similar to that proposed by those on the other end of the political spectrum as the "genres of power": Hirsch is right", says Gee, " that without having mastered an extensive list of trivialities people can be (and often are) excluded from 'goods' controlled by dominant groups in the society; he is wrong that this can be taught (in a classroom of all places!) apart from the socially situated practices that these groups have incorporated into their homes and daily lives" (Gee 1990, p. 149). Furthermore, if the markers of separation are indeed often trivial, then it is not very difficult for those in power to change them as new cohorts of 'outsiders' learn the spelling, grammar and phonology of the dominant groups. Treating academic literacies simply as 'genres' and assuming that anyone can gain access once they have been made explicit, is problematic not only in terms of pedagogy, as Howes points out, it also runs counter to current understandings of power relationships and of the role of discourse in them (Street, 1995).

Shirley Franklin also addresses the relationship between academic literacies and genres. Like Howes, Lea and others, she is critical of my title: there is not one 'academic literacy' but many. Most students arrive in the education system with a limited repertoire of literacy genres and need to be taught a range of them, across different disciplines and functions. She appears to suggest that these genres do not run as deeply as I implied: student identity may not necessarily be bound up in learning new ways of writing, they may simply take them on board but maintain their 'own' identity, rather like Ivanic's data on students seeing the whole process as a 'game'. However, as her examples show, for many students playing games like that is itself a moral issue that challenges their identity as 'honest' and straightforward. Again the writing process is implicated in other domains — moral, ideological, political — not just a set of technical skills. Franklin argues that learning the genres is a form of empowerment in that, once students have learned them, they can 'reconstruct and create their own generic structures'. This is an intriguing idea and might provide an answer to Howes' question about *how* students learn: once literacy practices are modelled for them, they are in a position to use the rules of construction like Levi-Strauss's *bricoleur* to create new ones.

Sally Mitchell's response develops the notion of learning and argues for a focus on learning based on discourse rather than on knowledge. Like Lea and many of the other contributors, including myself, she locates literacy learning in issues of authority and adds other rhetorical notions such as persuasive purpose and strategic value. Like Howes, however, she notes that simply making discourses and their underlying authority explicit is neither simple nor necessarily effective. The meta discourse that I constructed for helping students deal with Lienhardt's text, for instance, is not innocent: one reading of it might help students become simply cynics, challenging this and every text; another might simply help select the already 'good' student thus reproducing the very discourse and power structure I set out opposing. Other meta discourses would have other results.

So what are the aims of making discourse visible and does it make any difference to the balance of power? Like Lea, she is suspicious of my implied claim that students can simply take on critical discourse — they already know implicitly and frequently explicitly just what the boundaries of their own critical rights really are and soon learn the penalties if they overstep. Mitchell's own research on *argument* raised similar issues. Transgressive as opposed to reproductive uses of argument — that is argument across disciplinary boundaries to make new connections — is a risky business. Nevertheless, she seems to believe that training in exercises which reveal both potentials of specific literacy practices can help students reflect and change as well as just consolidate. Like me, she attempts to use a text 'transformatively', to extend and develop its original meanings and help students learn how to do this. This perhaps answers Howes' question about the ways in which students learn but does not necessarily resolve Gee's point about the arbitrariness of power over discourse forms.

A few themes, then, emerge from these responses. Most contributors agree that academic literacy is multiple, varying across disciplines and contexts; that the rules for acquiring it are often hidden and arbitrary, and that they involve assumptions about authority, legitimacy and power. But some responses challenge the notion that simply making these implicit conventions explicit will make much contribution to empowerment. Firstly, the ways in which students learn need to be addressed not just the form or content of what is learned. Learning may be transformative if it includes dialogic and alternative views of text but the boundaries of such views are still held by tutors rather than students and by institutions rather than individuals. Secondly, power may reside precisely in the arbitrariness of the conventions so that simply learning them may not provide access to power positions if those in control can alter them relatively easily. Thirdly, those of us attempting to help students reflect and comment critically need to recognise our own boundaries — at one extreme simply producing cynics and at the other reproducing the 'good' student as one who does like we do.

If these are the issues raised by a closer look at the question of academic literacies, then as in the study of literacies more generally, we find ourselves quickly moving away from the surface issues of reading and writing themselves and involved in more general issues of discourse, ideology and power. That the academic world should be one of the last to see that this is what is involved in addressing literacy may seem ironical to those who believed its claims to 'scientific' and critical authority: but as with any institutions, applying our insights to ourselves rather than others is frequently the last and the most difficult task we face. It is that recognition of the mote in our own eye that, I believe, finally justifies the novel form taken by this 'article': the multiple voices, styles, genres, formats etc. taken by these short pieces reinforces the theoretical argument about multiplicity in a way that would be lost if one author simply summarised in a single format text all of the contributions. It thereby fulfils, I believe, the condition I set myself at the outset of drawing attention to the genre itself; it allows the dialogic nature of all discourse to penetrate more evidently into academic discourse from which it has often been excluded — or disguised; and it makes a whole that is greater than the sum of its parts. I look forward to further responses ...

References

Chiseri-Strater, E. 1991. *Academic Literacies: The public and private discourse of university students.* Portsmouth, NH: Heinemann.

Cope, B and Kalantzis, M. 1993. *The Powers of Literacy: A genre approach to teaching writing.* London: Falmer Press.

Delpit, L. 1988. "The Silenced Dialogue: Power and pedagogy in educating other people's children." *Harvard Educational Review* 58(3): 280–298.

Gee, J. 1990. *Social Linguistics and Literacies: Ideology in discourses.* Brighton: Falmer Press.

Hill, C. and Parry, K. (eds). 1994. *From Testing to Assessment: English as an international language.* London: Longman.

Hirsch, E. D. Jr. 1987. *Cultural Literacy: What every American needs to know.* Boston, MA: Houghton Mifflin.

Street, B. 1995. *Social Literacies: Critical Approaches to Literacy in Education, Development and Ethnography* "Real Language" Series, Longman; London pp184.

Index

A
academic community/culture   5, 17–9, 37–41, 61, 81–4, 106ff, 127ff, 173–4, 208
academic essay   xvii, 17ff
   assignment   85–98
   essay-text   194, 209, 222
   question   130ff
   value system of   154–5
academic genre(s)   20–31, 108, 150–1, 198, 206–7, 214–5, 219, 220, 221, 223
academic literacies   xix, xxi, 8, 13, 15, 107, 155–56, 193, 195, 209–10, 221, 223, 224
academic literacy   xvii, 64, 103, 148–9, 155–6, 159–66, 191, 193ff, 211, 221ff
   essayist   128–143
   practices   8, 10, 40, 110–6, 156
academic socialisation   8, 10, 42, 96
academic writing   xiii-xv, 7, 15, 38, 61, 81, 83-4, 195, 196, 219
   as a resource   65
   conventions   129ff, 69, 84, 86–7
   perceptions of   84–99
   process   xiii, 40
   support   xiv, 91–8
   students'   196
access (to HE — Higher Education)   127–8
addressivity   128, 140ff

agency and subjectivity   xvi, xviii, 126, 169–189
anthropology   209, 212
   social   202–5
anxiety   71
approaches to student writing   8, 9
argument   17, 69, 154–5, 171–73, 218ff
assessment   41, 109, 110

B
Bakhtin M. M.   125, 127, 143, 166, 175, 180, 198

C
communities of practice   104
competence   176
   communicative   3, 9, 10
   strategic   42, 65, 66, 71, 73
composition   160–66
critical thinking   171, 179

D
dialogue   139ff
discourse(s)   7, 9, 10, 13
   academic   8, 15, 105, 191, 149–50, 217–8, 224
   critical   224
   critical discourse analysis   175–77
   dominance   xx
   of transparency   xviii, 125, 147, 150–1
distance learning texts   109

E

English for Academic Purposes (EAP) 20, 38, 160
error analysis 71–4, 88–90
evaluation 22
   evaluation criteria xxi, 221–2, 46, 85

F

Fairclough N. 8, 12, 177–178
familiarisation 44–5
feedback 31, 51–3, 109, 113–4, 120–2
Feynman R. 75–8
Foucault M. 7, 151, 178
Franklin S. 198, 212–4, 225

G

Gee J. 13, 130, 131–2, 144, 151, 224–5, 226
Grice's Cooperative Principle xviii, 75–78

H

Halliday M.A.K. 18, 41, 97
Heath S.B. xxi
Howes D. 207–10, 223–4, 226

I

identity/-ies xv, xx, 6, 7, 8, 15, 83, 100, 104
   shifting 7, 14
   and ownership 99–100
   and self 108, 109
institutional practices 5, 6, 7, 8, 12, 13
interlanguage 87–90
Ivanic R. xxii, 6, 14, 83, 108, 150, 194, 197, 225

K

Kress G. 18, 179–80, 182

L

Laurillard D. 105, 119–20
Lea M. xix-xxii, 7, 8, 11, 32, 39, 42, 83, 106–7, 150, 155, 194, 197, 204–5, 222–3
learning
   approaches 112–123
   domains 110–112
   as reformulation of texts 112–4
   as challenging texts 114–6
   as a social practice 7, 15
   second language 41
Levi-Strauss 225
Lienhardt G. 195–6, 197, 200–3, 221, 223, 224, 225
literacy
   literacies 224
   models 106, 211
   perspectives 195, 211, 212
   practices 213, 224

M

meaning making 8, 9, 10, 11, 125
Mitchell S. 17, 99, 175, 215–20, 225–6
motivated sign 125, 177–80

N

New Literacy Studies xix, xxi, 105, 106

P

Post-Graduate Certificate of Education) PGCE course 81ff
performance 174–75
phenomenography 104
plagiarism 30
power relations 7, 8, 13, 14, 15, 63

R

rhetoric 161–5

S

skills 161, 165, 166
  study xvii-xix, 8, 9, 42
Social Anthropology 192, 194, 198–201
Special Needs 93
Street B. xix-xxii, 7, 8, 11, 32, 39, 42, 65, 83, 106–7, 152, 155, 174, 194, 199, 225
students
  adult distance learners 110–122
  international/overseas 17ff, 37ff, 54–57
  Japanese 17–32, 47–54, 62–79
  'non-traditional' 82–96, 129
  PGCE 81ff
  student teachers 81–101

Swales J. 17, 38, 151, 175

T

taken-for-grantedness 98–100
task-based learning 38–56
topic and comment 24, 26
Taylor G. xxi, 194, 198
Turner J. 83, 154, 206, 223

V

voice (writer's/student's) 19, 96, 126, 206–7

W

Writing Across the Curicululum (WAC) 42, 160

In the STUDIES IN WRITTEN LANGUAGE AND LITERACY the following titles have been published thus far:

1. VERHOEVEN, Ludo (ed.): *Functional Literacy: Theoretical issues and educational implications.* 1995
2. KAPITZKE, Cushla: *Literacy and Religion: The textual politics and practice of Seventh-day Adventism.* 1995.
3. TAYLOR, Insup, and M. Martin Taylor: *Writing and literacy in Chinese, Korean, and Japanese.* 1995.
4. PRINSLOO, Mastin and Mignonne BREIER (eds): *The Social Uses of Literacy. Theory and Practice in Contemporary South Africa.* 1996.
5. IVANIČ, Roz: *Writing and Identity. The discoursal construction of identity in academic writing.* 1998.
6. PONTECORVO, Clotilde (ed.): *Writing Development. An interdisciplinary view.* 1997.
7. AIKMAN, Sheila: *Intercultural Education and Literacy. An ethnographic study of indigenous knowledge and learning in the Peruvian Amazon.* 1999.
8. JONES, Carys, Joan TURNER and Brian STREET (eds.): *Students Writing in the University. Cultural and epistemological issues.* 1999.
9. BARTON, David and Nigel HALL (eds.): *Letter Writing as a Social Practice.* n.y.p.